# Shakespeare and Material Culture

OXFORD SHAKESPEARE TOPICS
Published and Forthcoming Titles Include:

| Oxford Shakespeare Topics

# Shakespeare and Material Culture

CATHERINE RICHARDSON

OXFORD
UNIVERSITY PRESS

# OXFORD
UNIVERSITY PRESS

Great Clarendon Street, Oxford OX2 6DP

Oxford University Press is a department of the University of Oxford.
It furthers the University's objective of excellence in research, scholarship,
and education by publishing worldwide in

Oxford New York

Auckland Cape Town Dar es Salaam Hong Kong Karachi
Kuala Lumpur Madrid Melbourne Mexico City Nairobi
New Delhi Shanghai Taipei Toronto

With offices in

Argentina Austria Brazil Chile Czech Republic France Greece
Guatemala Hungary Italy Japan Poland Portugal Singapore
South Korea Switzerland Thailand Turkey Ukraine Vietnam

Published in the United States
by Oxford University Press Inc., New York

British Library Cataloguing in Publication Data

Data available

Library of Congress Cataloging in Publication Data

Data available

Typeset by SPI Publisher Services, Pondicherry, India
Printed in Great Britain on acid-free paper by
MPG Books Group, Bodmin and King's Lynn

ISBN 978–0–19–956227–5 (Pbk.)

5 7 9 10 8 6 4

*for Justin*

# Acknowledgements

I think, in retrospect, that I've been wanting to write this book for at least ten years. But I didn't know that until Stanley Wells happened to suggest that I might like to do so in Church Street in Stratford one evening. My thanks to him and to Peter Holland for making that suggestion are profound, as is my appreciation of their encouragement, helpful criticism and good humour in the face of my incredible typographical mistakes. And this is a book which I would certainly never have written in this form had it not been for my six years at the Shakespeare Institute. My time there was a very special one which leaves its mark on more than just what follows, and I have to thank John Jowett, Peter Holland, Russell Jackson and Kate McLuskie for the place's distinctive atmosphere and for countless influential conversations, and Martin Wiggins for that too, and for so much more besides. My wider work on material culture has also influenced what follows – an AHRC network on clothing run by Evelyn Welch, through which I worked with the collections of the Victoria and Albert Museum (as well as trying to make ruffs), helped build my confidence in talking about objects. Discussions with Evelyn, with Chris Breward, Hilary Davidson, Maria Hayward, Ros King, Giorgio Riello, Ulinka Rublack and Jenny Tiramani both then and since have helped to sharpen my ideas. At Birmingham and at Kent, likeminded colleagues have been unfailingly generous. Talking to Tara Hamling about material culture has been an enormous pleasure, as well as a steep learning curve about all things visual, and she has read several chapters. Jennie Batchelor at Kent has read a good half of what follows, and discussed it in generous detail. The University of Kent gave me the study leave which I needed to finish this book, and the staff and students of its wonderfully interdisciplinary Centre for Medieval and Early Modern Studies have influenced its final shape considerably.

Personally, for unfailing and unflappable help with admin and life in general, I must thank Rebecca and Juliet at the Institute and Claire at the Centre. Madaleine and Isaac are the adventure of a lifetime, an adventure which looks set to reach new horizons. And this book is for Justin because we met over two different kinds of material culture and a car park at art college. The things he makes are spectacularly beautiful and I hope he'll take this object, despite its imperfections, in the spirit in which it is offered. 'As hands do shut so hart be knit'.

# Contents

# Note on Texts and Abbreviations

All references to Shakespeare are to *The Complete Works*, ed. Stanley Wells and Gary Taylor (Oxford: Clarendon Press, 1988). Throughout I have silently modernized the spelling of quoted texts.

# List of Illustrations

# Introduction: early modern material culture

Gimmal or divided ring, shown both open and closed, Museum of London, sixteenth century. The inscription reads 'As hands do shut so hart be knit'.

In 1589, just before Shakespeare began his writing career, George Puttenham's comprehensive treatise *The Arte of English Poesie* was printed. The first of the three parts of the book lays out the different forms in which poetry was consumed in early modern England, including 'interlude, song, ballade, carol and ditty... comedy, tragedy, ode, epitaph, elegy, epigram, and other more'.[1] Puttenham's chapters range from 'In what form of Poesie the amorous affections and allurements were uttered' (one encompassing 'sorrowing, weeping, lamenting...with a thousand delicate devises, odes, songs, elegies, ballads, sonnets and other ditties, moving one way and another to great compassion'), to 'In what form of Poesie the evil and outrageous behaviours of Princes were reprehended' ('in plays and pageants'). Puttenham, in other words, puts plays in context – they are seen as one kind of poetic writing amongst many.

Last of all, Puttenham puts a chapter 'Of short Epigrams called posies'. These posies, he says, 'were sent usually for new years gifts' or, alternatively, they were put on 'banqueting dishes of sugar plate, or of march paines [marzipans], & such other dainty meats [foods] as by the courtesy & custom every guest might carry from a common feast home with him to his own house'. As a parting gift from an elite banquet then, guests might take with them a piece of sugar or marzipan with a short poem written upon it – 'the shorter the better' – presumably as a reminder of the hospitality they had received and the skill and wit of the host who had caused such a thing to be constructed. Puttenham suggests that such customs belonged to the past, i.e. to Classical times. In his own days, however, he tells us, we 'paint them...upon the back sides of our fruit trenchers of wood, or use them as devises in rings and arms and about such courtly purposes'. Posies had become more permanent then. No longer written into the mutable surfaces of food, in early modern England they were carved into the trenchers from which food was eaten, or engraved into the rings which people wore. In half a paragraph at the end of his list of noble uses of poetry, then, Puttenham gives a little space to a kind of writing which is perhaps the least like the type of poetic expression we would expect in this period – it has been called a type of graffiti.[2] And in describing this kind of writing, Puttenham links plays to things by means of the way they communicate through poetry.

Many of Puttenham's posies are an explicitly elite kind of writing – they are to be found at banquets and concern heraldry and other 'such courtly purposes' as he puts it. But writing on things went much lower down the social scale too, as his example of rings suggests. The gold gimmal (or two-halved) ring above, now in the collections of the Museum of London, for instance, is not one of the great 'Renaissance jewels': it is a love token passed between fairly ordinary Londoners. Its inscription, 'As hands do shut so hart be knit', is spread across the two halves of the ring, and can only be read once they are opened. On top of the two sections, keeping them together, is the pair of interlocking golden hands which can be seen in the right hand; lower image above. It is these hands to which the words refer, and the uppermost has a small heart on it which brings the two halves of the poetic conceit together visually. The ring is likely to have been given as a token in the way of marriage – an object which moved a couple closer towards a binding union. Its material form and the words written on it share the same message: the basic circular shape symbolizes the eternal nature of the bond of marriage; together, the words and the form of the hands make the ring 'work' – opening and closing it reveals and conceals its message, and hence performs the text which lies within.

The posy is a perfect example of two issues crucial to this book: the way early modern men and women used objects, and the way writing and material culture were related to one another in the period in which Shakespeare was producing his plays. People are surrounded by things in every period – we certainly are today – but in early modern England those things were seen to be useful, thought-provoking, marvellous and entertaining, capable of being surprising in senses which this ring suggests in its own modest way. Even in such a comparatively cheap and simply made object, there is a sense of ingenuity and a clear understanding of the way objects could perform emotions. So these were not just rarefied ideas about objects, they were meaningful ways of communicating in everyday life. Because above all, things were good for thinking with in early modern England – the physical form of objects was always a starting point for considering the nature of humanity, its sorrows and joys and the strength and quality of its relationships. That is why objects given as tokens of affection in the lead up to marriage had a legal validity. Their gift and acceptance was seen as a valid language of negotiation. The ring – a round thing made of precious metals which made it valuable and enduring – offered a circular space for thinking through the intensity of love and friendship and their place within the twin certainties of death and eternal life. The 'bracelet of bright hair about the bone' ('The Relic') by which John Donne imagines he and his beloved will meet again on the day of resurrection is a similar kind of token, one to which he gives a description whose poetic intensity is matched by contemporary perceptions of the prominence and durability of objects. It would not have surprised their wearers, I think, that these objects were dug up centuries later by metal detectorists to speak their intimate poetical conceits once more.

Because there can be no doubt that objects spoke in early modern England. Sometimes they spoke through their form and shape, their decoration and the materials from which they were formed. Every ring was potentially a symbol of infinity. But a surprisingly large number of objects spoke more literally through the words which decorated their surfaces, word and thing animating one another. If, as has been suggested, the various kinds of early modern 'graffiti' represent 'an inscriptional action whereby the intelligence of the maker registered itself in matter',[3] then the matter was the medium through which one intelligence made contact with another. And theatre is of course essentially, before anything else, a physical medium of performance which communicates with its audience through what words mean in relation to the gestures of the actor, the props which they use and the material space within which all come together. Looking at the material culture of the theatre necessarily promotes a sensitivity to performance and its relations to its audience – to the consumption of drama. If we want fully to understand the way Shakespeare's plays work then, we need to explore how he thinks with things as well as words.

The chapters which follow this introduction focus on a series of ways in which material culture is used in Shakespeare's plays, sensitive at all times, I hope, to the specificity of meanings within individual plays and genres: Chapter 2 considers things within webs of discourse, exploring, through the detailed example of the rings in *The Merchant of Venice*, how objects draw the language of the plays into themselves. Chapter 3 investigates how the material qualities of visual display communicated relationships of status and gender, looking first at the way the opening sequences of *Hamlet* rely upon clothing to make their meaning, and then at the significance of dress and the body in *Twelfth Night*'s gender confusions. Chapter 4 examines the way things formed a part of the linguistic texture of space, considering the uses of chairs on stage, first in *Richard II* and then in the closet scene in *Hamlet*, and comparing Shakespeare's practice here to the way he stages space in *Othello* and *Cymbeline*. Chapter 5 explores the role of objects in the construction of a set of social practices which brought units of offstage meaning onstage in order to explore their dynamics, taking as its example the generic differences between the banquets staged in *Romeo and Juliet*, *Titus Andronicus*, *As You Like It* and, in most detail, *The Tempest*. Finally, Chapter 6 works through the way things operate within the early modern theatre's forms of mimetic display – the part they play in its representations of reality. It considers the illusionistic pictures drawn in words in *A Midsummer Night's Dream* and *Hamlet* and the language of objects developed in these plays and *The Merry Wives of Windsor* alongside *Cymbeline's* troubled relationship with mimesis. In conclusion, I argue for the significance of the different relationships with material culture outlined in this Introduction for an understanding of how these plays functioned, for the centrality of things to the telling of stories, and for the way they offer themselves to a different kind of engagement with the stage which is closer to how we watch than how we read – less of linear, narrative connection with drama than one which respects its parts, its material elements, as a richly experiential way of coming to terms with the plays of Shakespeare.

## Talking About Things

But first this introduction explores the role of things in early modern England. The intimate conversations which, as we have seen above, objects effected between host and guest, lover and beloved are only one aspect of the peculiar nature of material communication in early modern England. Individual material dialogues took place within a national context of writing and talking about things: material culture was not only meaningful as a mode of communication between individuals, it also had a national profile and a significant prominence in political, moral and religious debate. Material conversations were carried on at the level of national legislation and printed moralizing. We need to get our heads around that way of thinking – to enter that distinctive world of goods and appreciate the potential transgressions involved in eating food, furnishing homes and wearing clothes for instance – if we are to understand the way Shakespeare's plays negotiated meaning between words and things.

This kind of state interest in the consumption practices of individual households is a feature of pre-modern attitudes towards material culture. Sumptuary laws in force throughout Elizabeth's reign and still frequently discussed in James's aimed to control the relationship between consumption and social status. Although this legislation had originally dealt with many different kinds of expenditure, on food and jewellery for instance, by the sixteenth century it was directed at the regulation of clothing according to degree. A 1574 proclamation began thus:

The excess of apparel and the superfluity of unnecessary foreign wares thereto belonging now of late years is grown by sufferance to such an extremity that the manifest decay of the whole realm generally is like to follow (by bringing into the realm such superfluities of silks, cloths of gold, silver... as of necessity the moneys and treasure of the realm is and must be yearly conveyed out of the same to answer the said excess).[4]

'Excess', 'superfluity' and the 'extremity' of 'unnecessary' consumption were seen in this alarmist rhetoric to threaten the nation itself, having a profound impact on its economic health through their influence on the balance of imports and exports.

But alongside those fiscal concerns, and intimately tied to them, the legislation went on to lay out more moral considerations:

particularly the wasting and undoing of a great number of young gentlemen, otherwise serviceable, and others seeking by show of apparel to be esteemed as gentlemen, who, allured by the vain show of those things,... run into such debts and shifts as they cannot live out of danger of laws without attempting unlawful acts, whereby they are not any ways serviceable to their country as otherwise they might be.

Again, it is the nation which is under threat, as serviceable, useful young men are enticed by 'the vain show of things' into a life of crime necessary to finance their habits. In a period which saw the development of significant antithetical discourses of 'covetousness' and 'commonwealth', these were powerful and unsettling arguments about a fracturing of communal responsibility. The arguments ran along these lines: excessive consumption set in train by the desire for fashion pulled thought, energy and finances away from what was seen as an undivided public good, and dispersed it into the multiple avenues of individual taste and fancy. It atomized national economies into their constituent individual consumers whose passions for things disrupted their sense of communal enterprise.

Although in theory any kind of consumption might become excessive and thereby threaten both individuals and their communities, clothing, perhaps the one unavoidable material possession in the English climate, seems to have caused a particular kind of moral concern. The status it is given in moral treatises is astounding. For instance, Philip Stubbes, in his *Anatomie of Abuses* (1583), outlined three types of pride: pride of heart, pride of mouth and pride of apparel. But it was not a proud heart or proud words which 'offendeth God more', it was pride in clothing: 'the pride of the heart, and of the mouth, are not opposite to the eye, nor visible to the sight, and therefore cannot entice others to vanity & sin'.[5] This brings out very strongly the performative nature of material culture which the ring above suggested. Pride in apparel – in the excesses of number and quality of items which fashion encouraged – was a visual provocation to sin. In relation to the staging of clothes in the early modern theatre, the perceived impact of the visibility of material culture within communities and the effects of display in multiplying discussion of consumer goods is especially significant. Much of clothing's perceived power came, then, from its embodied quality – the sins of excessive and provocative dress were literally brandished before the eye as their wearers walked by.

The language of these works is strong: Stubbes describes ruffs, invented as he says by the devil himself, as 'great and monstrous', but he warns that 'if Aeolus with his blasts, or Neptune with his storms chance to hit upon the crafty bark of their bruised ruffs, then they go flip flap in the wind, like rags flying abroad, and lie upon their shoulders like the dishclout of a slut'. But discourses which share this moral outrage, if not the offensive similes, can also be found in national attempts to address morality through the pulpit. The Elizabethan state produced a 'Homily Against excess of Apparel' – a 'state-sponsored' sermon, written to be read in church on a regular basis, along with its counterparts on Rebellion, Whoredom and Adultery, Swearing etc. Here too, parishioners could hear lamentation: 'But alas now a days how many may we behold occupied wholly in pampering the flesh, taking no care at all, but only how to deck them selves, setting their affection altogether on worldly bravery, abusing GODS goodness, when he sendeth plenty, to satisfy their wonton lusts, having no regard to the degree wherein GOD hath placed them.'[6]

The shared vehemence of this kind of condemnation was at least partly a feature of Protestant discourses about materiality more generally, discourses which were especially concerned with the relationship between a sound inner spirituality and its expression in fitting outer behaviour. Excessive clothing was particularly unsuitable for reformed Protestant communities because it drew attention to the body, and hence away from the soul. Its origins made it the subject of especial condemnation – it was necessitated by the Fall of Adam and Eve, whose stirring awareness of their full human nature took the form of a sudden consciousness of their nudity – 'And the eyes of them both were opened, and they knew that they were naked; and they sewed fig leaves together, and made themselves aprons' as it says in the King James Bible (1611), or 'breeches' as the Geneva Bible (1560) has it (Genesis 3:7). The translations tellingly choose items of clothing very familiar to early modern men and women. Adam and Eve's first more permanent suit of clothes, 'coats of skins', was given to them by God as a parting gift from Eden, a gift which encapsulated their post-lapsarian nature and acted as a marker of God's displeasure as well as his enduring care for mankind. Clothing carried traces of original sin from the moment of its inception, then: it mediated between God and man, between sight and the body. Objects which carried information about bodies, which mirrored them and touched them and in so doing revealed them outwardly, if not to the sight then to the imagination, had a double dose of both spiritual and moral danger.

For Protestants, however, the tactile properties of all objects were potentially troubling, and investment in material goods was problematic. Their religious practices were of course partly divided from Catholic ritual by a different attitude towards materiality: because Catholicism's investment in ecclesiastical art was said to encourage confusion between images and statues and the saints which they represented, Protestantism shied away from pictorial representation in the church; and whereas for Catholics the bread and wine of the Eucharist *became* the body and blood of Christ, for Protestants this crucial moment was only a memorial, a re-enactment involving no material change. In these ecclesiastical contexts, Protestantism gave greater emphasis to the more general position of material culture within Christianity, which sets worldly goods in opposition to the fruits of the spirit, and this attitude to an extent pervaded daily life. It was for this reason that individuals on their deathbed were advised to make a will – to deal with worldly things so that they could concentrate their attentions on the infinitely more significant heavenly ones: in Thomas Becon's influential book *The Sicke Mans Salve* (1561), a dialogue with a dying man, his friend advises that 'they whom the Lord hath endued with the goods of the world should before their departure set a godly order and quiet stay in their temporal possessions', because 'the world passeth away, and the lust thereof, but he that fulfilleth the will of God abideth for ever'. Hearing this, the dying man immediately asks 'Where is the pen, ink, and paper?', and assures his audience that he has always made his goods serve him, and never the other way round.[7] Denigrating the things of this world was a way of elevating the things of the next – the one made exceptional in relation to the mundaneness of the other.

But material objects were nevertheless essential to early modern thought processes, condensing complex concepts and ideas into resonant images in the mind's eye. The playwright John Lyly, for instance, demonstrates the way materiality could figure less concrete issues: 'Traffic and travel hath woven the nature of all Nations into ours' he complains, 'and made this land like Arras, full of devise, which was broad-cloth, full of workmanship'.[8] Not only the complicated cultural circulations between nations but also their crafty divisiveness is reflected in his contrast between simple English broadcloth and the foreign complexities of tapestry. But material culture also spanned the gap between the earthly and the spiritual: as Othello enters the chamber where Desdemona sleeps, he explores his murderous intentions by musing on the candle he holds in his hand: 'Put out the light, and then put out the light' (5.2.7). In a very common early modern train of thought, he moves from material object to eternal soul, making the former one term in a metaphor, and hence in some ways an equal partner in meaning. This interdependence between the earthly and the heavenly in post-reformation England is slightly uncomfortable. It is as though Protestantism cannot quite let go of the direct connections which Catholicism perceived there – the way things could hold this world and the next in a physical conjunction – like the glass through which St Paul imagined seeing darkly, which left human beings only a material sliver away from seeing 'face to face' (1 Corinthians 13:12).

The angry moralistic, anti-material discourse of Stubbes and those like him had a particular polemical aim, then. It was an attempt to define appropriate godly Protestant behaviour in opposition, by showing what it most certainly was not. Responding to the time, contemplation and money invested in dress, the hectoring expression of Protestant, often Puritan, disgust with social practice aimed to separate the writer and his readers from the ungodly through sheer outrage and abhorrence. For instance, the possession of 'two or three paire' of expensive and 'curiously knit' nether stockings by those 'having scarce forty shillings of wages by the year' is an example of 'impudent insolency, and shameful outrage', proof that 'Satan, Prince of Darkness and father of Pride, is let loose' in England.[9] Again, material culture gets caught up in a set of supposed binary oppositions. This morally polarizing use of objects is an extreme example of their wider facility for social distinction: the morality of goods was always in the end tied back to the concerns of sumptuary legislation because it was considerably more immoral for those of lower social status to indulge in excessive display than their betters.

But this essential discriminating function was perceived to be under threat. Fashion – the desire to alter set patterns of consumption by acquiring an additional something, different, new or in other ways distinctive – threatened material culture's ability to uphold the systems of social signification which divided society, and as a result tended towards chaos. So much of the outrage caused by consumption stems from the fact that writers perceive the wrong type of people to be consuming inappropriate kinds of things: people on small incomes who wear expensive stockings, or parishioners who satisfy their 'wanton lusts' willy-nilly, 'having no regard to the degree wherein GOD hath placed them.' Despite the Sumptuary Legislation setting out what one could wear dependent upon rank, 'one can scarcely know, who is a Noble woman, who is an honourable, or worshipful woman, from them of meaner sort'.[10]

And it is in the perceived threat to the fundamental categorizing capacity of material culture that national and local attitudes towards things connect most clearly to attitudes towards the early modern theatre. In addition to concerns about the blurring of status groups, dress provided the primary division between men and women: although 'apparel was given us as a sign distinctive to discern betwixt sex and sex, and therefore one to wear the apparel of another sex is to participate with the same and to adulterate the verity of his own kind', this was just what the moralists claimed was happening, in a theatre in which men played the female parts. For some scholars, the question of 'adulteration of kind' is a signal that clothing was seen to have the capacity to alter gender. In her work on anti-theatricality, Laura Levine sees these problems as being at root concerned with 'the fear... that theater could structurally transform men into women'. In one early modern view, ' "doing" is constitutive ... one becomes the thing one is imitating'. On the other hand, rather than becoming women, men who dress as women cease to be men and become instead monsters, things 'which have no essential nature – because [they] have no essential gender'.[11] In playing a woman you might lose your masculinity or even your humanity – it might be swallowed up in some way by the shape of the clothes which you wear, and the gestures which you imitate. Literary critics Peter Stallybrass and Ann Rosalind Jones, talking about Hal's speech in *The Second Part of Henry the Fourth* on grief ('I will deeply put the fashion on,/And wear it in my heart' (5.2.52)), say, 'the notion that 'Fashion' can be *'deeply* put on' or, in other words, that clothes permeate the wearer, fashioning him or her within... undoes the opposition of inside and outside, surface and depth.[12] William Prynne, whose 1633 *Histriomastix* marks the pinnacle of lurid early modern writing on this subject, states, in a cryptic reference to a passage in Deuteronomy, 'he who puts on a woman's raiment.... though it be but once, is doubtless a *putter on of women's apparel.'*

But if we look towards a marginally less vituperative early modern voice we get a rather different view: in *The Christians Sacrifice* (1622) Thomas Stoughton asked rhetorically 'How therefore have men and women changed their sex, (as much as they can) one with another? Men wearing long hair like unto women, and women cutting off their hair like unto boys, or beardless young men, wearing nothing thereon but hats... Oh monstrous, oh monstrous.'[13] Still the lament of the unheeded prophet of moral doom, but here a sense of the boundaries to the debate 'as much as they can', i.e., presumably, in appearance of clothing and hairstyles, on the outside rather than the inside; *'like unto* women'. The clothing historian Susan Vincent is nicely forceful on this issue: 'internal identity was permanent and essential' she says. She shows that what is actually being criticized in these debates is what we might call 'high fashion' – the kind of clothing worn almost exclusively in London and at the peripatetic court by the elite – which challenged the way gender was expressed through dress by borrowing elements of one sex's clothing to adorn the other.[14] The range of accusations aimed at the theatre, then, fits within the discourses of moral outrage which circled around the damaging effects of material excess on individuals and nations, and the two meet most forcefully over the question of theatrical costume.

So things were at the heart of important processes of social and moral categorization in an early modern society subject to social and moral change, and as such they were much talked about both in print and from the pulpit. Clothing was in many ways the most prominent form of material culture in this respect, but the same issues of patterns of consumption applied to other kinds of object, because those patterns demonstrated – materialized – social distinctions and made an individual's position in society palpable to both themselves and their peers. The material culture of the household, of which those peers also had experience, was therefore similarly significant. William Harrison, in his *Description of England* (1577), explores the relationship between social structure and the quality of household goods. In noblemen's houses there was 'abundance of arras, rich hangings of tapestry, silver vessels, and so much other plate as may furnish sundry cupboards to the sum oftentimes of a thousand or two thousand pounds at the least'. The household stuff belonging to 'knights, gentlemen, merchantmen, and some other wealthy citizens' is slightly less impressive, although still very fine: they possess 'great provision of tapestry', as opposed to 'abundance of arras', and they also own 'pewter, brass, and [fine] linen' – less valuable items made from cheaper raw materials are distinctive of their status. Their 'costly cupboards of plate' are 'worth five or six hundred or a thousand pounds' – about half of the value of the silver plate of the nobility. And recent change has led to similar goods being available even further down the social scale. Whereas 'in times past the costly furniture stayed there', now 'it is descended yet lower even unto the inferior artificers and many farmers'. Even labourers have apparently 'learned also to garnish their cupboards with plate, their joined beds with tapestry and silk hangings, and their tables with carpets and fine napery'.[15] Although the evidence does not bear this out, the way in which Harrison sees domestic objects as defining and yet blurring social boundaries is clear.

For Harrison, this improvement in domestic materiality down the social scale offers evidence of God's blessings of plenty on a favoured England. And this indicates that there is a morality associated with household things too – England has more of them because her subjects have done something to deserve it. For the writers of household manuals, the material and the spiritual household formed a pair in which riches should be matched with sober and godly behaviour. As they suggested, it was the relative weight given to the two parts of the whole of good household governance which distinguished good protestants from the rest of the world: 'For if Parents and Householders shall perform no further duty to their children and servants, than to provide for them meat, drink, and apparel, and to pay them their wages: then Papists, Atheists, yea, Turks, and Infidels, do yield this duty as well as they'.[16] The material household was, of course, of secondary importance to the domestic functions of spiritual nourishment and scriptural teaching.

The morality of household goods also had a significant gendered aspect. Scholars have argued that the early modern period sees the start of a fundamental shift in the function of the household, in which women's work changed in its value and meaning. Household tasks and processes at a certain social level and in some areas were more frequently 'outsourced' – brewing, baking, washing and spinning, for instance, might now be performed by skilled male professionals, and the goods which kept the house functioning were increasingly likely to be bought, rather than made within the home. In addition, the household became the repository for ever-growing numbers of household objects, as Harrison's description partly suggests. And as a result, as literary critic Natasha Korda has argued, 'relations between subjects within the home became increasingly centered around and mediated by objects.'[17] The role of a housewife of sufficient social status might not be to produce things, but rather to keep an eye on them – to marshal them for the benefit of outsiders. Early modern objects, then, were unavoidably implicated in placing their owners and users socially and morally, and those moralities in particular were explicitly gendered.

## People and Their Possessions

In order to understand how Shakespeare's audiences might have responded to material culture, then, this introduction has considered the nature and status of the debates about it which were circulating alongside his plays – how significant it was to the economic and moral health of the nation. However, as it has also become clear that the quality of things underpinned social relations, we need to know too who owned what type of objects if we are to understand the access different kinds of audience members had to material knowledge – to familiarity with things. And to do that, we need to find a way of imagining ourselves in different households.

I could say that a quantitative analysis of probate inventories – the records made of people's possessions at their death – shows that the number of tablecloths owned in provincial houses rose more sharply between 1560 and 1600 than possession of any other household object, and that the median number of tablecloths in each house at the start of the seventeenth century was four.[18] This is a useful fact – it might help us to understand, for instance, how banquets in Shakespeare's plays appealed to a growing middle-status urban element in their audiences by displaying the kinds of dining goods which were becoming central to their exhibition of status. But it does not really help us to understand what that status felt like – how it would have surrounded one materially with a particular range and number of goods which shaped daily life, and which were different to the goods owned by one's poorer or wealthier neighbour. And if we want to understand Shakespeare's audience's response to the material culture of the stage it is that experiential, visceral appreciation of early modern possessions which we need to investigate, to see how knowledge of objects might have been brought into play by the electrifying connections between words and things in performance. That takes a very different kind of writing about things – a less quantitative, more qualitative, experimental and 'novelistic' writing – because it means connecting things to one another around the types of people who would have used them.

This section of the Introduction, then, explores the connections between the smaller or larger number of objects which were owned at different points on the social scale. It considers them as groups of things which in their combination expressed the status of their low, middling and upper status owners. These three categories are the absolute minimum which it is possible to consider and, as will quickly become obvious, there are key distinctions within them. Nevertheless, this approach makes it possible to assess the nature of material status relatively economically; it does make it harder, however, to deal with those aspects of status which cut across social boundaries – the changes brought about by different phases in the lifecycle, and the effect which gender had on social identity. As far as the former is concerned, individuals below the level of the elite might rise in status across their active working lives, and their possessions would diminish once they stopped working, in the absence of pension schemes. But individuals who had had direct experience of a particular way of living at some stage in their lives appear to have regarded themselves as belonging to the highest status they had managed to attain, and for our purposes it is the fact that those experiences were part of their memories which is significant, as they could be brought to mind in the theatre.

Women's relationship with objects was, in a less positive way, similarly enduring. They were very rarely owners of household items – property belonged to men, so only as widows did they actually command those things which they regularly used, often more frequently than did their legal owners. This curious relation to objects – being in constant physical contact with them and having deft and skilful knowledge of their operation but unable to control or dispose of them in any executive sense, meant that women's relation to the material world was in many ways analogous to that of servants – expert and dextrous but lacking in authority.

*Lower status.* With these differences in mind then, rather than beginning with a statistical analysis, I'll start again with this image of a group of pins found on the site of the Rose Theatre on the South Bank of the Thames in Southwark, where plays such as *Titus Andronicus* might have been seen. These pins were found both beneath the stage and in the area where the groundlings would have stood, and their

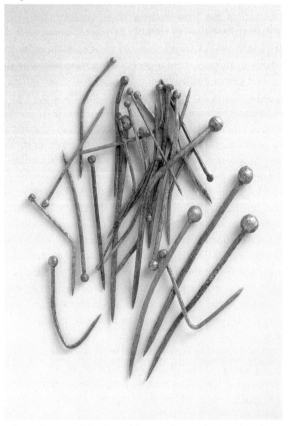

Pins found on the site of the Rose Theatre, Bankside, London, late sixteenth century, Museum of London Archaeology Service.

location suggests a material connection between stage practice and everyday life – both costumes and clothing depended upon pins to keep them together.[19] We might say that they stand for the most basic level of possessions in early modern England. Pins were, perhaps, the most fundamental object, without which it would not have been possible for anyone to leave the house. For the elite, large pins fastened great swathes of cloth into Farthingales (hooped petticoats); small pins gathered lengths of linen into the structured splendour of ruffs. For those below the level of the elite, they might hold sleeves onto bodices or doublets, or hold head coverings in place.

The image above shows pins of several sizes, several thicknesses and made from wire whose handmade alloys varied sufficiently in their mixture to produce diverse colours. Their differences suggest small-scale producers employing a common method slightly differently: although you can see that the heads of most of the pins here are made of pieces of wire wrapped round the central shank, they are wrapped in a variety of ways. This method had probably altered very little over the thousands of years during which forged metals had made it possible to join pieces of fabric together. On the other hand, pin making had recently been a topic of hot debate in Elizabethan England: 'In 1609 it was claimed that £60,000 worth of pins were used in England every year,' but the bulk of them came from Holland ('In 1597 £40,000 worth of pins and needles were said to be imported'), despite the fact that foreign pins were regularly banned in the period.[20] Alongside other government-inspired and private enterprises, 'stocking knitting, button making...nail making...knife and tool making, tobacco-pipe making, pot and oven making...ribbon and lace making, [and] linen weaving',[21] pin making was also developed as an English venture in the sixteenth century.

These debates about the economics of the trade must have made pins 'visible' around the Rose Theatre. The technical innovations which allowed the native industry to grow in the 1560s–1580s, and led to between 2,000 and 3,000 people being employed in London and the suburbs by the start of the seventeenth century, were probably made possible by the knowledge which Dutch immigrants brought with them. Usually, however, these are the kind of objects you are not meant to see. They are in the service of outer clothing, literally underpinning the shapes of fashion. In 4.3 of *Othello*, that intense, intimate scene in which Desdemona discusses men and marriage with her maid as Emilia prepares her for bed, Desdemona asks her, 'Prithee unpin me' (20). The close and personal nature of the scene comes partly from the focus on the careful skill needed to unpin her garments. Pins are essential things, things with which servants were so skilled that they probably used them instinctively and without giving any thought to their handling of them. They pinned their own clothing together into the relatively simple shapes of working dress, and they pinned their mistress's clothes or those of the men and women whose garments they laundered dexterously, in order to produce the fashions of which Stubbes and his like complained.

Even if you had very little clothing, you still had pins with which to fasten it. And, to return to Adam and Eve as the gates of Paradise closed behind them, how ever little you had, you still had clothing – a common refrain of poor women giving evidence in court was that they owned 'nothing but their apparel'. So we can start to imagine the most basic level of possessions above those of the indigent poor, putting them together a piece at a time around the concerns of their owners.[22] William Creake, a labourer from the town of Sandwich in Kent, for instance, owned only a purse, an old leather doublet, an old pair of breeches and a little old chest. He was still better off than the poor, whose clothes were charitable donations, and William's chest was an important possession – a kind of portable house in which those who had no home of their own and little furniture could keep the few things which they did own, safe from rats and damp. Beyond clothing and a chest, just above the bottom of the social scale one might own some basic kitchen equipment such as a frying or dripping pan, 'an old dabnet [cooking pan] and a little kettle'. And then perhaps, in towns where straw was less plentifully available to sleep on, a 'bolster and a pillow', even if one did not own a bed.

Owning very few things gives one a different relation to them, and underlines their association with uses crucial to sustaining the body. You might not think in terms of the generic meanings of objects – doublets and their differences from jackets, for instance – but think rather of the individuality of things and the way they relate to the body – my old leather doublet, with its unique marks of wear and the length of its association with my changing body whose shape it bears.

If men like William Creake's relationship with the world was negotiated through these very few possessions, then those a little further above him also possessed such basic items and additional goods – more, different and better quality things. Those people who lived in their own home, however humble, rather than a room in someone else's, owned more furniture – perhaps a stool and a trestle table (which could be taken down to make space): maybe a bedstead and a mattress. They might have owned some ironwork for a fireplace used for both heating and cooking – an 'iron grate and gridiron'; a 'spit and a pair of pothooks' perhaps. They might have wooden items from which to eat – 'two wooden platters, 6 dishes'; or just one 'treen [wooden] platter'. And a little further up from the bottom, they might have kitchen equipment for making food – a 'great dough keever [wooden tub]' maybe. The wooden goods are likely to have been made within the home, the metalware perhaps bought at local fairs, or from peddlers.

So the focus would be on the routines and processes associated with food, after the essentials of clothing and a little bedding. But these are still utilitarian objects, functionally formed and generic in the sense that their differences from one another were signed by the marks of use and the vagaries of hand manufacture rather than the decisions of a design process. At this level in particular, things were reused until no drop of their original substance remained: possessions included 'a woman's gown, turned and old'; a pair of vamped [patched] hose, made of old materials, and an old patched bed in the chamber where the owner died.

*Middling status.* But this was an increasingly polarized society in terms of its social relations, and those polarities can be seen now as they were experienced then by the sheer volume of goods owned. Above the social level of a basic, functioning household without servants, items were owned in relatively large numbers, including several of the same kind of thing. Such an expansion is indicative of a growing 'middling sort' of people who worked for a living, which distinguished them from those above them, but whose possessions made clear their distinction from their less prosperous neighbours. The historian Keith Wrightson defines them as 'a composite body of people of intermediate wealth, comprising substantial commercial farmers, prosperous manufacturers, independent tradesmen and the increasing numbers who gained their livings in commerce, the law and the provision of other professional services'.[23] The farmers, manufacturers and tradesmen in particular lived in households that were often powerful units of production and consumption which included a body of servants. If one could walk into one's kitchen and see, for instance, 'two dabnets [cooking pans], three chafing dishes, two frying pans, a dripping pan, two spits, a skymmer and a little ladle', or 'a brass pot, an iron pot, a dripping pan, five kettles, two posnets [little pots for boiling], a fryingpan, a pewter dish, a brass ladle and a jug' on the shelves and around the fire, and in it a 'pair of cobirons [to support the spit], three dripping pans, two frying pans and two gridirons'; if you could bring out a 'dozen saucers, six plates and eight porringers [bowls]' to hold food for your family and servants, then your house was a thriving location of domestic consumption. And you could expect to have a decent range of pewter vessels, maybe for use when guests came to share food – a generous collection might include a 'double salt, a little single salt, three porringers, four fruit dishes, two plates, nine saucers . . . a little drinking cup, a quart pot and a pint pot' – and you might keep this displayed on a court cupboard in the hall, or in a room such as a buttery, set aside for provisions and objects not used every day. And the production which took place in such a house necessitated another array of objects – you might also own, for instance, a 'steep fat [steeping vat for brewing or washing], three kevers [brewing coolers], two pails, two powdering tubs [in which to cure meat] . . . and two meal hives' for soaking malt and salting meat and fish or a 'woollen wheel and two linen trendles [wheels]' for the production of yarn to make cloth, a 'vice to twist silk', or an 'old wheel to point needles'. These kinds of households were traditionally self-sufficient in many of their processes, but it is here that the changes in the acquisition of objects from outside the house were perhaps most clearly felt. This does not mean, of course, that the householders went into shops and purchased domestic objects, but rather that they had a joiner make more of their furniture, perhaps bought more and finer cloth from local mercers and paid a local tailor to make it up, and bought more of the things which could not be made within the home such as jewellery and pewterware.

And with this wider range of possessions come other indications of increased status. At the top of this social level, those describing objects in inventories begin to record aesthetic details of the things which they list, such as a 'christening sheet with two broad seams of raised work', a 'woman's gown laced with velvet lace', or a cupboard cloth, 'wrought and fringed with black silk'. The men to whom these objects belonged can be traced in other records, suggesting that they were well known in their communities, serving as aldermen of the town for instance, or becoming freemen of its guilds. A variety of rooms in their houses catered for different kinds of leisure activity – a hall offered a more public space for eating, perhaps with servants, whereas a parlour presented a more intimate room for private dining. And the experience of middling status was one of abundance which expressed status through closely packed furniture and very full spaces. In a parlour in Canterbury in 1589, for instance, there was a table, and around it five 'wrought stools for men' and two for women, all 'covered in the seats', and three forms, or benches, a short settle and a chair, all of the more expensive joined work. There was a carved cupboard with a desk (rest) for a book on it, a joined chest and a pair of playing tables and their men, probably for chess. The seating in particular is extensive and must have packed the relatively small urban room. Perhaps most significantly, textiles of various kinds provided a level of comfort which must have made its occupant's domestic life feel qualitatively different from his less fortunate peers': carpets covered the table and cupboard, five cushions softened the benches, and window curtains and hanging cloths on the walls provided protection from draughts, the former offering a degree of privacy too. This room, as well as others, was heated, so these cloths could keep the warmth in as well as keeping the cold out.

And at such a level of status many of the most expensive goods which were owned were kept in storage. In the owner's bedchamber in that same house, for instance, were three 'deep' chests, and inside them a dizzying array of soft furnishings. They include tapestry coverlets, a Bruges satin cupboard cloth, a dornix [coarse damask] cupboard cloth lined with blue fabric, two pieces of tapestry hangings, short and long tapestry carpets, cushions including six tapestry ones, window cushions of wrought damask churchwork and green velvet and damask, window curtains of dornix and green say, cupboard cloths including one of turkeywork, and a wrought diaper towel of birds-eye work. The items are not listed in this order, rather as those taking the inventory pulled the array of extra furnishings out of the chest, and their sheer volume is definitive of upper-middling status, as is the variety of types of applied work here – turkeywork, churchwork, tapestry, birds-eye work – and of fabrics. Very expensive, such goods were kept even when worn out because their raw materials had an intrinsic value which meant they could be reused – a valance made of an old boughton work [worked cloth] coverlet, for instance – but at that stage they were often moved out of the most prominent areas of the house: a 'dornix covering, full of holes' in the servants' chamber.

There are some connections between the kind of additional objects owned at the very top of this social group and the possessions of the elite, for instance in terms of silverware, jewellery and portraits. One man's plate collection included, amongst other pieces, a great standing cup with a cover valued at £8 10s, a coconut with a silver foot, goblets, salts, cups, pots with lids, a silver bowl, a mazer (drinking bowl) and some wonderful spoons including: eight gilt ones with lions' heads, one with the image of Christ on the end, and 12 with squirrel knops, or knobs on the end. He also owned a reasonable amount of jewellery – seven rings including a gold ring with a turquoise – worn, no doubt, with his 'best gown faced with foynes', one of four from which he could choose, and the fabric of his clothes was velvet, damask, red striped taffeta, and crimson satin. This man's possessions were probably as far from William Creake's as it is possible to be in the small provincial urban societies of England.

These upper-middling status objects are connected to one another in economic, aesthetic and social terms, by the level of detail in which they are described. And we could take the coif shown on page 23 as epitomizing the physical qualities of the most impressive objects owned by this middling social group. It is made of linen, embroidered, and edged with bobbin lace. The raised branch motif connects floral sections which show a wide variety of stitches and design elements – complex work involving sections of cutwork and raised stitching in chain, ladder stitch and French knots. The pattern draws the eye around the coif, from the top of the head downwards towards the neck and shoulder, emphasizing the shape which it covers. The lace edges the face, providing a detailed and finely worked outline for it. The complexity of the overall pattern is best seen when the coif is set over a woman's hair, the colour showing through the cut sections and giving life to the whole.

This paradoxical relationship between concealing with fabric whilst revealing with the drawing of the gaze by decorative detail is common to many different types of middling status clothing, where

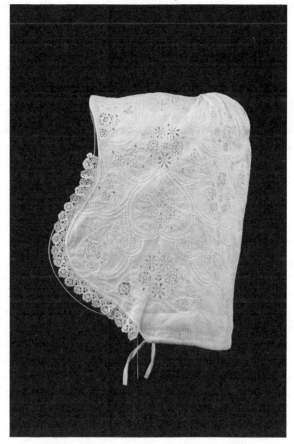

Linen coif, embroidered with linen thread and edged with bobbin lace, early seventeenth century, Victoria and Albert Museum.

fastenings, edgings and coverings formed the focus of the ornamentation in a way which problematized the act of concealing. It is use which is elaborated at this social level then – the objects are not intrinsically frivolous, rather their utility is celebrated and attention drawn to it through the addition of extra elaboration. And they are connected to the economic discourses of material goods discussed above. The key distinctions made amongst imported goods (which

Bed valance, tapestry, woven in silk and wool with some silver thread, Sheldon Tapestry Workshops, Warwickshire, 1600–10, Victoria and Albert Museum.

took money out of the country) were between essential ones, those 'arguably essential for a civilized life', and finally those 'that might be 'clean spared'.[24] The goods at this social level were largely of the 'arguably essential' kind.

*Elite status.* The kind of rooms already described for the lower and middling groups also existed in elite houses for the various levels of servants – those who were retained in large numbers in the sixteenth century in particular in order to reflect their masters' status and authority. The elite themselves, however, those whose wealth in lands and other property meant that they need undertake no profession or occupation, lived in rooms with a strikingly different level of decoration. Some objects at the middling level, usually domestic textiles, carried figurative imagery. Middling individuals often owned framed images of kings and queens or coats of arms, or painted cloths of biblical scenes, and they occasionally had portraits of themselves painted, and sometimes hung a curtain in front of them – a practice to which Olivia refers in *Twelfth Night*, as I discuss below, when she removes her veil, saying to Cesario 'we will draw the curtain and show you the picture' (1.5.223). These were likely to have been vernacular works, painted by local painter-stainers rather than the foreign-born artists who were the dominant force in London courtly painting. But higher up the social scale, pictorial domestic furnishings in the form of woven tapestries rather than painted cloths, or continentally inspired paintings, figured much more prominently. In a bedchamber in Warwick Castle, for instance, hung 'four pieces of fresh and lively hangings of the story of the Wooer' valued at a remarkable £80 (compare the £8 value of the middling-status standing cup).

The valance, which might stand for the higher social groups, is the valance from a bed – the part which hung down around the top, under which fell the curtains – probably belonging to someone near the lower end of this social group. It shows men and women in expensive clothing hunting with hounds, baiting bears and making amorous advances to the sound of music. These are all activities of elite leisure, and depicting them around the bed encloses the sleeper in the peaceful recollection of the repose his status allows him. The figurative work which is the main focus of the panel lays out the different activities, landscapes and architecture of elite pursuits in a way which guides the viewer from one side to the other. And it is a reflexive piece in many ways – intended to depict the kind of activities which might really be happening downstairs and outside. When Oberon and his fairies go to bless the 'best bride bed' of the newly married couples at the end of *A Midsummer Night's Dream* (5.2.33), these are the kind of hangings which the audience might have been expected to imagine around it, harking back to the sort of elite pursuits which the play has previously staged.

The valance's aesthetic form is detailed. It employs a rich array of flowers, classical heads and striped borders to surround what is in itself a busy scene, and even at this size – 25cm high – the detail given of doublets and hose, ruffs and the fenestration of the houses is considerable. It is woven in silk and wool, with some silver thread to give extra complexity and shimmer to the overall image. Like other early modern tapestries, it repays close, careful looking over a long period of time. And it draws attention to itself – its complexity and the brightness of its colours draw the eye.

These objects surrounded the elite man or woman in their bed, and the clothing which wrapped their bodies outside the house was no less magnificent. A scarlet suit owned by a Warwickshire baronet, for instance, must have been a striking sight: a cloak of scarlet lined in scarlet baize, and fastened with two dozen crimson ingrain buttons and loops, the doublet faced, and its skirts lined, with crimson taffeta and again closely buttoned, both suit and cloak laid on with 5½ oz of crimson ingrain silk galloon (or ribbon) lace; the outfit finished off with a pair of crimson taffeta ingrain garters and roses edged with silk lace, laced together with three dozen crimson silk ingrain and gold ribbon points and hung at the waist with a girdle of crimson ingrain satin embroidered and fringed with musk colour silk (a dark reddish-brown). The resplendent glory of the scarlet and crimson suit of clothing brought with it an imperative to act in a particular way – to exhibit the features of elite movement and gesture, not too hurried, slow and elegant, which befitted such stylish and physically restraining clothing. At other social levels there were no doubt different kinds of imperatives governing behaviour, but these tended to be negatively defined (sobriety as opposed to drunkenness for men, silent obedience as opposed to disorderly garrulousness for women) rather than self-consciously modelled by the subject.

At this elite level, objects were unique as a feature of their design. The scarlet outfit was of course bespoke and its fabrics carefully chosen; tapestries would have been woven to order for a specific room in a particular house, to which they would have given a unique identity. Rooms were often named – for instance the 'fresh and lively' story of the wooer at Warwick Castle hung in the 'silver bedchamber'. Things were very closely and explicitly linked to one another as an expression of a uniform and coherent identity. The furnishings of rooms were a part of this dynamic, often said to be 'suitable' to one another, meaning made of the same fabrics and colours so that they formed an aesthetic whole. Crucially, we can see other kinds of non-material purchase as fitting into this sense of identity. The purchaser of the crimson suit, for instance, also paid 'a company of Players styling themselves the Prince his' 2s 6d and 'the King, and Queen of Bohemia their Players' 2s, in addition to numerous small payments to fiddlers, tumblers, singers and Morris dancers. In other words entertaining travelling players (paying for household entertainment) was an integral part of the same pattern of behaviour as commissioning tapestries or crimson suits – it brought these various arts into the house, arts whose aesthetic connections to one another were clearly understood.[25]

And for these men and women, as was to an extent the case for their middling-status peers involved in trade, new patterns of commerce which linked the English economy increasingly closely and directly to the world economy brought exotic materials and objects from the Baltic, Iberia, the Mediterranean, the East Indies and the

New World. After the foundation of the East India Company in 1600, oriental spices and exotic silks began to enter the country in large numbers, showing that the elite must have generated some of the government's concern with the national balance of payments. English imports were rising in number, and it was at this highest social level in particular that the change was being felt at the turn of the sixteenth century: possession of exotic objects entering the country from abroad demonstrated the refined taste of their owners.

A china-work fruit table, or 'a dozen of Indian banqueting dishes' are likely to have been imported into London and then shipped to the provinces. At Warwick castle, for example, there were 50 carpets, mostly for tables, of which 10 were Persian, 16 Turkish and one 'very large stitched China carpet wrought in colours of silk upon Holland cloth and lined with striped China taffety [silk]'. These new and exotic goods took their place alongside more traditional markers of elite English identity. The owner of the Indian banqueting dishes also had a long cushion of black embroidered gold stuff with his arms embroidered on it and a pair of long cushions of purple velvet similarly embellished, materially stating his family's place within the ancient traditions of their country.

The differences in the quantity of possessions which these distinct groups owned, the range of goods, the materials from which they were produced and the way they were decorated not only show different economic strengths but also different aesthetic appreciations: it is the way the objects are linked to one another which epitomizes social status. Goods at the lower social level were closely connected to the body, and their uniqueness made marks of wear and change significant. Middling goods were linked together in terms of the processes of consumption and production, but they also had aesthetic qualities which came out in the descriptions which contemporaries gave of them. Upper-status goods were connected by the investment of their owners in a coherent sense of design made possible by commissioning all the furnishings for one room, for instance, at the same time. The patronage of various arts, as opposed to crafts, as a way of expressing status, wove the provision of entertainment closely into the decoration of the domestic interior.

This narrative of possessions is, of course, only one element of the story of early modern social relations in England. It is a material, rather than an economic, story – it could have been a tale of wage labour, or of spending power and the value of the estates managed by those at the top of the social scale. But these are the terms in which it was repeatedly expressed by contemporaries, who saw general issues in relation to particular things: early modern England was a socially polarized society where systems of social classification turned on the definition of material want. It was the difference between lack and plenty which both necessitated and facilitated poor relief; it was the palpable distinction between the many who had 'not so much as a poor flock bed to lie upon, but are forced to lie only upon straw and can hardly get that', and the few who had reserves of 50 carpets, which gave early modern social structures their meaning.[26] Political authority, economic influence and good social standing were all negotiated and expressed through material possessions.

## Words and things: Shakespeare's plays and material culture

Knowing what people owned and how their possessions defined their position within early modern society – their authority, outlook and expectations – helps us to begin to reconstruct some of the complexities of their engagement with objects on the stage. The lower-status audience members' unfamiliarity with some of the goods which appear in plays, for instance banqueting tableware or bed valances, is obvious from the biographies of possessions outlined above. Their distance from direct physical experience of them, or their knowledge of manufacture but not consumption of expensive objects, served to articulate their relative lack of political and economic authority.

Understanding the relationship between goods and social groups also makes it possible to see different categories of staged object. It enables us to appreciate the differences between essential goods common to all, like pins for instance, specialized objects which relate to skills, trades and professions such as buck baskets for washing, and expensive items like tapestries, which were largely the preserve of the rich. And connecting narratives of possession with discourses of consumption enables us to see the goods of the past not as a uniform field of objects where one simply needed more money to purchase more and better quality things, but rather as a series of objects made more or less prominent by contemporary debates about their morality, their novelty or newfangledness, their exoticness, or their perceived superfluous triviality. Some goods must have drawn attention to themselves in this way as unusual, because the like had not been seen before (those things associated with new activities such as smoking, for instance), and others must have been noticed because of the precociousness of their design as opposed to their form – familiar things in a different style like a 'China' carpet.

Once we begin to see material culture in terms of the lights and shades of contemporary opinion on goods, we can understand more clearly how it functions on the stage. And this gives us a fresh new angle on the relationship between drama and its reception and comprehension. Valuable scholarly work has traced audience familiarity with biblical quotation, echoes of language from prominent early modern texts such as the Book of Common Prayer, and direct narrative sources of plays as diverse as Ovid and contemporary ballads.[27] But we need to add to this an appreciation of how objects spoke to audiences, becoming sensitive to their familiarity with goods just as we have learned to appreciate their experience of the written word, conditioned by literacy and exposure to the rhythms of the liturgy. And if we can begin to see the way these complex verbal and material constraints upon responses to a play relate to one another, we will have a much richer understanding of what it meant to watch a play in the early modern theatre. We would then be placing our analysis somewhere between the desire to recover individual reactions which, with the odd exception like the astrologer and medical practitioner Simon Forman, who made notes on his experience of playgoing, are lost to us, and the blanket response of a 'whole audience's' reaction, which represents the fictitiously homogeneous responses of a deeply polarized society.

But understanding contemporary responses to the material culture of the stage is, of course, about much more than knowing what possessions the audience owned. First, the meaning of objects is only partly a function of their physical form. The fact that they signified differently depending on their perceived moral value, for instance, shows this quite clearly: a coif might be the same shape before, during and after a focus on appropriate covering of women's heads, but it will be perceived and understood differently. For the literary critic Jonathan Gil Harris, it is these contexts which actually 'produce' the object: 'is the object prior to and constitutive of the field of desire within which it participates (the object exists; the subject then chooses to consume or repudiate it)?', he asks. 'Or does this very field of desire, of temptation and renunciation, produce the object (the object is discursively constituted by the technologies of power that shape consumer desire and/or aversion)?' The object seen through the eyes of a desiring subject, like a window of pastries viewed by a hungry subject, takes on a particular form which links it to the qualities by which allure is judged. There is no 'thing' which can be studied dispassionately, outside these webs of meaning.[28] That is why this book is called *Shakespeare and Material Culture*, although it primarily focuses on objects rather than, for instance, the sounds or smells of the early modern theatre: because material culture is a term which 'encapsulates not just the physical attributes of an object, but the myriad and shifting contexts through which it acquires meaning'.[29] Subjects, then, 'make' objects in the image of patterns of desire and repudiation.

But objects also, it has been argued, make subjects – the process is reciprocal: 'Through their very materiality – their shape, function, decoration, and so on – [objects] have a role to play in creating and shaping experiences, identities and relationships.'[30] The physical form of things carries information about social practice which, once that thing has been chosen by the subject, remakes them to an extent in its own image. Having opted for a coif which seemed fitting for her, a woman's posture, gesture, physical appearance and interaction with her peers would then be shaped by the way she wore it. As the historian Sara Pennell puts it, '[m]undane objects are...not simply the evidence of practices, but the tools by which such practices are enabled, learnt and assimilated, and also by which the value of those practices, which may seem routine and meaningless to the outside world, may be understood as complex, consciously shaped and indeed owned by the people doing them'. Her example is the cooking pot, through the use and maintenance of which the 'value of domestic order...was realized'.[31] This book always begins with things, then, because information about identities, practices, ideas and ideologies – about people's lives – is contained in their form. But it is as a result, I hope, always about much more than the things themselves.

Studying objects on the stage, of course, lends a particular complexity to the question of how objects are 'produced' – whether we understand them as part of a theatrical narrative or as defined in relation to economic, social and cultural meanings offstage. We have to work out what role the information we have about the social life of objects outside the theatre has when they are employed as part of the illusion of a play. Literary critic James Calderwood discusses the changing identity of the joint stool in the banquet scene in *Macbeth* – the point at which Macbeth thinks he sees the ghost of Banquo and Lady Macbeth berates him: 'When all's done/You look but on a stool'(3.4.66–7). Calderwood sees the stool itself as moving from the King's Men's to Macbeth's possession in a process by which the audience fictionalize 'in their imaginations an object that remains incorrigibly what it was before the play began'. This discussion actually comes in the context of his views about literary language: 'The process is analogous to the absorption of language into a literary work. For the language the poet uses comes as drab and gross from the everyday world as Macbeth's joint-stool; but it has been transformed by the poetic imagination into a self-enclosed complex of meaning that abandons its referential dependence on the world outside.' Calderwood understands the stage as a self-enclosed arena for meaning which makes no reference beyond its fictionalized space. There is, he says, no 'route by which we can return from the language of *Macbeth*, whose meanings are uniquely contained in their own ghostly linguistic forms, to the language of Jacobean England from which it came'.[32] And similarly, 'there is no way back from Banquo's ghost to the joint-stool owned by the King's Men'. Arguing against this passage in the introduction to their book *Staged Properties*, Harris and Korda point instead to props' 'power to puncture the dramatic illusion by pointing to alternate social dramas of economic production, exchange, and ownership'.[33] Jonathan Harris says that props 'can draw explicit attention to their twin citizenship in a timeless world of formal illusion and a diachronic universe of material labor and transformation'. In other words they are capable both of playing a role in the drama and playing themselves – their offstage lives – at the same time.

Like language, props tie reality and illusion together, asking their audiences to see the one against the other and to make sense of the illusion in relation to the quality of their lived experience. And this too is a reciprocal process – just as subject and object were mutually constitutive, so the work that objects do on the stage alters the meanings of the drama in which they intervene, and the meanings of the objects are qualified and deepened by their participation within the narrative of the drama. Objects on the stage are held up for analysis, and their meanings change once they have had attention drawn to them in this way. So the on- and offstage meanings of objects will evolve at different rates – their cycles of significance intersecting with but distinct from each other. Andrew Sofer, for instance, explores the relationship between Shakespeare's staging of Yorick's skull, 'a scene unprecedented on the Elizabethan stage ... and the first scene in which skulls are used as stage properties', and the almost 'hundred years of *memento mori* tradition in the visual arts' which lies behind it. Although the *memento mori* image was an old and familiar one then, its emblematic qualities gracing painted and printed images and various kinds of jewellery from scent cases and toothpicks to mourning rings, the popularity of the skull as prop had a completely different timescale which began with *Hamlet*. And, as a thing on the stage rather than an emblem in a two-dimensional image, it has a very different meaning there – not, Sofer, argues, 'stone-cold metaphor', but rather 'hot property'.[34]

And, as the offstage meanings of objects can be seen as tied up in a long-term shift from feudalism to capitalism, from thrift to consumerism, or from Catholic to Protestant materialities, so the theatrical meanings of objects might be understood in the context of various shifts in the development of drama. Douglas Bruster, arguing that we need to analyse their contributions quantitatively if we are to fully understand the way they function qualitatively, suggests that plotting Shakespeare's use of objects on a graph would show 'a shallow "V" over the course of his career'. In generic terms, he points to the difference between the early comedy *Merry Wives* with 13.55 objects per 1,000 lines and the 'middle' period *As You Like It* with 5.36, or the early tragedy *Titus Andronicus* with 21 and the later *Hamlet* with 10.24 props per 1,000 lines – a distinction between 'display' and 'sparseness'. And he links this to changing theatrical tastes which move from the 'intensively visual theatre of the late 1580s and early 1590s' through a period of 'verbal preferences' at the end of the sixteenth and start of the seventeenth centuries, 'which in turn gave way to practices influenced by the spectacles of the Jacobean court'.[35]

Across Shakespeare's career, there was also a continuing shift in the dramatic mode from symbolism to realism. Despite the mimesis of interiority which Hamlet's soliloquies evince, early modern drama was still often a mode of symbolism, where actions and things took on a range of meanings above and beyond the literal referent of their day-to-day significance. In the broadest possible terms, it is impossible to put something on the stage and for that thing to remain meaningless – however mundane the object or the action, its presence on the stage gives it consequence because it implicitly asks an audience to consider its relevance to and value for the action which surrounds it. At the end of *A Midsummer Night's Dream*, for instance, Puck enters with a broom 'To sweep the dust behind the door' (5.1.390). In her book on *Staging Domesticity*, Wendy Wall calls the 'disposing of dirt left in domestic corners' a 'task usually too banal for representation'. Her 'usually' is crucial. It suggests that some actions and their accompanying objects carry less explicit social meaning than others, and that they are therefore less likely to be represented on the stage, where meaning must be communicated swiftly and intensely. It also assumes that, in this instance where the action *has* been represented, it *must* therefore accrue meaning, and she seeks out the potential extra-theatrical values and implications which it might bring with it into the performance.[36]

The meanings of staged objects are always quasi-allegorical then: the theatre gives a rich value to the everyday, lifting it above its quotidian significance and making out of it something new and strange. Richard Helgerson, talking about *The Merry Wives of Windsor*, suggests that it may in fact be those things which are most ordinary which mean the most metaphorically. He sees the play's central episodes in which Falstaff is shamed as devices which mark 'the intersection of the women's world of household and town and the playwright's world of literary kind and convention'. In other words these episodes of domestic process act as hubs around which the mimetic representation of everyday life and the energies and plot twists of familiar narratives both revolve. It is the buck basket (in which dirty laundry is usually carried out of the house and in which Falstaff is hidden), he says, which 'evokes a world of domestic labor'.[37] What does he mean by 'evokes'? Perhaps epitomizes, brings into play, brings to the forefront of the audience's memory so that they can apply that extra-theatrical information to the scene in front of them. This is the role which objects most often play on the stage.

What is it about a buck basket which makes it 'evoke', and how might it do so? It is partly the physical durability of objects which gives them a central function in accumulating and disseminating theatrical meanings. Their stasis of form in relation to the vagaries of human emotions and the respective confusions and frustrations of comic and tragic plots that gives them a sense of solidity. They become a conduit for the different kinds of meaning I have been discussing, a physical form around which words and ideas can cluster and to which they can become attached. Vibrant objects resonate with larger issues which have no material form of their own – economic questions of commodification and exchange, for instance. And this function makes it perfectly clear that a large part of the meaning of objects is contingent, always created by the context within which they find themselves – although they have a range of fundamental meanings, a ring or a handkerchief do not have a monolithic significance. Words draw *attention* to the meanings of things in a given situation.

Natasha Korda has said that 'If "the exploding availability of consumer goods in the early modern period" represented a thorough-going "cultural preoccupation", Shakespeare is too often seen as standing aloof from this preoccupation . . . Shakespeare's preoccupation, centuries of critics have maintained, is with the interior life of the subject, not with the world of goods.'[38] And Peter Stallybrass has outlined one strand of the history of this perceived aloofness: 'The process of divorcing supramaterial "culture" from its "mere" material supports begins in the Renaissance' he says, as part of an attempt 'to elevate cultural objects above material or economic value.' Instead, in the seventeenth century, the book 'becomes the immaterial support above which the mind of the reader communes with the mind of the author. And the author becomes a transcendental value who has no place in the material world.'[39] But drama, of course, is always embodied. There is only a Shakespeare if and when we attend to performance, and we can only write about performance as an embodied phenomenon, as a conjunction of bodies, properties and words consumed in a bounded space by a particular audience. Stallybrass and

Jones have argued in strident tones for the primacy of this material embodiment of Shakespeare. Clothes, they say, 'are central to what is staged', and 'if we do not understand the clothes, we do not understand the action, or the actors, or the theater, or the social formation' and, therefore, we do not understand the play.[40]

So the early modern theatre was a uniquely important place for the working out of the meanings of material culture. It was a place where words and things could be brought together prominently, and the meanings of each challenged publicly. And the way this took place is partly common to all drama – the bringing to prominence of things and the questioning of their identity. But it is also partly unique to the period in which Shakespeare was writing. In medieval drama, objects had either been involved in the embodiment of biblical stories, particular to the characters and families of the Bible whose status as human beings was seen in typological terms, or they had been employed in morality plays whose protagonists were allegorical elements of the human psyche. Early modern drama, however, displayed individuals – unlike the morality plays which preceded it, it gave its audiences Hamlet instead of Indecision, Falstaff instead of Gluttony. The things it staged were therefore objects which related to particularized subjects, subjects whose complexity necessitated interrelation in dialogue with other characters to draw it out, introspection in soliloquy in order to represent it, and relationships with objects which played a role in both the isolation and interactions of characters. Particularized subjects desire, renounce or own private property.

# Personal possessions

Gold ring set with turquoise, sixteenth century, Victoria and Albert Museum.

This chapter explores in detail the way Shakespeare uses one particular kind of object. It is intended as a case study in reading a play outwards from a thing – in this case the turquoise ring which Shylock's daughter Jessica steals from him and exchanges for a monkey in *The Merchant of Venice*: 'It was my turquoise. I had it of Leah when I was a bachelor. I would not have given it for a wilderness of monkeys.' (112–14).

The ring in the picture above is, aesthetically, fairly understated and unassuming. The setting around the stone is relatively plain work, designed to resemble the gathers of a piece of fabric caught up on each side and falling softly around the stone. This does not seem to be an unusual design, as there are similar examples of such rings extant from the fifteenth century too – it may be a conventional way of presenting such a stone. Concentrated in the middle is the blue-green turquoise, the focal point in its unadorned simplicity. The design makes it very clear that this stone has an intrinsic value – it is set in gold in the form in which it was dug out of the ground; it is not reshaped, evened up or faceted in any way, as if the naturalness of its irregularity gives it credibility.

The turquoise was a stone which had, since medieval times, been credited with a range of extraordinary powers. It was 'a Medieval conviction that certain stones became intimately familiar with the personality of their owners; that when the wearer of a turquoise fell ill the stone would change color out of sympathy, and if the owner came into the presence of disease, danger, or poison...the stone would warn him by changing color or otherwise manifesting alarm.'[1] These meanings seem to have been current well into the early modern period, making the turquoise the most valued of the semi-precious stones. Its closeness to its wearer and its subtle sensitivity to mood, to the constitution of the body and to that body's wellbeing, linked owner and stone in the most complex way. The stone is set in this ring, then, not to display its owner's wealth or taste in aesthetic terms, but rather to display the owner him or herself – to allow it to speak as loudly as possible of the natural properties which permitted it to reflect back its wearer's state.

The specificity of Shylock's ring, the fact that he particularly identifies it as a turquoise, suggests that the audience bring their knowledge of how such objects function into play – it is a call upon their memories. We do not know what kind of jewellery was actually used on stage, and indeed Shylock's ring does not even make an appearance, but these props like any other came into being in the audience's imagination through the discourses with which they were surrounded. And the identification of the turquoise makes reference to other kinds of writing about jewellery. It is implicitly linked to a romance tradition, as 'responsive' rings were so vital to the way narrative romances made their meanings. In the retellings of medieval tales of chivalry central to the tradition, rings made appearances in a variety of guises: offering their wearers protection, given as tokens of recognition which reunite people after a space of time, and turning pale if a beloved was in trouble. For instance, in the early fourteenth-century English romance *Ywain and Gawain*, Ywain is given his ring by his new bride as he embarks on a year's leave of absence from the marriage in order to uphold his knightly reputation. If he fails to return within the year he will lose his lady, and the ring is given to protect him from illness, imprisonment or other impediments which may prevent him from coming back in time. Unfortunately, he forgets to return and goes mad as a result. The crucial point in this story is the double meaning of the ring's magic. As Helen Cooper puts it in her book on English romances, 'Ywain will be protected by two things: the ring itself and his love for his lady. The ring's operation is guaranteed only as long as he holds her in his mind.' This gives it a value solely in relation to emotion: 'The magic of the ring has served no plot function in itself, and we have never seen it in action; but its very existence serves to highlight something in Ywain, to tell us about the nature of his failure and the nature of knighthood.'[2] Standing outside the action, Ywain's ring provides a metaphor for his emotional state – it has an epitomizing quality.

So in this kind of narrative, rings offer a way of discussing the quality of a relationship: Cooper refers to the use of a ring 'as a means of defining the *emotional statement* that shapes the story' (my italics). Given the familiarity of such tales in early modern England, and the particular significance of turquoises in gem lore, these meanings are likely to have been alive in more or less ironic ways within *The Merchant of Venice*, and the specificity of the mention of the turquoise suggests a ring with a particularly communicative nature.

In *The Merchant of Venice*, Shylock's ring appears only briefly, described in his lines quoted above, in a scene of curious confusions brought about by various kinds of loss. Act 3 begins with the news heard on the Rialto that Antonio has lost a ship on the Goodwin Sands, worrying because it suggests the possibility that he might not be able to fulfil the terms of his bond. But a little further into the scene it transpires that other news about loss is also being exchanged abroad. When Shylock is asked by Solanio 'what news among the merchants?' (22), his reply is bitter: 'You knew, none so well, none so well as you, of my daughter's flight.' (23–4). The conversation between Christian and Jew weaves its insults in and out of these two losses of ship and daughter and culminates in Shylock's famous assertion of common humanity, 'Hath not a Jew eyes?...' And then, in one of those curious moments in Shakespeare where characters enter and others leave almost simultaneously, the stage turns from a confrontation between Venice's opposing ethnic groups, with Shylock, Solanio and Salerio exchanging taunts, to the compelling meeting between the two Jews, Shylock and Tubal. The news that is exchanged now is even more vague and insubstantial, coming to Shylock at least third hand: carrying on the theme of rumour and report, Tubal confirms that he has not, in fact, found the missing Jessica in Genoa: 'I often came where I did hear of her, but cannot find her' (76–7). Tubal has been speaking to people who have spoken to others – he has had conversations with sailors who escaped the wreck of Antonio's argosy on its way from Tripolis for instance – he has experienced the wake and the consequences of events rather than the events themselves. All this gives the news of Jessica's elopement a strong narrative quality – it arrives on the stage as a story told and retold by individuals who are not close to her; the style of her elopement has had an impact, it has been noticed; she has stepped very far outside the bounds of her life with her father and the intimacy of his ethnic group.

The source of the information about Shylock's ring is not often paid much attention, but in fact it considerably extends that sense of the randomness of stories about Jessica. As Tubal relates the tale, 'There came divers of Antonio's creditors in my company to Venice that swear he cannot choose but break,' and it is one of these who 'showed me a ring that he had of your daughter for a monkey' (110–11). The fact that Jessica has swapped the ring for a monkey with one of Antonio's creditors, on their way to Venice to call in debts just as she is making her escape in the opposite direction, makes a curious kind of connection between the ring and Antonio, and that connection mirrors in material form the way the two losses are linked in 3.1. Do the creditors also trade in monkeys, or were the monkeys their pets? In either case, there is something chancy about this exchange which sets it apart from Jessica's other purchases and profligacy. It has the air of a whim about it, and of a trade almost comically unequal in kind regardless of the relative values of jewellery and animals.

Just as the source of Tubal's knowledge of this exchange turns out to be curious when probed, so does Shylock's assertion of the ring's identity. Why does he assume it is his turquoise? Tubal merely tells him that he has been shown 'a ring that he had of your daughter' and, as Shylock himself has already made clear, a diamond is gone with those other 'precious, precious jewels'. It is possible, of course, to imagine that the diamond was unset, and that only one of those jewels was a ring. But we are not told this, and there is something about the raw emotion of the scene and the way Shylock's mind darts from one aspect of his loss to another that suggests that the turquoise is his assumption, an assumption provoked, then, by the ring's status as the most painful and most inappropriate exchange which he can imagine his daughter to have made for a monkey. His mind is drawn to the ring in a way suggestive of the magical properties of connection which the turquoise held.

The audience's reaction to the ring is inevitably conditioned by their attitude towards Shylock, and that response is built up as a series of contrasts. His language in the part of the scene which he shares with Tubal is totally different to the impressive and moving rhetoric of his earlier set-piece speech of racial identity. The first has a rhetorical polish, a rhythm and poise which lend it its striking dignity: 'Hath not a Jew eyes? Hath not a Jew hands, organs, dimensions, senses, affections, passions; fed with the same food, hurt with the same weapons, subject to the same diseases, healed by the same means, warmed and cooled by the same winter and summer as a Christian is? If you prick us, do we not bleed?' (55–60). This kind of language asks the audience to respond to the circumstances of a fellow human being with empathy. But alone with Tubal in the second part of the scene, Shylock takes on the discourse of a comic character, and this distances the audience from any emotional investment they might previously have made in his situation. The language here is repetitive both in word choice and in subject matter:

I would my daughter were dead at my foot and the jewels in her ear! Would she were hearsed at my foot, and the ducats in her coffin! No news of them? Why, so. And I know not what's spent in the search. Why thou, loss upon loss: the thief gone with so much, and so much to find the thief, and no satisfaction, no revenge, nor no ill luck stirring but what lights on my shoulders, no sighs but o' my breathing, no tears but o' my shedding.

(3.1.82–90)

Although this is not the kind of near breakdown of language suffered by Othello, for instance – it retains its rhetorical flourishes such as the repetition of 'no' in the final clauses – it still sounds like a kind of frenzy. The repeated confusion of jewels and daughter robs it of any sense of a noble disintegration and gives it instead the topsy turveyness of comedy. The speech is uncomfortably close to Solanio's clearly humorous description in Act 2 Scene 8 of the passion 'so confused,/So strange, outrageous, and so variable' which 'the dog Jew did utter in the streets':

> My daughter! O, my ducats! O, my daughter!
> Fled with a Christian! O, my Christian ducats!
> Justice! The law! My ducats and my daughter!
> A sealed bag, two sealed bags of ducats,
> Of double ducats, stol'n from me by my daughter!
> And jewels, two stones, two rich and precious stones,
> Stol'n by my daughter! Justice! Find the girl!
> She hath the stones upon her, and the ducats!
>
> (15–22)

Shylock's speech comes to seem an embodiment of this comically excessive language, and it threatens to fulfil Solanio's assessment of him.

When Tubal comes to the matter of Jessica's spending during her elopement, then, the audience have recently experienced both sides of Shylock – the sophisticated meditator upon the nature of racial difference and the stereotypical comic Jew. And it is that brief description of the ring which mediates between them, which saves Shylock from appearing to body forth stock phrases by connecting the rhetoric of humanity with a capacity for deep emotion. Although Shylock's language has already been excessive – he has shaped the hysterical fantasy of his daughter dead at his feet, hearsed in her coffin with his goods – in relation to the ring, if metaphorically and potentially comically, he talks of torture: 'Out upon her! Thou torturest me, Tubal.' The reference to torture is interestingly physical, a pain suggestive of the close connections between his body and the stolen ring. The ring actually wounds him, as though it was used by his daughter as a weapon against him. Brief as it is, its mention is crucial to the tension Shakespeare maintains between the stock comic Jew who rants of daughters and ducats and Shylock the individual, the man with a past.

'It was my turquoise. I had it of Leah when I was a bachelor. I would not have given it for a wilderness of monkeys' (112–14). These brief sentences have a curious power. Despite the simplicity of their language which lacks rhetorical flourish or the kind of explicit call to empathy which his earlier speech had, they have an impact beyond their size. Three short sentences, each simple statements and building one upon another, not a word is wasted. Unlike his earlier speech which addressed the condition of the Jewish race in general ('If you prick *us* do *we* not bleed'), here Shylock uses 'I' and 'my' throughout. This is, then, his personal as opposed to his racial history. The latter was tied up with the 'Jewish gabardine' upon which Antonio spits, the former is encapsulated in this single personal possession. The mention of Leah underlines his closeness to Tubal, to whom he does not need to explain her identity. But perhaps it is the wilderness which gives the speech its most distinctive character. Its primary meaning is 'A wild or uncultivated region or tract of land, uninhabited, or inhabited only by wild animals'; 'a tract of solitude and savageness' (*Oxford English Dictionary*), but as used here it also has the suggestion of a couple of other meanings: the biblical curse of Numbers 14 would not be out of place for a character well-versed in Old Testament stories: 'And your children shall wander in the wilderness forty years, and bear your whoredoms, until your carcasses be wasted in the wilderness' (v. 33). This is a place which threatens all the bonds of human community, where one might be lost in every sense of the word, cut off from one's ties to other human beings and to God.[3] One other meaning seems significant in this context – 'A mingled, confused, or vast assemblage or collection of persons or things': in this meaning the monkeys make the wilderness, it is a wilderness because of the confusing number of them; suiting Shylock's frenzy of different losses, too many things cause desolation.

These lines have struck critics and actors alike as especially, powerfully important. The actor Patrick Stewart, writing about his experience of playing Shylock, comments on the significance of the single word 'bachelor': 'That word shatters our image of this man Shylock and we see the man that once was, a bachelor, with all the association of youth, innocence and love that is to come. Shakespeare doesn't need to write a pre-history of Shylock. Those two lines say it all.' The lines have also in some cases produced a prop, as some productions have added a physical ring when Shylock leaves Jessica on her own in Act 2 Scene 5, 'thus making sure that the audience already know how important it is for him'.[4]

Rather than a price, the ring is given a history, and the power of this fleeting allusion comes from the way the history of the object points to, concretizes, the history of Shylock – his previous life of which we hear nothing else. The lines draw attention to themselves largely *because* of their simplicity. The unadorned plainness of the stone in the ring above has a verbal echo in them which sets it against the much more elaborate rings which were popular at the time, carved and enamelled in complex shapes or embellished with filigree-work for instance. It was a commonplace of early modern writing on rhetoric that the complexities of words worked in a similar way to the embellishments on clothing or the decoration on domestic furnishings. This ring draws attention to its message rather than the medium of that message. Similarly, Shylock's lines about his ring are powerful in a totally different way to his famous speech – through what is not said rather than through their facility with language; through the space which their simplicity leaves for imagining emotion.

The ring unsettles the dynamics between characters because it deals with a back-story, letting history briefly and powerfully intrude upon the present of the play's action; bringing in other periods, events and characters which all alter the way the individuals on the stage react to one another and the way the audience responds to them. Precise value, like the 2,000 ducats (or around £180,000) which Shylock's diamond cost when he bought it in Frankfurt, is replaced by history, by a provenance which explains its 'sentimental value'.[5] Perhaps that is too Victorian a term, because what Shylock shows us here is the powerful and close associations between people which objects make. It is not sentiment so much as connection – to use the terminology of this play, bond – the physical relationship between body and body which the supposed properties of turquoise make explicit, but which every object to a certain extent has the capacity to cement.

In a book about Shakespeare and mourning, Heather Dubrow argues that the stories told about objects in Shakespeare – the diamond ring that Innogen gives Posthumus that belonged to her dead mother; Othello's handkerchief which belonged to his wife – bestow on them 'the talismanic preciousness often associated with relics of the dead'. They foreground the way things make connections with the absent-presence of the deceased. She goes on to point out what that does to the notion of presence within the play, suggesting that Leah is present in the characters' thoughts, 'but absent from their quotidian world'.[6] These things insist upon material culture as an embodied form, one which connects bodies, one which speaks loudly about memory and grief as a desire for presence. The caskets from which Bassanio chooses, for instance, link him to Portia's dead father, making a material (literally tangible) connection between two men which brings to the fore the value system which we are to believe they both share. It is their mutual view of the relative merits of the material stuff of the caskets which allows the father to give his daughter to a son-in-law, choosing him remotely through the quality of his response. And Leah is present in the play only through the responses to her ring as Portia's father is through his caskets – they are characterized by their investments of affect and care in objects. Both of these objects belonging to the absent dead ask characters and audience alike to value the past within the present, as a way of achieving or predicting the future. Memories of the giver can, discussion of these things suggests, be kept freshly close as long as the things which mediate them stay within one's possession.

The ring, then, works to characterize Shylock indirectly – it is a key part of our sense of the complexity of his character. Unlike the taunts of the Christians which Shylock addresses in the previous section of the scene and in conversation with Antonio earlier in the play, the meanings of the ring are not explicitly explored – the bold, simple statements of its identity do not draw out its significance for the audience, and no one else mentions it. The sparseness of its description opens up a multitude of questions about his role as bachelor, husband, and father to a young child which we cannot, of course, answer. And these questions play quite strongly against what we actually see of this man in the rest of the play. The ring makes the insistent claim that its audience try to form a trajectory from the past to the present Shylock, one which explains the loss of love and comfort and the souring of the hope that love brings. Although it is not actually present on the stage, then, this one small object creates the kind of loose ends which fire audiences' imaginations and therefore create the illusion of mimetic characterization. Shylock's turquoise, true to type, appears to reflect back the complexities of its owner's emotional state.

But the ring, of course, has implications beyond its reflections of Shylock's identity. If we want fully to understand its power, then we need to consider in more detail how it fits within the play's discourses of value, of romance and of racial distinction. By doing so, we will be able to see more clearly how those discourses work. In the course of his discussion of his loss with Tubal, for instance, Shylock prices his loss of jewels in very different ways – at 'Two thousand ducats' as well as in the words discussed above. The most commonly remarked-upon aspect of the play's language is the tensions between Jewish and Christian attitudes towards money. We feel the contrast most strongly at the start of Act 1 Scene 3, as Shylock's bald economics – 'Three thousand ducats' – replace Bassanio's elaborate language of riches – 'In Belmont is a lady richly left./And she is fair'. It looks as though it ought to be possible to make a clear dividing line between a straightforward, utterly pragmatic but grubby view of the power of money, and the language of romance which mystifies such financial considerations and focuses instead upon the rich aesthetics which they produce. Belmont is, after all, an island theoretically separated both physically and conceptually from the mercantilism of the city's endless bargains and repeated mentions of cash. In the former location is based a romance plot about choosing a wife through the selection of caskets, and in the latter a brutal bargain for exactly one pound of flesh.

Such clear dichotomies do not, of course, stand too much inspection as many critics have pointed out. Karen Newman argues that both locations deal in exchange, as do the plots which they generate. 'Though venturing at Belmont is admittedly idealized' she says, 'what is important is the *structure* of exchange itself which characterizes both the economic transactions of Venice and the love relationships forged at Belmont.'[7] Rather than a dichotomy between romance and commercial language then, the play presents a common system of value differently interpreted and expressed. Peter Holland traces money and its definition between the two locations as a way of connecting them and their discourses: 'the idea of what constitutes a lavish sum moves from Venice to Belmont and back to Venice' he says, and in doing so it provides a coherent context within which value can be judged and compared. He brings all those mentions of ducats up to date, so that we can hear their relative values more clearly: 'Antonio is borrowing a sum of about £270,000 to lend to Bassanio. Shylock refuses a repayment of £540,000; Portia offers extraordinary sums worth between £3.25 million and £5.4 million; Shylock's diamond cost about £180,000 and in one night at Genoa Jessica spent well over £7,200 on dinner.'[8] This alters our view of the characters involved and their actions: 'Portia's huge wealth does not therefore become a fairy-tale sum,' she is extremely wealthy, but not in ways which make her intervention in Venetian economics magical, in ways that mystify it – rather, she is a part of a consistent economics which stretches across the two locations and *should*, therefore, have been able to prevail in the courtroom.

Nevertheless, it does not – huge differences remain in the way characters respond to the value of money and the things it buys, and it is those differences which send the play spiralling down towards tragedy. The ring is caught up in terms which have a double meaning. One of Shylock's repetitions as he discusses the loss of his jewels runs thus: 'The curse never fell upon our nation till now; I never felt it till now: two thousand ducats in that; and other precious, precious jewels.' The double 'preciousness' of the jewels is partly, but not entirely, contained by the identification of the sum which they were worth. The repetition draws attention to the word and in doing so opens up the possibility that it is meant here as a way of exceeding the earlier value given – of gesturing towards a more emotive worth which is then clarified by the history given to the turquoise. Whether this interpretation characterizes Shylock or just opens up meaning for an audience (whether we hear it as intentional), it is these polyvalent words that draw attention to the different and to an extent conflicting notions of value that generate the play's productive and edgy tensions.

Historian Craig Muldrew's work on the social function of economic structures in early modern England is key to our understanding of the intersection of these discourses. He sees the meanings of wealth as drawing intricate and subtle connections between money and personal qualities. He maintains, for instance, that economic theory is 'insufficient' to understand 'the complex way in which the value of gold, gender and marriage are related within a modern market economy'. He advocates a more holistic approach to the question of value, stating that 'Today, the value of capital held in banks or as bank money is simply based on its buying power in terms of price, which is commonly thought of as being quite different from the way most people value love, friendship or compassion. But in early modern England it was impossible to make such a conceptual divide.' Central to this wider interpretation of worth is the kind of trust which formed between individuals in close relationships: 'reputation for honesty became a type of cultural currency which had an enormous value in terms of social estimation'.[9] And built upon such social estimation was a sense of credit-worthiness which facilitated almost all aspects of early modern life. This is Antonio's 'credit' which Bassanio is to try in Venice (1.1.180), for money which he will have 'of my trust or for my sake' (185). So reputation is a currency in an analogous way to the function of ducats as a medium of exchange, but that means that there is no easy contrast between a pure discourse of love and a sordid discourse of mercantilism – the two are perpetually interdependent. This interdependence is hard to analyse because it is implicit – it means that reckonings are made on subjective and unspoken understandings of individual reputations and connections, part of a concept of the 'common fame' of a person's character which is by its aggregative and memorial nature hard to pin down. In theatrical terms, it makes the relationship between characterization and interaction with different systems of value crucial to the representation of society. And objects, as we have seen, help to clarify such issues, offering a way of locating attitudes and understanding responses.

These different systems of value are, of course, central to the play's representation of the relationships between racial groups. Shylock's careful spelling out of the economic value of money is a sharp contrast with the Venetian tendency to talk a rather euphemistic language of materiality, of the things which money buys rather than the sums for which such things are purchased. This is set up in the opening scene, focused around the discussion of Antonio's melancholy: first he himself queries its source by asking 'What stuff [material]' tis made of' (1.1.4), then Salerio talks of Antonio's argosies' 'woven wings' (1.1.14) and imagines him imagining one 'scatter all her spices on the stream,/Enrobe the roaring waters with my silks' (33–4). Within the first 30 or so lines of the play money is dressed, through a series of elegant metaphorical elaborations, in the rich objects of mercantile trade. And it is this kind of language which is developed in Bassanio's request, not for money but rather for 'the means/To hold a rival place' with Portia's wooers. Antonio in turn offers to 'furnish' him to Belmont, meaning to equip him in a way suitable to such an enterprise, through the necessary material things. In the scene in which Shylock describes his ring, the Venetians cast everything in relentlessly material terms from Antonio's ship 'of rich lading' in the Goodwin Sands where 'the carcasses of many a tall ship lie buried' to the figure of the gossip, imagined in the action of knapping (biting or snapping at) ginger (3–9). 'I for my part knew the tailor that made the wings she flew withal' (26) says Salerio to Shylock, metaphorically exploring the technicalities of the escape through processes of manufacture, and then later, 'There is more difference between thy flesh and hers than between jet and ivory' (35–6).

For Shylock too, although negatively, the definition of Jewish attitudes towards money is made through his use of material display. His frugality with his personal money is shown most clearly in his household, and it is contrasted against the Venetians' profligacy. Lancelot says he is 'famished in his service. You may tell every finger I have with my ribs' (2.2.100–1), and Shylock's own assertion to him that 'thou shalt see ... | The difference of old Shylock and Bassanio... Thou shalt not gormandize | As thou hast done with me... | And sleep and snore and rend apparel out' (2.5.1–5) is to be taken comically. Shylock's domestic economy is, indeed, largely explained in relation to Lancelot's change of households. In 2.2, the servant quibbled on the 'old proverb' in relation to his old and new masters, saying to Bassanio that it was 'very well parted between my master Shylock and you, sir: you have the grace of God, sir, and he hath enough' (144–6), and Bassanio himself wonders why Lancelot will 'leave a rich Jew's service to become/ The follower of so poor a gentleman' (142–3). Nevertheless, it is Bassanio who is offering 'rare new liveries' (2.2.103–4) – Bassanio who feels the imperative need to display wealth through material culture in a way that can be read by all instantly. At some stage after 2.2 Lancelot must enter in a rare new livery, in his case one 'More guarded than his fellows' (2.2.150), more elaborately edged and trimmed, and the contrast between his two costumes and the way Shylock is dressed will give just the kind of visual cues of racial difference to an audience that Bassanio appreciates work so effectively in the fictive world of *Merchant*'s Venice.

The controlling discourse of Shylock's sense of the difference between racial attitudes towards materiality is that of the appetites: there is, for instance, his unpleasant assertion that he will go to Bassanio's house 'in hate, to feed upon/The prodigal Christian' (2.5.14–5). Christian feasting and hospitality are set against Old Testament notions of racial segregation. Jessica's discussion of the distinctions between Jewish and Venetian domestic life suggests a kind of soberness in her assertion to Lancelot that 'Our house is hell, and thou, a merry devil,/Didst rob it of some taste of tediousness' (2.3.2–3). Her choice of the word 'taste' draws attention to appetite and takes us back to Lancelot's accusation of insufficient food in the previous scene, and that phrase is immediately contrasted with Lancelot's new master's house at which there is to be supper. That lack of mirth might be a racial characteristic, but it could equally well be a personal one, a result of individual sadness. It might augment, in other words, our sense either of Shylock the Jew or Shylock Leah's widower.

The appetite for materiality which Shylock sees as an almost bestial craving is also made clear in the scene of Jessica's escape. In 2.5 her father tells her to

> Lock up my doors; and when you hear the drum
> And the vile squealing of the wry-necked fife,
> Clamber not you up to the casements then,
> Nor thrust your head into the public street
> To gaze on Christian fools with varnished faces,
> But stop my house's ears – I mean my casements.
> Let not the sound of shallow fopp'ry enter
> My sober house.
>
> (29–36)

Shylock's wish to keep out the noise of festivity takes material form in the use of doors and casements to draw a firm boundary between Jewish and Christian space and therefore a distinction between their modes of expression. Shylock's Jewishness begins to sound faintly like

Puritanism – like Malvolio's aversion to feasting and to the indecorous excesses of merriment. The verbs Shylock uses about Jessica's potential engagement with Christian masquing – 'clamber', 'thrust', 'gaze' – suggest eagerness, almost desperation to see, and then the long looking which in other places Shakespeare describes as feeding the sight.[10]

So how does Shylock's ring fit into these racially distinctive views of materiality? Usury is cast as the guiding principle of Jewish attitudes in the play, of course, but such an object calls attention to the tensions between attitudes to money and attitudes to things. If Jews were considered to belong to no country and if their social condition was therefore seen as one of 'wandering', then objects must both make wealth portable and preserve a crucial sense of dynastic identity which counteracts geographical mobility: both wealth and identity are at points kept close in the form of things.[11] Valuable possessions, rather than the flows of financial fluidity, might be central to Jewishness, and this is a crucial material context for Shylock's ring, a further suggestion of the nature of its closeness to his person. This one thing, then, weighs against the entirely pejorative language of usury.

Objects are more plentiful in Venetian discourses, and they are bought and consumed much more regularly, but they do not by and large endure. Venetian attitudes towards precious metals show theirs to be a generalized culture of consumption. They exhibit no sense of a separation between objects and money, both of which are used up in a constant stream. These discourses lend an edge to the play's racial oppositions, introducing two notions familiar from English attitudes towards Italian materiality outside the play: youthful exuberance and the wonder of pageantry and urban display vie against the immoral material over-indulgence of foreigners with their foppish attitude towards dress and accessories. Both notions come into being around *Merchant*'s central objects.

It is across this divide in the meanings of things which Jessica steps when she leaves her father's house at night with a casket containing the ring. Her conversion from Judaism to Christianity is figured in the play as a translation from one economic mode to another – theoretically from usury to provisioning for friendship but, as the stories we hear show it, more clearly from thrift to consumption. Literary critic Bruce Boehrer points out that 'Her betrayal of her father is very largely an economic one, an engagement with patterns of fiscal behavior to which Shylock is inveterately opposed and which align Jessica at once with the play's "prodigal" Christians.' Her spending habits, then, most clearly demonstrate her own sense of her conversion. The relative values which Peter Holland works out for the play's different sums make it very clear that Jessica's £7,200 on a night in Genoa is on a similar scale to Bassanio's loan of £270,000 for furnishing forth to Belmont, and that both have that essential sense of frippery, of both conspicuous consumption and of ephemerality, of a show which will not endure. Boehrer goes on to argue for the metaphorical significance of the monkey to our understanding of this difference: 'rare and expensive, exotic and difficult to obtain, and valuable not for its ability to perform useful household labor but rather for its participation in a logic of pet-ownership that presupposes and even esteems nonproductivity'.[12] The distinction between the ring and the monkey, in other words, is crucial to our understanding of the contrast between Jewishness and Christianness in the play, and their two different kinds of material engagement. It was linked, for a contemporary audience, to the morality of excessive decoration explored in the introduction above, and to the distinctions between goods 'arguably essential for a civilized life', and those that might be 'clean spared'.

And if the ring and its history are disruptive in the sense that they unsettle what we think we know about Shylock the moneylender, then they also intrude uncomfortably into our assessment of his daughter Jessica, disturbing her place within the festive celebrations of marriage in the latter part of the play, nagging at the audience's wish to read her in positive terms in line with the movement of the drama to comic resolution. She must, we must assume, have known its meaning, and that makes it impossible to interpret her deed as anything other than heartlessly cruel and intended to be enormously destructive of family ties. But with no discussion of her action at all, it comes to look both casual and calculated at the same time; at best the deed of a person ignorant of anything but the moment. If Shylock's description of the ring is the cornerstone of our sense of his emotional life, his capacity both to experience love and to be wounded by it, the subjective embodiment of his rhetorical assertions of Jewish humanity, then surely our experience of his pain reflects negatively upon our understanding of Jessica as a character? Rather than accusing her directly, however, Shylock's statement haunts our image of her. The more human it makes him the more it raises questions about her humanity which sour the play's celebration of her 'salvation'. Reading the play from the ring outwards means giving the characterization of her that a material object offers equal weight to the rather bland speeches that she herself is given in the play.

Looking at how the ring is placed within the play's discourses of materiality helps us to understand its value as an object, and seeing how it operates within the emotional dynamics of the drama makes it possible to explore how small things can stand as metaphors, as epitomes of or focal points for the kind of undermining uncertainties of emotion and meaning which Shakespeare's dramas so skilfully bring into play.

In order to understand Shylock's ring fully we also, of course, have to see how it is related to the play's other prominent objects – Portia's and Nerissa's rings. These rings sit rather differently from Shylock's within the shape of the play as a whole. They form the zenith of the romance plot of the three caskets, concluding and sealing the successful choice of casket, but then providing the material for the potential unravelling of the marriages, and therefore the play's development towards a comic conclusion in marriage, as they are given away. The rings first appear at the head of the celebrations which follow a series of scenes which address different value systems. We initially hear of the casket plot when we see Portia and Nerissa for the first time in 1.2; it develops through 2.1 as we meet Morocco, and then offers its three vignettes of choice in 2.7, 2.9 and 3.2. In the first, Morocco chooses the gold casket, in the second Aragon selects the silver one, and in the third, of course, Bassanio chooses the lead one containing Portia's picture. In this trio of scenes questions of value and its relation to objects are addressed explicitly, and together they stage the conflict between the opposed value systems of urban elites and questing romance lovers. Morocco's view is a hyper-masculine one, and his discourse is suggestive of a chivalric ideal of praising a woman by relating her to goods of the greatest price. 'Is't like that lead contains her?'Twere damnation/To think so base a thought. It were too gross/To rib her cerecloth in the obscure grave.' (2.7.49). His assessment soars above the base and gross. Aragon's brand of masculine hazard desires to separate itself from the multitude and thereby to show itself as uniquely worthy: 'I will not choose what many men desire,/Because I will not jump with common spirits/And rank me with the barbarous multitudes.' Less interested in what might represent Portia than how they might represent themselves – which choice would be fitting for princes adverse to obscurity and the common view – they both lose the contest. In the way in which *Merchant* links objects of the same kind to one another, these caskets appear together for the last time in the scene after Jessica throws her father's, with the ring in it, from his window – all four pleading some kind of judgement of worth.

The more worldly, less aristocratic (although still elite) Bassanio muses to himself before the caskets in strikingly different terms. His speech examines the connections between precious metals and coins in order to build a different system of value to his rivals': 'Therefore, thou gaudy gold, /Hard food for Midas, I will none of thee' he states, and then of silver, 'Nor none of thee, thou pale and common drudge/ 'Tween man and man.' But this section of the play produces a kind of disconnect between material discourses and characterization: Bassanio's opening lines are most disturbing: 'So may the outward shows be least themselves,' he says, contrasting inner with outer, and yet, 'The world is still deceived with ornament' (3.2.73–4). 'Thus', he concludes, 'ornament is but the guiled shore/To a most dangerous sea' (97). This homily on the deceits of ornament sits rather uncomfortably with Bassanio's attitude to material culture in the rest of the play – it is a moralizing language of renunciation which is in many ways closest to Shylock's, although much more warm-spirited. It connects back problematically to Bassanio's actions, for instance to his own assertion that Lancelot should have a new livery 'more guarded than his fellows', and it picks up on other characters' views, for instance Jessica's suggestion that she 'make fast the doors, and gild myself/With some more ducats' (2.6.49–50). Bassanio's rejection of ornament seems rather to call for an understated aesthetic like that of the ring with which this chapter began. Such a switch from Venetian investment in the materials of display to the renunciation of the appealing aesthetics of exteriors which he preaches in front of the caskets is tricky to reconcile – it perhaps pushes the limits of the audience's investment in the transformative power of love too far.

Literary critic Steve Patterson argues that the play does not 'allow for a complete mystification of [Bassanio's] turn to romance'. Rather, his 'facility with rhetorical flourishes and with suiting behavior to the needs of the moment undermines an audience's ability to completely invest in the romantic fantasy orchestrated at Belmont'.[13] It is not quite clear, in other words, how the different discourses which surround Portia's ring fit together – there seems to be some conflict between them. The moments of theatrical triumphalism to which Bassanio's correct choice belongs and on which comedy thrives are often undercut by the quiet yet persistent presence of objects which call attention to such clashes of meaning.

This is the context within which Portia gives her ring then – the cumulative discourses of ways of relating the value of a human being to the value of objects and their constituent materials. And the actual form in which she bestows it is equally significant. Portia counters her new husband's careful assessment of value with the language of excess: 'Though for myself alone/I would not be ambitious in my wish/To wish myself much better', she says, 'yet for you/I would be trebled twenty times myself,/A thousand times more fair, ten thousand times more rich/That only to stand high in your account/I might in virtues, beauties, livings, friends/Exceed account.' (3.2.150). Her giving of herself is as infinite as Antonio's, as total and all-encompassing, and like his it is a part of a romance language which refuses to make social qualifications. Nevertheless, just as Antonio's 'extremest means' (1.1.138) are in the end translated into something more palpable – Shylock's bond for Bassanio – so Portia's greatest imaginings and her still impressive self are given to him in the form of the ring. She 'converts' herself and all she has, 'This house, these servants, and this same myself' into it. 'I give them with this ring' she says, mimicking not only the words of the marriage service, which make the gift part of a formal contract of matrimony, but also the style of an early modern deed of gift in which one object was often given as a part which came to symbolize the whole of property. The ring, in other words, comes to stand for both her body and her material goods.

But it also manages the audience's imagination of her wealth – we do not see the 'fair mansion' of which she 'was the lord'; we see only representatives of its domestic routines and servants, its bounty and hospitality. The ring must come to stand for what theatre cannot show, it must deliver fantastic wealth in microcosm and in doing so stimulate the audience's imagination. It does so not as a consequence of its material qualities (it is too small for an audience to see in detail, whatever the prop actually looked like), but rather as a function of its narrative position. In the interplay between the small ring and the huge fortune; between the object of lesser value (as Bassanio asserts when he offers to buy 'Balthasar' a more expensive one) and the peerless Portia, who has caused princes to leave their kingdoms to hazard all for her, a material object can be seen to stand as a metonymic piece of the whole.

Portia is also explicit about the ring's role in binding the couple together. Having woven her gifts into its material form, she continues, 'Which when you part from, lose, or give away,/Let it presage the ruin of your love,/And be my vantage to exclaim on you' (171–2). Although it obviously has the whiff of prophecy about it, at this stage in the play the powerful equation of the ring with a contract of love ties it most clearly to Shylock's ring, and to that similar moment which we have perhaps imagined which translates singleness into doubleness – the Jew's bachelorhood into marriage. Bassanio's response also echoes Shylock's. The metaphor he chooses in his reply to Portia seeks to express the settling of his many thoughts and emotions through an analogy to a diverse audience who respond individually but with one accord. It is one of like things: 'Where every something being blent together/Turns to a wild of nothing save of joy.' A 'wild' of joy – in its now unusual nominal use as a 'wild or waste place; a region or tract of uncultivated and uninhabited land; a waste, a wilderness',[14] it is of course close to Shylock's identification of the wilderness of monkeys – the place made wild by so many of the same things. Bassanio's response to the gift of his ring reworks in comic mode Shylock's reaction to the loss of his. At stake in the connection between these two rings is an echo of past practices which insists on a common ground amongst racial difference, just before Bassanio receives the letter which asserts Shylock's fundamental inhumanity: 'A *creature* that did bear the shape of man' (3.2.273).

Bassanio's reply to the ring also stresses the way that objects simultaneously produce and channel excess. There was, he says, 'such confusion in my powers/As after some oration fairly spoke/By a belovèd prince there doth appear/Among the buzzing pleasèd multitude'. He is initially struck dumb, bereft 'of all words'. Having offered his simile, however, he continues, 'But when this ring/Parts from this finger, then parts life from hence', a sentence in which 'but' means *despite* the wild of joy. It is the ring, in other words, which organizes his thoughts and brings him down to earth, as Olivia's gift of a pearl to Sebastian does in *Twelfth Night*. The sentence actually suggests a range of gestures: if Portia has not already put the ring on his finger, then Bassanio must do so at this point, and if she has then he clearly gestures towards it here and, we might imagine, moves his other hand from the ring, up the vein which was thought to run from that finger straight into the heart on 'then parts life from hence'. The ring, in other words, organizes Bassanio's thoughts sufficiently to make it possible to move from the statement of his momentarily overwhelmed condition to a more appropriate response in a vow of his own – Portia's ring (self, wealth and house) for his faith and truth (he has, after all, little else to offer). Shylock's ring focused his losses into one palpable thing which could represent his response fully; Bassanio's, if rhetorically, organizes confusion into a way forward. Both objects provide a stopping point to the energies of the emotional escalation of the scene, a pause for reflection: they take on the quality of a boundary which encloses the spaces of excessive emotion.

Objects, then, control emotions, and they can offer a space for working things out around which it is possible for many different narratives to cluster. Rings have an important social role in signalling and mitigating difference of course, because their function is to bind two disparate beings together into the one body of marriage: their empty centre negotiates distinction and brings two parties into an intimate relationship. Like Desdemona's handkerchief in *Othello*, the rings in *Merchant* are capable of holding different and often conflicting stories, meanings and discourses of value in relation to one another. The powerful tales told about the handkerchief in *Othello* do not add up – they conflict with one another in ways which demonstrate the differences between characters: their outlooks, value systems, priorities, assumptions, even mental states. The discontinuities between these stories are given meaning, in other words, by their common focus on the same object. And such a process gives that object a prominent status within the play. The difference in *Merchant*, of course, is the connections the play draws between similar objects and the meaning it derives from their different narrative status. The three rings in the play and the four caskets achieve a different kind of prominence to *Othello*'s single handkerchief. As a group they ask to be read in relation to one another, but they also draw attention to the fact that the rings in particular attract different levels of narrative attention: Shylock's ring has just that one brief mention, whereas Portia's and Nerissa's are endlessly and explicitly discussed. The late seventeenth-century literary critic Thomas Rymer's famously damning assessment of *Othello*, 'So much ado, so much stress, so much passion and repetition about an Handker-chief,'[15] is a well-celebrated response to this kind of over-determined meaning which things attract. But his sense of perspective, and the notion of things as the hub around which stories and actions congre-gate, is much more widely applicable. Writing a chapter in this form, as an analysis which grows out from an object central to the narrative, is replicating in more positive terms Rymer's sense of the work things do in Shakespeare's plays.

But objects reveal those questions of value most clearly when they move – they bring all the elements explored above into particular focus. They move from one place to another, on the fluid early modern stage which can become Belmont or Venice between an exit and an entrance. And as they move, so attention is drawn to them – characters become suddenly, explicitly aware of their worth, and as a result the value systems which underpin their meaning are revealed to the audience. At this point objects often become a focus of crisis. Shylock's ring left Venice for Genoa and in doing so entered an uncontrollable and riotous kind of economics, and Portia's ring leaves the miraculous and shining world of Belmont for the extended exchange networks of Venice, which are altogether less controllable. It is through these shared things that we are forced to examine similarity and difference.

Objects connect scenes together visually – in the present of the drama's action. Steve Patterson's sensitive reading of the trial scene in 4.1 imagines the impact of Antonio's and Bassanio's words within the stage space: 'the proclamation of devotion between Shakespeare's two men . . . is set against the comic presence of disguised wives, so that the amorous vows ring more of betrayal than loyalty. These friends seem histrionic and loose-tongued . . . The females standing by seem cheated, not invited into some endlessly generous circle of amity'.[16] And we can add to this clash between the plot of homosocial friendship and the triumph of Bassanio's heterosexual success at Belmont the physical presence of Portia's ring, attention drawn to it on his finger as he tells Antonio 'I am married to a wife/Which is as dear to me as life itself,/But life itself, my wife, and all the world/Are not with me esteemed above thy life' (4.1.279–82). The ring physically puts Bassanio's two pledges of his life ('I would lose all, ay, sacrifice them all . . . to deliver you'; 'when this ring/Parts from this finger, then parts life from hence') up against one another. The constancy of the ring's shape and the durability of its material challenge and are challenged by the doubleness of Bassanio's commitments. This is cheap and uncomfortable. In contrast, the audience must be increasingly prepared to read Shylock's turquoise as representing a true sentiment, contrasted as it is against the damaged unconditionality of the play's other rings. To entertain such a thought during the trial scene is simultaneously to appreciate and to dread Shylock's absolute and inflexible purpose. The presence of this ring in contrast to the absence of Shylock's is deeply troubling to the audience's sense of the play's governing morality.

It is that ring of Portia's which moves most frequently in the crucial closing stages of the play, as *Merchant* drives towards its comic resolution. The final phase of its meanings begins in the emotional high of the aftermath of the trial scene, as Bassanio speaks to Balthasar in the elaborate terms of politeness to near-strangers of similar status:

> Dear sir, of force I must attempt you further.
> Take some remembrance of us as a tribute,
> Not as fee. Grant me two things, I pray you:
> Not to deny me, and to pardon me.
>
> (4.1.418–21).

The token he offers is a 'remembrance', meaning a thing whose physical presence brings to mind an absence, so here again the ring links two situations, past and present, and two bodies, present and absent. But wearing another's ring means touching the thing which they have touched, and Portia's response to Bassanio's reaction is telling: 'I'll take this ring from you./Do not draw back your hand.

I'll take no more,/And you in love shall not deny me this.' This is very suggestive of the potentially troubling physicality of the gift, as well as the reluctance of its giver. The closeness of the exchange is underlined in her response to his recoil, with the nearness of the parties to one another: a curious combination of physical intimacy and social distance. The awkwardness of the situation points up the potentially illicit transfer of such an intimate object as a ring.

The exchange of personal objects, then, is always potentially risky in social terms as it enables them to make illegitimate intimacies. Bassanio is eventually persuaded to give Balthasar the ring by Antonio: 'Let his [the doctor's] deservings and my love withal/Be valued 'gainst your wife's commandement' (447–8). The meanings of Portia's ring are suddenly altered from a gift from wife to husband to a gift from one man to another at the instigation of a third man. Love for Antonio is again here explicitly set against Bassanio's betrothal, in a speech which must take away some of Portia's triumph at winning the ring. Back in Belmont, it is again Antonio who finally brings the ring to rest, declaring that he 'dare be bound again,/My soul upon the forfeit, that your lord/Will never more break faith advisedly.' Calling him Bassanio's 'surety', Portia gives it to Antonio who duly gives it to Bassanio: 'Here, Lord Bassanio, swear to keep this ring' (256). Rings, intended to be given to seal the intimate contracts between two – worn to advertise the unavailability of the unique receiver – are suddenly moved around by a third party.

Steve Patterson argues for an essential similarity between Shylock and Antonio. Pointing out that they are the 'two characters who believe deeply in values outside the marketplace,' he suggests that they 'have no place in Venice'. And it is the ring which he points to as proof: 'Shylock's relationship to money is, like Antonio's, not reducible to self-interest, as becomes evident when the Jew bemoans the loss of Leah's priceless ring.'[17] The rings link Antonio to Portia and Shylock, across the play's widest chasm of meanings. It is Antonio's love which ties them together, and both touch him in the sense that they connect with the narrative of his bond, but they do not do so directly, physically, and that sense of his complex involvement with Portia's ring, but his distance from the processes of wiving and thriving, delineates the isolation in which many productions of the play leave him. Although they circulate amongst wider discourses, in the end rings are material surrogates for caresses and physical intimacies.

Because of a ring's close connections to the body, its material movements also have a moral dimension. Portia's accusatory speech to Bassanio on the 'knowledge' of his illicit gift speaks a distinctive language:

> If you had known the virtue of the ring,
> Or half her worthiness that gave the ring,
> Or your own honour to contain the ring,
> You would not then have parted with the ring.

'Virtue', 'worthiness' and 'honour' are the language of reputation – crucial as we have seen to the construction of credit, but also essential to female sexual fidelity. Containing the ring means keeping it between the couple for whom it originally had meaning, accruing honour by ensuring it does not pass beyond the intimacies of giver and receiver. This discourse of female virtue and male honour is linked to the inalienability of personal property and the intimacy of the wearing of rings. It is the negative side of Portia's explicit gift of both property and body with the object in the first place; it flirts with the possibility of adultery by using a material substitute. Following the connections a ring makes between expected and unexpected people shows how dangerously open *Merchant*'s ending is, how compromised its smooth path of marriage.

It is at their points of exchange that *Merchant*'s rings are explicitly held up for evaluation, their values sharpened as attention is concentrated upon them. The final discussion of value in the play, Graziano and Nerissa's dialogue at the gates of the Belmont house, is instructive. He says that they are arguing 'About a hoop of gold, a paltry ring/ That she did give me'. The paltriness of the ring, its insignificance and worthlessness, appears to lie in the posy which is written upon it: 'For all the world like cutlers' poetry/Upon a knife – "Love me and leave me not"'. This ring is not, in other words, an elite object of aesthetic value. It is a common-or-garden love token of just the kind with which this book began, and one which mirrors the more expensive version given by Nerissa's mistress in a typical comic plot/subplot way. Nerissa, however, is not lured into argument on these grounds and lets the matter of its abused message lie: 'What talk you of the posy or the value?/You swore to me when I did give it you/That you would wear it till your hour of death,/And that it should lie with you in your grave.' The posy may have been couched in the language of cutlers, but the sentiment – the vow which accompanied its giving – means that it was, as Portia puts it, 'stuck on with oaths upon your finger' and 'riveted with faith unto your flesh', immoveable as the love it is to signify. Nerissa's and Graziano's very different perspectives on the same object worry at the extent to which sign and signifier are linked to one another; the way that material and affective qualities might or might not map onto one another. Undoing Thomas Rymer's identification of a 'fetish-like' obsession with objects (in his case the handkerchief) as an end in themselves, the play's last dialogue on value moves away from the material obsessions of a tragic investment of emotion in tokens.

And with this argument, *The Merchant of Venice* finally gives up its quest for the meaning of objects in favour of a more explicit comedy. Extending its consideration of the rings past the point of productive investigation of value, it comes out the other side into farce. Although the characters lose interest in their capacity to signify, they increase their verbal focus on them. Mentions of Portia's ring chime through the closing speeches in a comic sequence reminiscent of Shylock's litany of grief. Bassanio implores:

> Sweet Portia
> If you did know to whom I gave the ring,
> If you did know for whom I gave the ring,
> And would conceive for what I gave the ring,
> And how unwillingly I left the ring
> When naught would be accepted but the ring,
> You would abate the strength of your displeasure.

(192–8)

The ring rings out – comedy of repetition lightens the mood around the pain of loss here by resisting emotional engagement, as it perhaps did for the early modern audience's appreciation of Shylock's torture, producing, uncomfortably for us, slightly relieved laughter? Here, the balance is clearly in favour of the comic as the situation was a counterfeit one of a bogus exchange, but the final movement of the play still sounds troublingly like a diversion tactic: laughter is the only way forward which avoids outright conflict, and all this serious talk of rings turns, eventually, into a joke. It is down to Graziano, as usual, to reduce this complex relationship between women, men and objects to its basest possible level in the play's closing couplet by alluding to his husbandly protection of his wife's genitals: 'Well, while I live I'll fear no other thing/So sore as keeping safe Nerissa's ring' (306–7). Nevertheless, paradoxically, the comically obsessive verbal focus on the ring does bring into play its troubled trajectories. Every one of the marriages which wrap up *Merchant*'s concerns is in some way compromised by the illegitimate exchange of rings. It is rings, in other words, starting with Shylock's, which draw into themselves, which focus, all the uncertainly comic moments of this play from Jessica's compromised character, to her and her new husband's rehearsal of failed loves in 5.1, to the threat to Antonio's life and his exclusion from the concluding couplings.

By the end of the play then, the ring has been emptied out of its more serious meanings and has become a comic no-thing, part of a pretty bad joke. Its changing status points up the different timescales of words and things in plays – while the things remain constant in their material form, their meanings shift in and out of different webs of discourse and through the shades of different generic emphases. And those emphases also cohere in a variety of ways around different types of thing. Maybe the distinction between handkerchiefs as objects associated with the practices of personal hygiene (however socially significant) and rings as signifiers of eternal contracts was behind Rymer's disgust at the prominence of Desdemona's lost possession in *Othello*. Rings have their own lore and their own significance in other kinds of narrative – they come into plays bearing a greater heritage of story than many other things, and that is one of the reasons why they are such useful comic properties. On the enduring, precious circularity of *Merchant*'s rings rests the emotional life of her characters.

# Dressing and cross-dressing

Cutwork and needle lace border, Italy, 1600–20, Victoria and Albert Museum.

Costumes were the early modern theatre's most valuable asset. In contemporary terms, they were worth more than the theatres in which plays were staged, and companies often paid more to tailors to dress their actors than they did to playwrights to write their texts. In a particularly excessive case in 1598, George Chapman was paid a maximum of £6 for a play called *The Fountain of New Fashions*.

Theatre historian Jean MacIntyre argues that costuming the play may, however, have cost as much as £60, expenditure including 'a Riche cloak' bought for an incredible £19, and a 'jerkin of velvet laid with broad . . . silver lace'.[1] If these figures are right then these costumes, admittedly ones intended to stage a visual encounter with the variety and curiousness of contemporary fashions, necessitated investment at the rate of ten times the cost of the play itself.

Such huge sums make it clear that this was a theatre of spectacle. Whilst it did not use elaborate sets and scenery, the display of sumptuous fabrics, ornate trimmings and diverse designs in clothing was clearly an important part of its appeal to the audience. But the detail in which these purchases are recorded suggests something more. It connects to the discourses of the sumptuary legislation discussed in the Introduction above, and in doing so it indicates that the spectacle of staged fashion was not a homogeneous one, but one through which audiences could distinguish between different characters' status.

So this chapter is about the many ways in which drama uses clothing to make distinctions and connections between the characters who constitute the play. Looking at Shakespeare's theatre from this material angle gives a very different perspective on his work to a more text-based approach. Jean MacIntyre argues, for instance, that 'the number of characters a small company could play was limited not so much by how many belonged to it as by how many costumes it owned',[2] as character was defined by the actor's costume rather than his body. Peter Stallybrass and Ann Rosalind Jones have suggested that 'the commercial theater was crucially shaped by the market in clothes. Or, to put it another way, the theater was a new and spectacular development of the clothing trade.'[3] They put the clothing first, then, and see the theatre as developing out of the opportunities which the circulation of dress in early modern London offered.

This chapter begins with a piece of lace. Or rather a part of a decorative border made up of two different kinds of lace. The deep band along the top is made of cutwork – the earliest form of needle lace, it was worked on a piece of cloth (usually linen) from which sections were cut away and the remaining threads bound together with fine stitches. The incredibly delicate structures of elaborate patterns grew from the places where the cloth was removed, leaving only traces of the warp and weft structure of the original fabric which held the lace together. But below the top border grows an even finer form, the 'punto in aria', or 'stitches in the air', which were worked without the support of a linen base and took their own form as a kind of fabric in their own right. The band retains the geometric outline of the linen warp and weft on which it is grounded, whilst the points of the edge break free into more organic and daring shapes. It is the balance between the stitched areas and the spaces in between which gives lace its unique aesthetic superiority; the apparent fragility of its delicate design suggests the refinement and gentility of its wearer. And the finer and more complex this balance between fabric and space, the more time and skill can be seen to have been invested in its manufacture, and the greater the value of the piece.

This kind of lace was most prominently worn around the neck and the wrists, where it was gathered and starched into ruffs and cuff bands or worn flat over the shoulders. The piece shown here was probably part of a collar. It set off the extremities of those whose faces were shielded from the sunlight and whose hands undertook no manual labour. Less impressive lace embellished the clothing of the middling sort too – a cap edged in lace epitomized their most impressive possessions as discussed in the Introduction, and it was just the kind of ornament which set them apart from those below them. It drew attention to the point at which white skin met the rich dark colours of expensive outer fabrics, and it indicated the presence of the finely woven undergarments to which it was often connected. As it was these linen undergarments which were washed on a regular basis, rather than the gowns, doublets or kirtles which covered them, the whiteness of linen and lace became a metaphor for cleanliness and therefore wealth – the capacity to provide enough pieces of linen to change it regularly. From the 1570s when the commercial theatre took a firm hold on London's leisure market until shortly after Shakespeare's death, lace reached the height of its popularity for fashionable men and women. Lace and theatre, then, grew together in fashion. At the same time, increasing urban wealth made people sensitive to minute variations in status – to whether one's neighbours were even slightly more wealthy or fashionable than oneself – and these variations were expressed most visibly in the trimmings of clothing, in the furs, fastenings and, of course, lace, with which they were edged and embellished. Because lace was made domestically in England as well as professionally – ladies of the middling sort in particular were encouraged to produce it to adorn both clothing and household linens such as pillowcases and table cloths – so its processes and complexities were familiar to those who understood the challenges of its various methods of manufacture and were sensitive to the aesthetic effects which those techniques produced. Shakespeare's audiences would have been able to tell cutwork from needle or bobbin lace at quite a distance. And they would immediately understand the information about status and wealth which the diverse qualities of different kinds of design signified. The lace pictured here was a world away from the audience's skills – above the capacities of even the professional domestic market, it would have been imported from Italy.

Lace was crucial to the staging of early modern plays because of the intricacy of social information communicated by the amount of it, its breadth, the way it was made, the stuff from which it was manufactured and the way it was worn. The differences between the clothing of masters and their servants, between different ranks of servants, or between the various characters in a large state scene, for instance, would all be instantly comprehensible from their clothing and the way it was embellished. Modern productions at 'Shakespeare's Globe' (the reconstructed Southbank Theatre in London) which have used costumes produced by early modern methods have shown how effectively social information can be communicated by styles of clothing and amounts of lace, both to actors in their roles and to modern audiences with less sensitivity to the qualities of cloth. Costumes make actors move and interact with one another differently, and have immediate visual impact.[4] Such cues to the audience help to place actors' speeches in relation to the status of their character, adding layers of complexity to the formality of modes of address, the intimacy of information communicated or the violence of insults thrown.

Whilst lace made from linen and silk thread defined those of middling to high status in their 'best' or 'holiday' clothing, courtly dress was embellished with silver or gold. Gold lace was tremendously expensive, being made from silver-gilt thread. On the stage, however, such finery was often (although not always) replaced by the considerably cheaper copper lace, made in the same way but with copper in imitation of precious metal. As a form which mimicked courtly splendour in a way which was intended to deceive the viewer – to pass substitute inferiority off as something which it was not – 'copper-lace' became a pejorative by-word for theatrical illusion, for an industry built upon deception and the pretence which dressed commoners as kings. Real courtly clothing was rarely worn, both in the sense that individuals would not need to dress themselves so magnificently every day, and in the sense that a courtier could not afford to be seen in the same outfit too often. In addition, it was worn in a different way: these clothes were carefully placed upon their wearers by servants skilled in such actions, and once on they glorified individuals who demonstrated their social superiority by moving slowly and gracefully. Staging aristocracy, on the other hand, often demanded quick changes, the exaggerated ranting of tragedy, the physical antics of comedy or the battles of history, and this strenuous exertion exhausted not only actors but also their costumes. The wide gap between frenetic theatrical practice and the more stately lives it emulated can be seen in the evidence for repairs which we can trace through the accounts of Philip Henslowe, owner of the Rose Theatre, in which he records the frequent visits of 'the copper lace man'. It has been estimated that 'Between December 1597 and March 1603, the Admiral's and Worcester's Men between them borrowed £69 6s 9d from Henslowe to buy copper lace, including £20 towards their "old debts",' possibly representing as much as six pounds (i.e. the weight of a smallish new-born baby) of copper lace trimming for some suits of theatrical clothing.[5] Such extra weight would clearly affect the actor's movement.

The sources of this clothing were apparently diverse. The Swiss traveller Thomas Platter famously reported in his late sixteenth-century travel diary that the servants of the nobility sold the fine clothing which their masters gave or bequeathed to them because the sumptuary laws made it impossible for them to wear it. It is hard to estimate how common a practice this was, but actors certainly bought individual pieces: the rich cloak mentioned above as having been bought for the huge sum of £19 second hand was purchased from a certain Mr Langley (perhaps Francis Langley, owner of The Swan playhouse), for instance. Literary critic Natasha Korda has argued that clothes may have formed a very tangible connection between Philip Henslowe, owner of the Rose's activities as a theatrical entre-preneur, and his pawnbroking business: she suggests that unredeemed pledges found their way onto the stage as costumes.[6] Such close connections between London clothing and theatrical costume would underline the topicality of plays and their material continuity with the practices and prejudices of urban life.

So clothes were sourced from different markets created by the elite's need to be seen to be constantly in fashion and the substantial value which was inherent in the stuff from which fashion was created. But they were also made up from scratch: in a series of entries from 1601, for instance, Henslowe records 14d paid 'unto the tyer man' for 'money which he laid out to buy tiffany for the play of Cardinal Wolsey'; 20s lent 'for velvet & making of the doctor's gown in Cardinal Wolsey'; 30s to 'Dover the tailor to buy divers things for the 3 part of Tom Strowd'.[7] Individual costumes for each play had fabric purchased and made up for them when it was necessary to add to the stock already in the company's hands. And in some cases this made for a piecemeal approach to clothing. As Henslowe's inventory of costumes contains comparatively few garments for female parts, it is possible that those were supplied from the actors' own stores of costumes, and clothing Shakespeare's women, then, might have involved tapping several different sources of garments: 'company ownership of women's costumes coexisted with masters' ownership of such costumes for their apprentices, just as personally owned wardrobes like Alleyn's and Beeston's, and probably those of others, coexisted with company stock'.[8]

If the quality of costume was a significant element of the appeal of the early modern theatre, then how long did that appeal last? If, as I suggested above, early modern men and women possessed a sensitivity to the precise material form of clothing which is by and large alien to us, then they are also likely to have had an accurate memory for costumes, and been able to 'follow' them – recognizing them on the back of a different character in a subsequent play. But clothing could not simply be replaced because it was well known; as it was worth so much money it was often reused. This process is much easier to follow in the Revels Accounts, those detailed records of the monarch's own entertainments. The following, not atypical entry pursues the fortunes of a piece of particularly pricey fabric: 'green cloth of Silver translated into lining of the Almaynes slops [Germans' trousers] and again cut in pieces to payn [make up from strips of cloth] Fisher mens slops & bodies [bodices] and again translated into A Maske of Mariners and again translated into Torchbearers for a masque of

Turks'. Having been altered so many times, it was said to be 'so often showen and translated' that it 'was forworn and not serviceable nor chargeable': it was worn out in several different ways – physically worn through, repeatedly altered and, if you like, visually exhausted as seen too often.[9]

On the commercial stage the economics of spectacle clearly needed some very careful handling in order to preserve assets and yet maximize appeal. It was the playwright's job to use costume change sparingly and to pattern visual sparseness with spectacle. MacIntyre identifies two different approaches: once the Admiral's Men had paid for a production, she says, 'they would follow it with other plays which could use much the same costumes and properties'. On the other hand, for the Lord Chamberlain's Men, 'Shakespeare's care for costume economy is marked. His doubling schemes permit a maximum number of characters to be played by a minimum number of actors.' And over time, as the confidence of the commercial theatre grew and its investment in spectacle increased, growing costume stocks were put to increasing use: 'In 1588 the Queen's Men could hardly have imagined the wealth of costumes available for the spectacular processions in Shakespeare's *Henry VIII*, little more than twenty-five years after they had premiered the first known play on English history.'[10]

Because of the need for reuse, given the value of cloth, there are comparatively few costumes in Henslowe's inventories which are specific to a particular role: 'Gone and lost' from the Admiral's Men's costume inventory were, for instance, 'long-shanks [King Edward I's] suit' and 'Harry the fifth's doublet and velvet gown, but these are the exceptions rather than the rule.[11] The distinctions clothing made were by and large those of gender and of social status then, rather than of character. Amongst these less-specific clothes: 'A count of the "sewtes," hose, doublets, and jerkins listed in the inventory gives something over eighty complete men's outfits usable in many parts. These outfits seem mostly for one social class, the gentry' who it is argued needed further changes of clothing in order adequately to represent their engagement with fashion. With 12 actors, the Admiral's Men would have a minimum of six to seven suits each, which suggests that, on a rough count, a playgoer could have seen the whole wardrobe in a little over a fortnight.[12]

Exploring the meanings of intricate but tiny pieces of cloth such as the one with which this chapter began offers us an additional insight into the way those communities of diverse individuals which plays represent were structured for their audiences, an insight which attends to the fact that status outside the theatre was most commonly communicated through the cloth, cut and ornament added to dress. In addition to the forms of address, different modes of speech and physical familiarity at actors' disposal, the interrelationships between characters of high and low status and their exact rank in relation to one another could be gauged through clothing. But so could the nature of their role within the action. Imagine seeing *Hamlet* for the first time. The opening scene explores the impact of costume upon its onstage as well as its offstage audience. The Ghost appears to the soldiers on watch *in complete armour, holding a truncheon, with his beaver up*. The power of this character is a result of its material presence, its manifestation in the scene. Barnardo says as it leaves, 'Is not this something more than fantasy?' (52), and Horatio agrees that it has been physically, materially present in front of them: 'I might not this believe/Without the sensible and true avouch/Of mine own eyes' (55–7). It is its armour which gives it a measure of corporeality and hence credibility. And the Ghost's likeness to the dead king is also a feature of its costume – 'Such was the very armour he had on/When he th'ambitious Norway combated' (59–60) – this recognition gives him an identity and with it a purpose and a message. The armour makes the king a visual symbol of the nation's state in this distinctly martial scene: the young Fortinbras comes to 'recover of us by strong hand . . . those foresaid lands/So by his father lost' (101–3), a fact which Horatio offers to explain 'The source of this our watch, and the chief head/Of this post-haste and rummage in the land' (105–6). And yet full armour was old fashioned by the time Shakespeare was writing the play – it was mainly worn on ceremonial occasions rather than in battle where its enormous weight would have made soldiers dangerously inflexible. So this ghost in his armour offers just the kind of utterly tangible experience necessary for belief, making the past absolutely solid and substantial in the present.[13]

The other character who stands out in this opening scene as a result of his dress is Horatio, who enters with Marcellus to join Barnardo and Francisco, but who is not a soldier. He is addressed as a scholar by

Marcellus and it is as a scholar that he addresses the ghost in formal examination: 'What art thou that usurps't this time of night, /Together with that fair and warlike form/In which the majesty of buried Denmark/Did sometimes march? By heaven, I charge thee speak' (I. i. 44–7). Horatio has been specifically invited to join the watch so that, if the ghost appears again, he may 'approve our eyes and speak to it' (27). His verse is elevated and authoritative and, thus far at least, confident in its questioning, and it combines with what we must presume was the costume of a scholar – probably the sober black of learning – to mark him out from the others on the stage.

As I.I ends with the watch going to find Hamlet, so I.2 begins with his entry. But the audience are not told this; the initial focus is not on him, but rather on his uncle, and it is always an ironically present possibility that they will assume that Hamlet, son to the dead old king, is himself the man who enters first in I.2, crowned. In a full stage direction the reader is told *Flourish. Enter Claudius, King of Denmark, Gertrude the Queen, members of the Council, such as Polonius, his son Laertes and daughter Ophelia, Prince Hamlet dressed in black, with others.* This formal, courtly opening shows that the two scenes are intended to complement each other: in contrast to the confusion at night on the battlements in which a king in full armour appears, here Claudius enters crowned and robed as King, with Gertrude similarly regally attired as his wife, coming straight, we are given to believe, from their wedding. This pageant of rule is sustained on its own terms and without direct relation to the previous scene whilst the representatives of the court enter, but it is then explained and made pertinent swiftly in Claudius' opening speech: 'Though yet of Hamlet our dear brother's death/The memory be green' he begins, and continues in line 8 to introduce 'our sometime sister, now our queen'.

The contrasts of clothing are instructive in terms of the depiction of Denmark. Whilst the old king's armour identified him as a noble warrior, the new king's robes offer a contrasting focus on policy which is drawn out in the discussion of diplomatic response to Fortinbras's appeal for lands and the entrance and swift exit of Valtemand and Cornelius to old Norway with a letter suggesting he curb 'his nephew's purpose' (30). Claudius' current authority is underlined in the strongest possible visual terms by this extravagant entry, but the ceremonial is ironically undercut by the previous scene's suggestions of a question mark over his succession – its dubious underpinning in entitlement and its execution in less than heroic form calls it into question. The tensions between natural and legal justice and the edgy tautness of expression within Claudius' oppressive regime which develop in the rest of the play gain their force from the audience's appreciation of his absolute power, and it is a power expressed through the spectacle of sartorial authority. Mention of 'our last king' (1.1.79) or 'the king that's dead' (39) makes it clear that the audience are witnessing what is under any circumstances a nervous moment as power is transferred between one monarch and the next. Appropriate costume underpins these power dynamics in such fundamental ways that it might be said to produce them – to bring authority into being by giving it a fitting guise and to force its actors to adopt the movement and gestures befitting it – in analogous ways to the methods by which Shakespeare produces the ghost of Old Hamlet through his armour: an outside more convincing than the inside.

As Valtemand and Cornelius exit, however, Claudius changes the style and pace of the scene, moving from regal ceremonial to personal issues: 'And now, Laertes, what's the news with you?' (42). And it is in the context of the discussion of Laertes' leaving for France that Claudius turns to his final piece of business: 'But now, my cousin Hamlet, and my son –' (64). If we return to the opening of the scene once more we can perhaps appreciate how visually distinctive Hamlet's dress is at this point. All the other characters are supposed to have come from a royal wedding and are hence in their court clothes – dressed in similar weights of copper lace to those itemized in Henslowe's accounts we can assume. In addition to the splendours of such trimmings, formal dress was essentially colourful, which was why mourning clothes were such a strong statement intended to abjure status distinctions in favour of the advertisement of loss – in practice, of course, the distinctions between costly and cheap black cloths were considerable, although less instantly visually appreciable. Against this backdrop of majesty, Hamlet's black costume is incongruous in relation to the celebration, to the court setting and to his own status there. Although everyone else's status could be understood in terms relative to the monarch, Hamlet stands outside such an immediate frame of reference and his identity in this respect is relegated to his

suggested character as both a scholar like Horatio who has forgotten
to change clothes and a malcontent at the edges of the court. And
although Shakespeare is quick to have Claudius explain his own and
Gertrude's identity, no explanation is given for this interloper in an
atmosphere of festivity until line 64. Although recognizing the identity of the actor playing the part may well have suggested to an early
modern audience the significance of the character to the rest of the
play, the delay in answering the question which the entrance at the
start of the scene is intended to put into their minds builds suspense
whilst a richer context is provided for it by the ensuing action.

These opening scenes visually single out two young men as characters
who stand apart and interpret the action before them. They set up a
younger generation who must puzzle out and in a complex way resolve
the sins of the older one. Writing about representations of the ghost,
Reginald Foakes argues that its armour 'marks both the ghost's association with an old ethos based on violence, and also his cultural difference from young Hamlet, the student from Wittenberg'.[14] In a play
about deep thought and ponderous consideration of action, the material
delineation of Hamlet's difference is crucial. And his first speech longer
than a line is, of course, one about the nature of clothing:

> Seems, madam? Nay, it *is*. I know not 'seems'.
> 'Tis not alone my inky cloak, good mother,
> Nor customary suits of solemn black,
> Nor windy suspiration of forced breath,
> No, nor the fruitful river in the eye,
> Nor the dejected haviour of the visage,
> Together with all forms, moods, shows of grief
> That can denote me truly. These indeed 'seem',
> For they are actions that a man might play;
> But I have that within which passeth show –
> These but the trappings and the suits of woe.
>
> (76–86)

This speech takes us right to the centre of the relationship between
clothing and theatre's acts and illusions. It is the 'inky cloak' and its
accompanying gestures which must communicate emotion – must
allow it to pass from inner truth to outer show – and yet external signs
can be feigned because they are 'actions that a man might play', that

he might put on just as he slips on a costume. Hamlet's speech, then, is a metatheatrical meditation on the relationship between role and costume just as much as it is a consideration of ways of guaranteeing the authenticity of emotion.

Medieval theatre used costume change to echo and display an inner change in the character. As Mankind, the eponymous hero of a late medieval moral play, enters in a progressively shortened coat, the audience understand visually something essential about his diminishing virtue in the face of the constant onslaught of the vices' allurements. As the similarly eponymous Everyman reaches the end of the pilgrimage which represents his spiritual development, he is re-clothed by knowledge in a garment of sorrow. London's commercial theatre had moved away from the stark allegories of morality drama, however. Rather than capturing the wide symbolic universe of life and death, virtue and vice, heaven and hell on its stage, the early modern theatre chose to portray the exceptional experiences of individuals – specific people with their particular problems and solutions as opposed to inclusive characters whose journeys represented what all men and women had in common. Viewing the development of early modern drama chronologically reveals the shifting role of costume change from the demonstration of an altered state to, from the 1580s, the signalling of a different circumstance or activity (for instance going on a journey) as permanent theatres were able to offer more space for storing costumes. From 1594 onwards, 'costume change to fit a scene's occasion becomes more common', and after 1600 even begins to be more common than 'the traditional expressive changes'.[15] This suggests a gradual movement towards more mimetic uses of clothing which represented social situations rather than the inner states of characters – costume which contributed to the definition of action rather than character.

Hamlet as a character is tied up in these developments in complex ways. He has become the epitome of that particularizing process of the early modern theatre as it turns towards unique individual experience, often heralded as the archetype of theatrical interiority and 'modern' subjectivity. In that case, his discussion of the relationship between inner truth and material objects stands for the process of mental rather than physical articulation of identity. And yet, in the years around 1600 when *Hamlet* appeared, character realism was still to an extent being patterned against material theatrical devices which are non-mimetic, producing an alluring, thought-provoking tension. Talking about that opening speech of his, Stallybrass and Jones express some frustration with the simplicity of the smooth narrative of change towards a purely interior subjectivity. Hamlet, they say, 'has been misheard in our haste to find a modern subject, untrammelled by the objects that surround him ... If he claims something in addition to his mourning clothes, those clothes are still a necessary part of his memorializing of his father.'[16] Hamlet explores the relationship between inner and outer expressions of identity through his visual difference from the rest of his father/uncle's court, and the theatre simultaneously explores its own nature, because the relationship between the costume which signifies a role and the actor's body which it covers is always at heart one of disguise and falsehood. Costume change, then, gets to the nub of both this new theatre's precocious display of realism, and the dependence of that change of focus on the material culture of the stage. But the relationship between inner and outer truths is most problematic – the illusion deepest – when this theatre stages a woman's part.

In *Twelfth Night*, for instance, 1.2 begins with the question which Viola addresses to the sea captain and sailors with whom she enters from the shipwreck, 'What country, friends, is this?': the atmosphere established at the entry of this female character, played by a boy, is one of confusion and uncertainty. Coming after the play's opening scene during which Orsino explores his own excessive love pains, 1.2 introduces the haunting sense of loss which stays with *Twelfth Night* at least until its consummatory final scene. Viola's initial question gives the impression that the party are standing on the shore, recently washed up and coming to terms with their situation. The scene is relatively brief – it serves to explain what has happened and to set up a trajectory for Viola which will see her appear two scenes later in Orsino's court. So the captain introduces Viola to Illyria, its Duke and the woman whose love the Duke longs for, and they discuss the possibility of her brother's survival. With these three key characters in place in the audience's mind, Viola then begins to think through her situation, to work out her relationship to them, and to plan her intervention in the social life of Illyria: 'I pray thee – and I'll pay thee bounteously', she says to the captain,

Conceal me what I am, and be my aid
For such disguise as haply shall become
The form of my intent. I'll serve this duke.
Thou shalt present me as an eunuch to him.

(48–52)

With the captain's help she will 'conceal' and 'disguise' herself – he
is to help her to the masculine clothes which she will put on and then
to present her in them – and these clothes will become the 'form' of
her intent, its shape, its visual aspect or its image (*Oxford English
Dictionary*), as that intent can only be realized by material means.
And this change only ever conceals gender, it never disguises identity
or personality. Indeed in many ways it is Viola's preservation of both
and their occasional surfacing in her confessions of family details to
Orsino and status to Olivia which conveys her close to her master and
his intended mistress. Changing gender therefore allows her to bring
her personal female qualities into the court under the cloak of male-
ness. But Cesario's identity is, as a result, an interestingly confused
one: as she puts it to herself during her 'fight' with Sir Andrew, 'I my
brother know/Yet living in my glass. Even such and so/In favour was
my brother, and he went/Still in this fashion, colour, ornament,/For
him I imitate' (3.4.371–5). In other words she does not just become a
man, but rather the man she has lost, and she becomes him in a way
which in some senses recuperates that loss – she is both a masculine
version of herself and a feminine version of her brother, a combination of cross-dressing and resurrection which becomes a vexed issue,
as we shall see, at the end of the play.

So what exactly is at stake in *Twelfth Night*, in the boy actor's
assumption of female clothing and his subsequent adoption, as
Viola, of masculine disguise? Cross-dressing has been the object of
a scholarly fascination which has explored the nature of its effects
upon its contemporary audiences inside and outside the theatre. In
order to understand how dressing differently could be seen to alter
gender so effectively, critics have investigated contemporary medical
theories which propound distinctively pre-modern views of the relations between male and female bodily difference. In the 'one sex'
model which was enormously influential throughout the sixteenth
and seventeenth centuries, women's reproductive organs were seen as

inverted versions of men's, similar in shape and function but on the inside rather than the outside. Literary critic Jean Howard, in an influential 1988 article, asks whether male actors' cross-dressing might be 'an inevitable extension of a sex-gender system in which there was only one sex and that one sex male?' Will Fisher has pointed out that 'masculinity and femininity were often conceptualized as being malleable' in contrast to our own fixed view of gender identity, and he has explored the extent to which gender was constructed in terms other than those of anatomical distinction: 'clothing materialized gender along with other, more corporeal, features, and both were essential'. He insists on resisting the temptation to see clothes as either 'superfluous objects or as things that are unproblematically assimilated into the body and self', trying instead to 'emphasize the continuity between interior and exterior, as between nature and culture, sex and gender'.[17] In other words, for critics like Fisher early modern clothing was not only central to the construction of roles within the theatre, but also to the production of the gendered identities of men and women in their daily life. Indeed, for many of these literary critics the two processes are analogous to the point of blurring the boundaries between them.

Offstage, historians have found a confusing array of diverse and differently motivated practices by and large far distant from the fashionable activities attacked by moralists and considered in the Introduction. Some, for instance, have suggested that 'passing oneself off as a man was a real and viable option for women who had fallen into bad times and were struggling to overcome their difficult circumstances'. They argue that these women 'were part of a tradition of cross-dressing of which they were well aware' and one which was deep-rooted across Europe. On the other hand, in more festive contexts, gender change could go either way. Natalie Zemon Davis's work on the figure of the unruly female in general across fictive and non-fictive sources suggests that 'Whereas sexual inversion in literary and pictorial play more often involved the female taking on the male role or dressing as a man, the festive inversion more often involved the male taking on the role or garb of the woman.' In politically charged situations like riots, she found that the 'donning of female clothes by men' was 'surprisingly frequent'. David Cressy similarly argues that 'transvestism was limited, temporary, and pragmatic'. He examines the case of Thomas Salmon, a servant from Great Tew in Oxfordshire who 'hearing that there would be good cheer at the house of Eleanor Rymel who was then lately brought a-bed, wished that he might be there; whereupon his dame Elizabeth Fletcher said he should, and then fetched her apparel, and he put off his doublet and he came to the said house where the women met, and bid them say that he was Mrs Garrett's maid . . . and he stayed there in the room but a little, but he continued in that apparel about two hours'.[18] There is a strong sense of sport, of entertainment value, to this story and others like it, and it connects to Davis's 'festive inversion' to suggest different motivations for male and female cross-dressing.

These historians have found contingent uses of the trope of the cross-dresser, generated by specific sets of circumstances or problems in need of a solution, and largely temporary in their nature. The examples they study show that putting on the clothing of another gender was a definite possibility – one of the options to which the mind might turn when faced with a social problem which was insoluble in other ways. But they also show that the idea could have political implications as it was used as an oblique insult to authority and the status quo, and it involved its participants in a kind of 'merriment', a word with implications for both festive inversion and social protest which draws attention to the essentially comedic entertainment value which it can possess as a practice. Cross-dressing is by and large the action of lower-status individuals using dress physically to change places. Rigid gender divisions and hierarchies appear to have generated the desire to see and act from 'the other side of the fence' and the clothing differences which supported and defined those divisions made it possible to adopt a different social perspective by changing clothes. It is the material objects through which gender is negotiated, in other words, which focus the exploration of ideologies, and that makes changing clothes a potentially political act.

But there was also, of course, that rhetoric of moral outrage against cross-dressing which focused on the connections between onstage and offstage practice explored in the Introduction. Literary critic Laura Levine contends that this type of writing argues for the currency of magical beliefs that the actor 'himself can be shaped or unfashioned' by his costume. Dress historians have taken a different approach centred in fashion history rather than the exploration of identity construction, and traced the crystallization of the motif 'of women who apparelled themselves as men' out of the 'standard theme associating women with fashionable dress'. Susan Vincent has tried to establish the exact kinds of behaviour being attacked in satirical pamphlets, and she does so by separating out the form of garments from their design: 'wearers were not donning men's garments, but wearing clothes cut for females with alterations of decoration and form to *resemble* male attire'. Talking about the moralist Philip Stubbes' writing on clothing, Susan Vincent argues that 'it was but a small leap from bodices styled after men's doublets, to gender fluidity and transposition of sexual categories', but she is very clear that 'this is a discursive leap only and not one that was made anywhere but on the page'. In other words this is a totally different kind of cross-dressing to the lower-status politically inspired practice explored by historians. These wearers were the elite who were at the forefront of fashion: 'The clothing and comportment complained of were not serious attempts to mask gender but essays in chic and avant-garde fashion.'[19] The distinction between a form of disguise intended to deceive about gender or at least identity and a fashionable excess which pushed provocatively at gender boundaries is a crucial one.

We can see Viola's 'double' practice, then – the boy actor's donning of female attire in order to play a part and the female character's donning of male dress in order to survive – as caught between these historical customs, the one born of desperation and generated by generally lower-status responses to a need to do something drastic in order to escape circumstances, and the other a titillating bending of gender identity which was undertaken by those who did not desire to deceive so much as to provoke, and who fully intended to keep both genders in play at the same time. Jean Howard argues that on- and offstage practice formed an 'interlocking grid' through which we can read 'aspects of class and gender struggle in the period', and that 'the ideological import of crossdressing was mediated by all the conventions of dramatic narrative and Renaissance dramatic production'.[20] Whilst these connections between theatrical and non-theatrical practices are obviously key, stressing seamlessness risks running the two stages of the process together – the actor playing the part in woman's dress and the female character dressing as a man. *Twelfth Night*, on the other hand, keeps both processes separate but dependent, at points downplaying each in favour of the other.

The effects on their audiences of cross-dressing on the stage have largely been conceived in psychological terms – in terms of the erotics of male actors dressing as female characters, and of those characters in their turn dressing as men. The theoretical perspectives employed have been diverse – 'post-Foucaultian analysis of the discursive construction of sexuality, the poetics and politics of representation, materialist feminism, [and] queer theory' for instance, have been used to ask, 'Where is the locus of the desire occasioned by the transvestite? In the representation or the performance? In the (imagined or actual) unveiling? In what is unveiled? . . . [D]oes the beholder of the image *want* or *want to be* that image?'[21] The problem with psychological readings of cross-dressing is that they so often lose sight of the practice's material basis. Without the primacy of the material construction of cross-dressed identity on which Viola's description of the 'form' of her intent insists, as Marjorie Garber argues in her influential book *Vested Interests*, 'the plays' obsessive emphasis on clothing as a marker of difference is obscured, as the reader's (or director's or designer's) eye glides absentmindedly past lists of incomprehensible garments in search of moral or emotional (or even sexual or political) context'.[22] Reading materially, on the other hand, forces us to focus questions of desire: on, for instance, how the staged image of the cross-dresser would be read by the audience from a physical point of view, and in what way and on what level they might access some of these complex theoretical positions which are suggested for the character. The visual image is, of course, the first thing to be seen by the audience and the primary site of their appreciation of the uniqueness of characters; a material reading therefore starts with the clothes on which that image is principally based, and is grounded in them. Clothing is the quality of the essence which is desired and the governing aspect of its representation: it is the opening gambit of actor to audience in relation to which all other information about their character is read. And potentially, cross-dressing disrupts that process of revelation which pulls all out after the initial visual image, which uses it as a starting point for a journey of discovery, depending on the extent to which we are asked to probe the relationship between costume and the actor's body.

*Twelfth Night* is structured around two striking scenes which foreground the significance of clothing in the creation of gendered identity and suggest ways of reading the cross-dressed body. The first occurs in 1.5, when Viola as Cesario meets Olivia for the first time. The moment is set up as one of indeterminacy – a social situation which lacks clarity – Maria confirms that the person waiting at the gate is 'a fair young man, and well attended' (98–9), a drunken Toby insists he is a 'gentleman' but can manage no more sense than that, and even the precise Malvolio fails adequately to describe him. The latter answers a series of questions which he appears purposely to misconstrue: asked 'What kind o' man is he?' – what birth or disposition – he answers 'Why, of mankind.' When clarification is demanded 'What manner of man?' meaning both type and bearing or behaviour, he replies 'Of very ill manner' – he focuses on behaviour rather than status in each instance. Olivia asks finally 'Of what personage [character, status or appearance] and years?', to which question she receives a reply which denies all the social categories implied in her questions so far and focuses instead on the difficult question of age: 'Not yet old enough for a man, nor young enough for a boy... Tis with him in standing water between boy and man' (145–54). These entanglements of social status and behaviour set up Olivia's confusion and play out in comic form the audience's anticipation of a meeting between a female courtier acting as go-between with a message of love for a Countess.

But the indeterminacy of this first meeting is not only generated by the difficulties of describing Cesario, it is also a feature of the reception which s/he receives once Olivia has agreed to entertain the embassy. Olivia meets Cesario veiled and in the company of Maria and her attendants, forcing her visitor to ask 'Are you the lady of the house' (177–8). This confusion must partly spring from Cesario's nervousness at her entertainment by the object of her master's affections and her lack of experience in such situations. But it is clearly also engineered by Olivia, who apparently exploits the veils necessitated by the household's state of mourning and the relatively elevated status of an intimate servant like Maria (which might make it possible to confuse the quality of their mourning clothes). The confusion which is stressed as a result, and the lack of any clear social rules for such an encounter, produce an excitingly unstable meeting, one in which the possibilities of being misunder-stood, misrepresented and just plain wrong about another character foreground questions of social and, eventually, emotional judgement.

And then, almost magically, this indeterminacy is translated into what is probably the most direct social interaction in the play, despite, because of, ironically in relation to, the fiction of Cesario's gender. The frankness, the peeling away of the layers of propriety and the tortuous complexity of elite Elizabethan courtship negotiations, begins at the moment when Cesario lays aside the predictable 'method acting' of her embassy and, almost as a *non sequitur*, asks 'Good madam, let me see your face' (220). It is this moment, of course, which alters the dynamic from a formal embassy which presents information in a decorous way to a personal communication which embodies the message rather than merely presenting it. Communicating with Olivia's face allows Cesario to bring her empathy with the notion of love into play, and it is this personal approach to the role of go-between which causes Olivia to fall in love with 'him'. At that point, Olivia begins to engage with the messenger, to hear her rather than merely to permit her to speak, to focus upon her rather than simply ignoring her as a conduit for the message of another.

This moment works, on the level of the narrative, as a metaphor for self-revelation – it is susceptible to a psychological explanation. But in the material terms of performance what happens is that 'she' removes her veil, and that action is directly implicated in the play's construc-tion of gender: one of the clearest moments for an audience watching a male actor playing a woman can be when he is in love with a man playing a man. Such moments underscore the sense of differentiation which sustains the fiction of the drama – difference creates bonds between individuals. When Olivia raises her veil, the audience must believe her a beautiful woman if they are to invest emotionally in the plot which unfurls. Such a process usually takes its efficacy from the way it sets up stable binary oppositions – male and female, beholder and subject, lover and beloved. Here, the moment is a complex theatrical 'joke' about love and gender, as a man playing a woman reveals 'herself' to a man playing a woman playing a man in such a way as to produce for the audience the theatrical effect of respect for beauty. And yet we still have to believe in Olivia's beauty, even as we appreciate her misunderstanding of Cesario's appeal. In other words this moment holds half of those complex ideas about cross-dressing at bay, insisting that the present of this encounter is somehow separate from the audience's knowledge of the actors' actually very different situation. In doing so, it pulls apart the doubleness of Viola's cross-dressing, drawing explicit attention to what usually happens in the theatre, when only one of the characters is pretending to be something they are not. Like Hamlet's insistence on clothing as the illusion which produces the 'real' underneath – the potentially deceitful inky cloak as opposed to the truly, honestly grieving soul – here Olivia's veil represents the material excess whose removal produces an 'authentic' gendered image below.

And the way Olivia's words and actions frame this striking moment of intensity is significant. She offers both her on- and offstage audience a means of reading the confusions of dress on which both the power and the comedy of the scene depend. Her response to Cesario is to agree, grudgingly perhaps, 'we will draw the curtain and show you the picture'. And then, having removed her veil, 'Look you, sir, such a one I was this present. Is't not well done?' (222–5). In response to Cesario's question whether 'God did all' she assures ''Tis in grain, sir, 'twill endure wind and weather' (227). In other words Olivia describes herself, or more properly the experience of looking at her face which Cesario is having, as a picture. She imagines this for him as an aesthetic experience, and this suggests that the quality of his appreciation may perhaps not be so far away from Leontes' encounter with the statue of Hermione – a delight in the conceit of something which is both representation and reality, both the perfection of a painted image and the living and breathing referent who caused it to be brought into being.

This is a deceptively straightforward context to provide for a view which creates what is not really there, which sets a practice of viewing in place of the material fact of an actor's gender. It stresses Olivia's status as the kind of woman who is used to seeing her own painted image; it underscores the way that status is constructed in relation to the patronage of artists and the commissioning of objects of aesthetic value; it insists that appreciation of a woman's beauty takes place, for people of this status at least, in relation to the dual financial and artistic value of household things. Such a context joins Olivia and Cesario in an elite experience which confirms the latter's status as being, indeed, 'above her fortunes' (1.5.268) – as was shown in the Introduction, owning a portrait of oneself was a key marker of the borderlines of elite status. Olivia's next move is to provide an inventory of her face which is both an account of her 'value' visually and financially, and a blazon of her parts whose heraldic status slows the moment of appreciation to one of wonder for Cesario. But this first small yet significant moment also offers a way of reading character which is mediated through surface representation. The confusions of gender achieve a moment of clarity as the two resolve themselves into the stable, familiar positions of beholder and beheld, as a painting's subject and its audience, for long enough to generate the rest of the plot of the play.

And given that this moment of revelation is explicit about portraiture as a governing dynamic for the interpretation of the cross-dressed elite body, it is important to bring the interpretive practices of early modern image viewing to bear on the scene. Portraiture was changing: there was a general trend across Elizabeth's reign towards the depiction of 'feeling', away from something much more symbolic which suggests the representation of lineage and the symbolism of elite virtue. These two modes of portraiture, the symbolic and the mimetic, had one thing in common: they both used clothing to express the sitter's identity. It was on clothing that the powerful energies of painterly skill and intricate technique were expended and through it that the artist's talents were displayed. But there were differences: the palpable reality of earlier, more symbolic modes of portraiture – their very material presence – was generated by the enormous detail in which clothing was depicted. The 'new sensibility', however, expressed mental states such as 'the humour of 'melancholy' through a disruption in the sitter's dress – in deliberately 'untidy, negligent clothing'.[23]

The art historian Ellen Chirelstein explores the connections between these two different pictorial conventions in a portrait of Lady Elizabeth Pope painted in the 1610s. Here, she sees the modern influence of Italian painting in the depiction of both space and the body and traces it to Inigo Jones's drawings of the female form produced as vehicles for the costumes he designed for court masques. His costume drawings, she argues, 'reflect a conception of the figure in which the bodies of the performers move, have weight and volume, and display the contours of a classical figure'. However, although present, such 'Italianate elements' of the spatial positioning and three-dimensionality of the body 'do not fundamentally reorder [the artist Robert Peake's] conception of the painting'. Rather, it is *structured* 'as a flat heraldic field influenced by the non-illusionistic ordering of heraldic shields', and it is this two-dimensional field whose 'references to volume, space and motion lie on the surface' which 'appears to control the display of Elizabeth Pope's body'. Meaning, then, is generated by the contrast between 'the heraldic flatness of Elizabeth Pope's body and the sensuous physicality of her costume'.[24] This painting might stand for the turning point in English portraiture. The indications of a naturalistic tendency began to be seen around the turn of the sixteenth century, but they did not win out until several decades later, and the mixtures of old and new styles continued until as late as 1620.[25] Until at least the time of Shakespeare's death, then, English portraiture retained elements of its concentration on the relationship between the face and clothing as the dominant focus of the viewer's attention, rather than the connections between the body and the clothing with which it was covered, as was the case in Italian art.

The persistence of this anti-mimetic concentration on heraldic ways of making meaning is instructive for our appreciation of the way stage costume might have been understood, as the controlling dynamic of the representation of women's bodies in a different medium. The beauty of the cloth with its very fully represented pattern lies on the surface, drawing the audience's attention away from the body underneath. Instead, the tensions between the gaze of the sitter which invites engagement, suggests depth, and indicates presence and the relentlessly enticing fabric of her dress which forms a kind of eddy of looking, an end in itself to the viewer's enquiry, give Lady Elizabeth a sense of enigma, of partial invitation matched against reserve but also of personal appeal contrasted with a statement of the material richness of elite identity.

Dress history tells an interestingly analogous story of a change in visual concentration from face to body towards the end of Elizabeth's reign: for women, the gradual disappearance of 'a bizarre silhouette created by extensive stiffening and padding, and so encrusted with decoration that the natural female form entirely disappeared,' for

Lady Elizabeth Pope, attrib. Robert Peake, *c.*1615, oil on wood support, 775 × 610 mm, Tate Collection.

men, the end of an extreme artificiality of shape, in which a 'ruff encircled the head, effectively isolating it from the body, a padded doublet curved into a point below the waist, the hose were minimal and the thighs were encased in tightly fitting canions', creating an unbalanced upper body. Until at least the end of Elizabeth's reign, 'fashionable costume referred not so much to the forms or comfort of the three-dimensional body hidden underneath, responding instead to the dictates of portraiture and constant display, becoming itself a canvas or panel for the loaded plant, animal and architectural forms described through the flat patterns of blackwork embroidery, woven silk and applied jewellery'.[26] Elite dress in Elizabeth's reign separated clothing from the body underneath.

The fascination with material complexity as the way of expressing elite identity brought clothing very close to the two-dimensional art of painting. It was most pronounced in courtly clothing, suggesting that increasing levels of formality meant increasing abstraction and a more marked concentration on surfaces. This kind of material identity provided an exterior which stood for the body, which gave through the flawlessness of fabric what the body could not offer, in a period where the skin bore the very obvious marks of illness and disease. Bodies were corruptible, mutable and frail; fabric achieved the monumental perfection necessary to represent enduring power, drawing attention away from the body and towards its substitute self.

Olivia's comment about the portrait, then, opens up a series of different discourses of elite identity which are firmly tied into the way clothing stands for the body – detracts attention away from it. Obviously it is a brief conceit, but it does indicate how dress created the dynamics of interaction which underlined authority. The majority of the audience in the public theatre did not, of course, own portraits. On the other hand, they would have been familiar with the kinds of languages of clothing through which the painted subject exerted his or her influence – public portraits of mayors and mayoresses and civic benefactors, or prime wardens of London livery companies, for instance, would be familiar to the majority of urban dwellers.[27] So the process does signify lower down the social scale, but in a way which perhaps draws attention to the differences between looking at a portrait in a public space and viewing one in one's own home. Listening to Olivia's description of herself, written at the very end of Elizabeth's reign before the changes outlined above, meant bringing into play portraiture's focus on dress as the key signifier of the beauty – the aesthetic finery – of gender and power, rather than any more bodily thoughts.

The second of the play's commanding visual images created by cross-dressing comes at the end, when the status dynamics which govern *Twelfth Night*'s largely uncontrollable passions are clearest, and the black mood of violent passion caused by an illicit love across social boundaries reaches its deepest point. When Olivia and her attendants enter in 5.1 and the two central households around which the play is organized stand face to face on the stage for the first time, Orsino begins to talk violently in terms of sacrifice, rather than in the formal terms of embassy, suggesting he might 'Kill what I love' (117). He seems, at this point, to be talking of Olivia, but then, having confessed that 'I partly know the instrument/That screws me from my true place in your favour', he offers to tear Cesario 'out of that cruel eye/Where he sits crownèd in his master's spite'. His fantasy of revenge lays bare the shocking status implications of Olivia's love for Cesario. Orsino's is the true place because he is the highest status man in Illyria; Cesario has been crowned by Olivia, been raised to that point by her love for him, because s/he was brought into a position of intimacy by her dress. This movement of the play reworks in considerably less comic terms Malvolio's fantasies of social elevation and the new costumes through which he imagined his elite identity in his 'branched velvet gown...' (2.545–6).

The mood is dispelled by the prolonged sequence of wonder which attends the revelation of the twins' identity, a sense of awe which must cancel out and resolve the wounded violence and Sir Andrew's, and Sir Toby's violent wounding in the opening part of the scene. Orsino sums up the picture with which on- and offstage audience are confronted:

> One face, one voice, one habit, and two persons,
> A natural perspective, that is and is not.

> (213–14)

The 'natural perspective' refers to a Renaissance 'distorting glass' which produces an optical illusion which doubles a picture. It is, in other words, a thing of artifice, an unusual optical effect which invites the audience to see this scene too as a visual image, as an experience whose marvellousness is generated by a similitude which is visual, material. Despite being two persons, Viola and Sebastian have one face, voice and habit. But it is the latter which guarantees, which secures the former two similarities in the case of a pair of parts played by, we presume, two actors whose physical characteristics were not identical. And in any case, with boys playing female parts, it is only dress which can produce the illusion of male and female twinning as it must be seen here – more layered replication than even twin actors could hold out to their audience.

The extended sequence of question and answer which the twins share explores correspondence in a variety of senses. 'Do I stand there?', Sebastian initially asks. He foregrounds his confusions of identity by investigating the relationship between outer image and inner essence – the person who faces him looks like him and wears his clothes, and it is that which secures both his conviction that he knows them and his assurance that he does not. The outfit both insures affinity and denies recognition. Knowing that he had no brother, there follows a series of further questions: 'what kin are you to me?/ What countryman? What name? What parentage?' (228–9), and these permit the lyrical antiphon of growing conviction, 'My father had a mole upon his brow./And so had mine' (240–1). The question and response echoes in language the visual image of similarity, and the two together give the scene its distinctive emotional quality of the duplication of wonder. By prolonging, blissfully, the moment of recognition between brother and sister, this dialogue slows it right down to the pace of amazement, and it focuses all eyes on the image of similarity on the stage. The fascination with correspondence in this emotional centre to the scene is a focus on the surface, on the fabric which covers bodies and is the only possible source of the kind of total similitude of twins of different genders which *Twelfth Night* calls for. It is the explicit artifice of identical outfits which creates a wonder sufficient for romance, one which aims to prevail over psychologically convincing explanations for the swapping of genders and partners by stressing the strength of the emotional response to material duplication. It is, of course, a convention of disguise in romances that even close family members fail to recognise one. Comedies, with their close associations with romance, give great weight to the material qualities of identity, and this scene in *Twelfth Night* plays with such a convention. It examines the captivating intensity of the interplay between costumed surface and inner reality, between image and self, but it finally insists on the outer, holding off the problem of what lies inside past the end of the play.

Because in the end, with all questions answered satisfactorily, one issue is left:

> If nothing lets to make us happy both
> But this my masculine usurped attire,
> Do not embrace me till each circumstance
> Of place, time, fortune do cohere and jump
> That I am Viola
>
> (247–11)

Literary critic Yu Jin Ko writes about that curious injunction 'Do not embrace me' as an echo of the *noli me tangere* moment between Christ and Mary Magdalene in the garden on the resurrection morning. He points out the way the moment brings together the deepest spiritual joy with the greatest physical pain – the pain of absence in this world caused by and yet generating the deferred joy of presence in the next.[28] It is, in other words, the materiality of presence which generates both joy and pain. Christ and Mary are in two different states of being – their distance is enforced by difference – whereas Sebastian and Viola are in many ways too similar. Sebastian cannot touch Viola because they are the same, because of that curious over-similarity which is generated by the shared gender their doubled outfit suggests, which is duplication more than twinning. But there is also a sense of loss in this doubleness, because if Viola is not herself then she cannot be there: the essential gendered essence which separates her from her brother is missing.

But of course *Twelfth Night* avoids that probing of the differences which lie under identicalness – it does not ask her to undress. Instead, it spends its energies pursuing a material remnant. Cross-dressing is sometimes talked about in terms of a residue of meaning, in which 'representations, even when framed in ways that limit their transgressiveness', must leave something behind: something of the possibility of transgressing gender boundaries which cross-dressing opens up for an audience and on which it cannot entirely close the lid. But *Twelfth Night* makes it clear that there is also a material surplus to deal with: 'I'll bring you to a captain in this town/Where lie my maiden weeds'(251–2), Viola says, but the total revelation which her earlier lines promised is held off, its conclusion tied up in some complicated way with the provision of her rightful dress. 'Give me thy hand,/*And let me see thee in thy woman's weeds*' (270–1) Orsino says: the satisfaction of the shared marriage celebrations which Olivia suggests is delayed, deferred because of Malvolio's oblique involvement. Orsino is not motivated by his sense of the need for a concluding harmony in restitution of wrongs when he sends men to 'Pursue him, and entreat him to a peace' (376), but by a sense that it is only with Malvolio's help that Cesario can become herself again, a self bound up entirely, it seems, in the self-same dress in which she left her gendered identity. This focus, whilst obviously serving to tie the subplot of the gulling of Malvolio to the main plot's conclusions, also has the effect of increasing the significance of those original articles of clothing immeasurably. Viola's female outfit now has the power to restore a lost identity which she earlier put aside in the process of dressing as her brother; her male outfit, which insured her physical and emotional proximity to Olivia and Orsino, finally holds her apart from consummation with both Orsino and Sebastian.

Clothing, then, is at the heart of the play's explorations of distance, closeness and desire. But in that case to what extent are the audience asked to think about the role of the body in this drama of emotions, surfaces and cloth? How much force might those controlling dynamics of aesthetic response have had in managing the audience's propensity to look beyond or beneath clothes? We need to bring other, non-elite discourses to bear at this point, in order to establish what the audience might have considered to be the relationship between dress and the body, and the contexts in which people imagined or touched what lay beneath. In historian Laura Gowing's groundbreaking study of discourses of touch in the alehouses and streets of England, she makes it clear that she does not intend 'to propose a history that gets at "real" bodies, without discourse'.[29] Similarly, a reading of theatrically spectacular bodies does not tell us about how real bodies were touched, imagined or dreamed about, and knowing that (if it were possible to know that) does not help us understand theatrical practice. But such a focus does take us beyond purely literate discourses of gender, adding to our understanding of the stage a non-literate, material history of the body. And thinking about 'real' and staged bodies alongside one another, as a set of material practices which reflect and shape a very different mind-set to our own, suggests different routes for the early modern imagination.

Laura Gowing's examples show that at least part of the dynamic of elite portraiture was applicable further down the social scale: at all social levels, clothing stood for the body. She says that 'Chastity was guaranteed and represented by the making and keeping of firm boundaries around the body, solid control over access to the private parts', and it was clothing which provided the boundary, denied access to the eyes and the hands: as 'a bodily boundary, as a metaphor for the body itself, as a marker and evidence, and as a narrative focus'.[30] For women telling stories about rape in particular, talking about clothes instead of bodies offered a material substitute which maintained a vestige of honour and self-respect, enabling them to avoid making public once more in the court that which had already been too open. Clothing was part of the discourses of decency because it left the body out of the debate.

Conduct literature often focused on partial undress, suggesting that the public tying of the points or laces that connected early modern clothing could only indicate a recently completed bodily function. This kind of sartorial 'unreadiness' asked the viewer to complete the process by imagining the action which has just taken place. Such emphasis on action as an element of body – the call to imagine bodily functions rather than the bodies which have performed them, suggests that undress may not usually signal nudity – may not signpost the body at all in these public discourses. Early modern courts were especially sensitive to descriptions of undress, accepting them as material proof of carnal states. For instance, William Breamer accused Richard Smith in the following terms: 'I found thee in my own ground with my wife, thy hose untrussed, thy doublet unbuttoned.' This is the usual proof of sexual liaison offered in the courts, a focus on partial dress which stands for the partial nudity which is its pair, and the action which both together suggest. But Breamer goes one step further, telling how he saw his wife: 'her clothes . . . so high I took her white skin to have been the white of a cow'. The visceral shock of the sight of flesh has a powerful image-making quality, but it is not common in such court material. More usually in stories about sexual intercourse, clothing provided the point of negotiation, the final layer of protection. And both in and out of court, in the way these often slanderous stories circulated, they generated humour – a seventeenth-century jest ran that 'A wench came to Sir Henry Nevill, and made a pitiful complaint how such a man had ravisht her . . . upon examination . . . the fellow confessed he had carnally known her, but not without her consent; for if it please your worship said he, she took up her smock very willingly; O Lord Sir, says she, if I had not done so, he kept up such a Wimbling, as he had bor'd a great hole in my smock presently.'[31] The jest itself here is complex – the story she tells is rooted in the manufacturing language of 'wimbling', of boring holes with a wimble or awl, and it suggests that she is forced into the position of having to consent to sex in order to protect her clothing. The language of material damage put onto the smock is instructive – another deflection which avoids her body and her sexuality to comic ends. In lower status judicial and comic contexts too then, clothing stands for the body and permits the discussion of honour in material rather than corporeal terms.[32]

These metaphorical uses of clothing also show, however, how contingent ideologies of the 'closed body' were on gender and social status. Laura Gowing argues that 'single women's and servants' place in their community was defined by a lack of autonomy over their own bodies, enforced by women as well as men', and that there were unofficial searches of servants' bodies in rural communities by mistresses and neighbours. *Twelfth Night* raises the issue of the prospect of ordering Cesario to change clothes – it would be unthinkable that such a thing should be said to Olivia. Although the 'peculiarly intimate and tactile nature of women's public authority over the female body was disappearing' at the end of the early modern period, while Shakespeare was writing, searches of the body for marks of witchcraft and pregnancy, for instance, were still legally valid.[33] Although at all points on the social scale clothing offered a crucial line of protection, especially for women, the legal sanctions which could result in its legitimate penetration were far stronger against those of lower status. Negotiating the clothing of the elite was physically harder, because their dress was more complex, but it was also conceptually more difficult because fewer people had the authority so to do. Watching Olivia remove her veil as a servant woman in the audience might have brought with it some subconscious sense of a potentially open body viewing a habitually closed one – a visceral appreciation of differences in bodily control.

And those moralized vestimentary notions of 'open' and 'closed' were in themselves subject to degrees of meaning, because there was an important category in between dress and nakedness: the crucial early modern distinction between inside and outside dress, between public and private sartorial conventions. 'Undress' habitually referred to a less formal type of clothing, rather than nakedness, for those who could afford several sets of clothes. Rather than being about the body, it involved the articulation of items of dress; the loosening of that perfection of public image into a studied informality. And that informality was heavily inflected in status terms – only those of equal status or in a position of service were likely to see one in such an informal state. Onstage, in *Othello*, Dedemona asks Emilia to fetch her nightly wearing. Emilia asks whether she should fetch her nightgown but is told not to. 'In fact', Stallybrass and Jones argue, 'the absence of the nightgown makes all the more insistent the fact that we are witnessing Desdemona/a boy actor undress'.[34] But seen from the perspective of the history of elite dress, Desdemona's distinction is actually one between a nightgown – an informal gown worn in the house after the formal public attire of the day – and nightly wearing, the smock in which she will sleep. Desdemona is choosing between an 'evening in' with her husband and the end of the day, as a measure of her resignation and defeat. Again, clothing's complex layering deflects attention away from the body.

What was the material process of undressing? It is possible to perform the task of early modern elite dressing by listing the sequence of garments worn by men: the shirt, then the waistcoat, on top the doublet and finally a jerkin. The doublet was fastened to the hose by passing points or laces through eyelet holes made in the waist of both and tying them together. Then a girdle with dagger and rapier attached would be fastened around the waist, and netherstocks (stockings) held up with garters covered the legs. Finally, a gown or a cloak was worn on top, and shoes, hat, handkerchief and gloves completed the outfit. Female dress began with the smock, on top of which was worn a skirt called a kirtle, sometimes divided by a contrasting and decorated 'forepart', a triangle of cloth at the front. Above was the boned bodice with sleeves tied into it and perhaps a partlet or decorative yoke filling in the area of the chest and cleavage. On top of all was worn the gown.[35]

Stallybrass and Jones argue that, 'in bed scene after bed scene, what is staged is a tableau in which we are about to witness the *female body* (and most particularly the female breast), even though it is a *boy* who is undressing'. They do not believe that 'the convention of the boy actor meant that the physical body of the boy was subsumed by the conventions of femininity signified by costume and gesture'. Such subsumptions, they say, were 'played with to the point of their undoing'.[36] But the way gendered clothing was organized suggests a complication of the notion of 'the brink of undress'. The final layer was the smock for women and the shirt for men. These were famously similar items, borrowed between the sexes as attested to by historical accounts and satirized by Ben Jonson in *Every Man in his Humour*. Undressed, then, in a way appropriate for bed, men and women were at the point in their clothed identity where they were most similar, where gender differences had given way to status similarities expressed in the quality of linen and the addition of embroidery and lace. If these are the meanings of undress, then the bodily location of gender becomes suddenly less important.

Partly this is again a question of clothing standing for the body, and deflecting attention onto itself. In her analysis of Lady Elizabeth's portrait, discussed above, Ellen Chirelstein argues for a particular mode of desire. 'Elizabeth Pope's figure is not', she says, 'an object of desire or a vehicle for the expression of emotion.' Rather, 'her heraldic body restricts the play of erotic meaning to the voluptuous display of wealth and status'.[37] Despite the fact that she is shown in an informal mode of dress which reveals most of her chest, the play of desire is not linked to that imagined connection between cloth and skin. Rather, a different kind of eroticism is suggested here, a material desire rather than, or perhaps as a form of, a sexual one. Clothing's crucial roles in the definition of both gender and status are here brought together then, into an erotic of status, of wealth, which has the potential to short circuit the body as a location of desire, or at least to play down its role in the generation of longing for another person. And this in turn indicates that status generates desire as a lust for power which finds its location in the material expressions by which people show their status on their bodies – the rich complexities of their clothing. The truly shocking thing about the way this trope of potentially erotic viewing works in *Twelfth Night*, of course, is the fact that it positions a servant (although admittedly an elite one) as the viewing subject.

But this evidence also suggests that the similarity of male and female undress outside the theatre played with the notion of surfaces in a way which made fabric into the body to be desired. Linen was thin, thinner the richer one was, and placed over skin 'the boundaries blurred between the two, and the second skin of cloth became meta-phorically indistinguishable from the body's "natural" covering'. Such an argument can be extended to bands, cuffs and ruffs 'found at the visual borders between body and clothing, thus helping to separate public from private space. Being neither wholly textile nor entirely skin, their lacy texture mediated between the two.'[38] It might be, then, that it was the lace with which this chapter began which signified the body on the stage, just as much as the scenes of near-nakedness which were staged. Lace suggested the fineness of linen, the alluring social status of the body's identity as much as its potentially tactile presence underneath.

Freud argued that 'The progressive concealment of the body which goes along with civilization keeps sexual curiosity awake. This curi-osity seeks to complete the sexual object by revealing its hidden parts.'[39] Clothing, in this formulation, is always a metonym, always merely an indication of a whole which cannot be shown. But early modern clothing reads more like a metaphor for different states of dress and undress and their corresponding levels of intimacy and formality, or for the desires stimulated by status through cloth – more like a visual substitute for what is not to be seen than a small suggestion which guides the imagination through layers of cloth to the body beneath. This period's focus on the quality and the imper-meability of clothed surfaces militates against the applicability of Freud's view to early modern England. Elite clothing in particular, but all clothing to an extent, might hold the eye in a richer way than the imperfect, diseased body, discouraging and diverting the imagin-ation towards a perfectible material exterior. Stage clothing might, the majority of the time at least, be drawing attention primarily to itself.

# Household, rooms and the spaces within

Armchair, wood, gilt and painted, with silk velvet upholstery, early seventeenth century, Victoria and Albert Museum.

This chapter explores the way Shakespeare uses material culture to create the illusion of a household interior on the stage. It starts with a chair to make the point that the interiors which Shakespeare's audience saw were not produced through stage sets or scenery, but by the generation of a unique series of spatial dynamics which connected objects to the plays' emotional discourses and to a complex atmosphere of moral and judicial interest in space outside the theatre.

This is a magnificent chair in every sense of the word. Its dimensions are large – it stands a metre high, 70cm wide and almost as deep, but it appears proportionally broader, partly because of the bold richness of the silk velvet fabric with which it is covered. The dark stripe across the centre of the back shows where a thick fringe was attached, and further fringes would have dropped from the base of the back and the seat, all helping to emphasize the width of the area left for the occupant. The painted decoration on the flat part of the front legs to which the seat is attached follows the line of the velvet in a similar colour, extending it out to the very edge of the frame. The stretchers – the pieces of wood which connect the legs to one another near the ground – reinforce the horizontal lines of the seat in their sturdiness.

The chair's angles suggest a particular kind of seated pose – the arms slope downwards but rise just at the end in a scroll to provide a natural resting place for the hands, which would expose jewelled fingers to those facing the sitter; the back slopes backwards, unusually for a chair of this period, in order to provide a slightly more relaxed posture, one which assumes respect. And the front legs are turned whilst the rear ones are square and plainer, suggesting that the chair was intended to be viewed from the front as that is where its decoration is concentrated. Sitting in a chair like this meant expecting to be addressed directly, and to hold the attention of others in the room.

Despite the monumental heaviness of the wood from which the chair is made and its style of manufacture, the decoration is light and subtle. It is still possible to make out the gilt paint which forms the ground of the ornament, and some of the floral imagery which has been applied to the legs, stretchers and uprights. The flowers and leaves are formalized in design and would originally have been very brightly coloured, well set off against the gold. And the chair would have had gilt finials at the top of the back uprights, one in each corner.

Its visual appeal, in other words, is the glint of precious metals in daylight or candlelight, against the rich deepness of velvet. It draws attention to itself and its occupant.

Painted, gilded, carved, turned, joined and upholstered, this is a very luxurious piece of furniture, and it clearly demonstrates elite status. Houses of the middling sort contained perhaps one or two wooden chairs. In a sample of 1,650 early modern inventories, only just over 1,000 properties contained chairs. Of that 1,000, only 10 per cent had more than three and just over half had only one, for the head of the house.[1] The decoration of such non-elite chairs was provided by carving rather than painting, and they were very rarely upholstered, having detachable cushions which could be moved around as needed. They were used around tables with a set of stools, or for seating by the fireside with benches. Upholstered furniture, however, was often made in matching sets, in this case perhaps a set of smaller chairs without the arms. Seating, in other words, materialized both the interconnectedness of individuals within a household and their relative status, the head of the house being seated in the most impressive chair. Putting one's arms over the arms of a chair was one of the gestures through which domestic authority was practised, was made material, palpable for both superior and subordinate.

Of course we do not know what kind of chairs actually appeared on the stage in Shakespeare's plays, but there are several scenes which call for this kind of elite object, two of which will be considered in this chapter. It is perhaps part way between the 'Chair of State' or throne called for in court scenes and the more regular chairs widely used either to carry on the sick or to indicate, for instance, a meal.[2] It may well be that the same kind of furniture was used in all these cases, its status altered by the cloth of state which hung over a throne, or by cushions for a domestic scene. The power of playing can turn an ordinary chair into a throne in the audience's imagination – as Andrew Sofer argues in his book on the prop, it 'springs into life as much in the imaginations of spectators as in the hands of actors or the words of the playwright'.[3]

In all cases, however, bringing a chair onto the stage provides a sort of theatrical shorthand for an interior space. Immediately and economically, its presence defines the scene as taking place inside and, apart from the case of the throne, within a household interior. In

*Richard II*, for instance, John of Gaunt enters in Act 2 Scene 1 'sick', the actor carried onto the stage in a chair. The chair is crucial to the scene because of the spatial dynamic it creates. Its meanings are nicely paradoxical. First, the way Gaunt is carried in takes away his physical autonomy, and his need to use the chair underlines his failing strength and his bodily frailness. His age and his impending death are stressed throughout in the dialogue, and the chair is an important part of making visible the decrepitude of a healthy actor – bodying it forth for an audience. And the precariousness of Gaunt's life is a significant ground for the words he speaks to the King – the words of dying men were and perhaps still are taken to be not only utterly true (as the moment for guile has now passed) but also, therefore, to have a prophetic quality, 'they say the tongues of dying men/Enforce attention, like deep harmony' (5–6) as Gaunt puts it.

And as his impending death gives his words a powerful context, so the chair itself gives to the actor who inhabits it a striking performative power. It creates a particular kind of space around itself – the focused space which separates onstage actor from onstage audience, but which simultaneously holds them in firm relation to one another. Gaunt's chair orders 2.1 – localizes it – insists upon its status as an interior scene linked to a domestic space. The more the closeness of Gaunt's death is insisted upon, the more, fixed in his chair, the royal party are forced to organize themselves around him. As the posture suggested by the shape of the chair is one of authority, so the King must be forced, at least at points, to stand in front of a seated man in order to hear the uncomfortable words which Gaunt addresses to him. In such a situation, the chair has interesting resonances with a Chair of State in the sense that it sets its occupant apart from the other characters in the scene, providing a constant perspective of power upon events. Gaunt's vulnerable power in relation to his weak king can be played up by the way an actor uses the prop.

Gathered around Gaunt in this scene are his 'courtly neighbours' we might say, both the King and Aumerle are his relatives and the others are of his community. And here again the chair makes a very precise kind of social meaning. As it organizes the characters around the dying man as their focus of attention, so the action becomes visually reminiscent of an early modern deathbed. This social trope was a very recognizable one, familiar to Shakespeare's audiences from the church courts' investigations into the validity of testaments, from the *Ars Moriendi* tradition of writings about a good death, and from their own personal experiences of being called upon to bear witness to the wills of friends, relatives and neighbours. In this trope the words of the dying man have to be closely attended to because they have executive power, and for this reason those who are to bear witness gather closely and attentively around the testator, their concentration sharpened by the importance of completing earthly tasks in time: 'Will the king come, that I may breathe my last' as Gaunt asks in the first line of 2.1. The prop brings with it, then, a social unit, a piece of theatre which is also a recognizable ritual of offstage life, and these units are powerful imaginative triggers for an audience.[4]

And if we see the chair in this scene as providing a visual clue to this very specific kind of social practice, then the words Gaunt speaks from it represent his last will and testament. A great deal of his discourse in this scene is about inheritance, and the scene develops, extends and gives point to a sequence of speeches about property. In 1.4 Richard talks about Gaunt's property, setting the audience up to receive the old man's description of England in relation to their knowledge of what is going to happen to his own estates. Richard sees private property as a transmutable commodity, saying 'The lining of his [Gaunt's] coffers shall make coats'(60) to clothe soldiers for the Irish wars. Clothing was often given in the early modern period to be made into something else, but this is a gross parody of the creative reuse of worn materials. What Richard does in taking away Bolingbroke's patrimony, of course, is to disrupt all the laws of inheritance on which his kingdom stands. As York says to him after Gaunt's death,

> Take Hereford's rights away, and take from Time
> His charters and his customary rites:
> Let not tomorrow then ensue today;
> Be not thyself, for how art thou a king
> But by fair sequence and succession?
>
> (2.1.196–200)

Gaunt's speech in 2.1 is a central moment in the play's thinking about the relationship between private property and the country of England as a form of inheritance. In 1.4, Richard says of Bolingbroke that he acts 'As were our England in reversion his' (34), meaning that, were Richard to die without heirs the kingdom would, like a piece of property bequeathed in a will, pass directly to him. And Richard also explains his financial position with reference to the country: 'We are enforced to farm our royal realm,/The revenue whereof shall furnish us/For our affairs in hand' (44–6). 'Farm' here means to rent, or lease, rather than to plough. It is what commoners might do with their land, and it directly echoes Gaunt's accusation that 'This land of such dear souls, this dear dear land,/ . . . Is now leased out – I die pronouncing it –/Like to a tenement or pelting farm' (2.1.57–60). The domestic significance of the chair in this scene makes explicit the connections and disconnections between personal and national events, personal and national tragedies. By bringing domestic space into play, the prop sharpens the meanings of the discussions of land and lineage, of patrimony and the passing of the generations – it gives them an added significance which raises the audience's awareness of their meaning in relation to those discussions which came in the first act and those which are to follow.

At the centre of *Hamlet* is another such chair, one which is part of the furniture of Gertrude's closet. After Hamlet has said that he does know she is his mother but wishes it could be otherwise, when she threatens to leave him in her closet and to 'set those to you that can speak' (3.4.17), he makes her stay: 'Come, come, and sit you down. You shall not budge./You go not till I set you up a glass/Where you may see the inmost part of you' (18–20). And again, as she presumably rises up when he stabs Polonius, he insists 'Peace, sit you down' (33). The chair secures her presence, and thus the focus of the scene.

Gertrude's chair, like Gaunt's, is a chair that bespeaks status – standing for one of a set of chairs in a queen's closet it might be read as being of just such imposing quality as the one at the head of this chapter. As with Gaunt's chair, of course, it might actually be represented by a much less impressive piece of furniture on the stage, but the logic of the repeated identification of this room as a royal closet demands that the audience imagine a stately piece of furniture suitable for a queen to sit upon: the closet was part of a suite of rooms forming the royal apartments which were often accessed through one another – the final room, it was attached to but separate from the bedchamber and came perhaps closer than any room to offering the monarch private space. But in this scene, as in *Richard II*, the sitter's authority is compromised, not because of physical weakness this time but because of the moral frailty of which Hamlet accuses Gertrude while she sits in the chair. And unlike the way Gaunt's seated position organized characters around itself in *Richard II*, in *Hamlet* the only other character on stage enforces Gertrude's sitting. Making her sit down underlines the physical and emotional power which Hamlet's anger gives him and it puts her relative physical and moral weakness into tension with her status as a queen, as the occupant of the closet for whom such a chair was designed.

The closet scene is at the centre of *Hamlet* in the sense that it comes approximately half way through the play, but it is also at its emotional heart. Its combination of strong emotion and secluded space is enormously powerful, and it interacts in interesting ways with the kinds of political power which are displayed in the surrounding scenes. Stephen Greenblatt talks about *Hamlet*'s 'magical intensity', and this scene is a significant part of that impression with which the play leaves us.[5]

The interior space developed in the closet scene takes a great deal of its meaning from contrast – it is given its physical qualities and its significance in relation to the way space is developed in the play as a whole. Other plays build up their sense of family and the mutual relations of the household through a mimetic relationship between different domestic spaces within the same house, shown sequentially to the audience with the illusion that they and the actions that take place within them are linked together. In *Romeo and Juliet*, for instance, scenes of preparation for Capulet's feast generate frantic speeches of comic confusion: Peter enters at the end of 1.3 saying 'Madam, the guests are come, supper served up, you called, my young lady asked for, the Nurse cursed in the pantry, and everything in extremity. I must hence to wait. I beseech you follow straight' (101–5). His mention of the guests to whom supper is served and the pantry from which the provisions come brings a whole household into relation with the room that the stage itself is taken to represent, and stresses the interdependency of spaces and different domestic activities.

The logic that space gives to the action in *Hamlet*, however, is by and large that the rooms of Elsinore are disconnected, that the actions which go on in each fail to come together to form the kind of productive sense of household which comes across in Peter's speech. Inside space becomes a general environment in the sense that it is shaped and given its uniquely oppressive quality by the politics of surveillance in Claudius' court. The play fails to differentiate between rooms: whatever space events take place in is much the same as another, overlooked and filled with the foreboding of 'rotten' Denmark. Claudius entreats Rosencrantz and Guildenstern 'That you vouchsafe your rest here in our court' (2.2.13); Hamlet tells the players 'You are welcome to Elsinore' (2.2.549). The pervasive political atmosphere of Denmark is echoed in the non-specific terms in which the castle is opened up to strangers.

The striking paucity of named spaces in this play immediately makes the closet stand out. There are some suggestions of location – in 1.3, for instance, Laertes is 'stayed for' to go 'Aboard, aboard, for shame!'(55–7), indicating that he might be on a quay. But he could just as easily still be in the castle and running even later for his passage as no one takes the trouble to locate the scene precisely by saying the equivalent of 'here on this quay...'. Laertes' passionate speech to Claudius accuses him over the matter of his father's 'means of death, his obscure burial –/No trophy, sword, or hatchment o'er his bones' (4.5.211–2), which suggests a location where he has been able to visit Polonius' tomb, but one that he does not name. Hamlet, unable to reason with Rosencrantz and Guildenstern, says 'Shall we to th' court?' (2.2.267), suggesting somewhere which must be a location within Elsinor, but which is being used primarily here as an event, a political context rather than a room.

And much of the spatial language in the play operates metaphorically. 'Denmark's a prison'(2.2.246), Hamlet tells Rosencrantz and Guildenstern, and he reflects on this idea in a way which develops our sense of his spatial understanding: 'I could be bounded in a nutshell and count myself a king of infinite space, were it not that I have bad dreams' (256–8). 'I'll be placed, so please you, in the ear/Of all their conference' (3.1.187–8) says Polonius, obscuring physical location with a sense of its value for observation. The ending of 4.4 in the second quarto has the Norwegian Captain explain his campaign in terms which express the futility not only of war but of spatial identity: 'We go to gain a little patch of ground/That hath in it no profit but the name' (9–10). Laertes says that he will cut Hamlet's 'throat i'th' church' (4.6.99), but he means something like 'the most sacred and therefore inappropriate place' rather than a specific ecclesiastical location for a slaughter.

Those spaces which are named therefore stand out. There is the area outside the castle: Marcellus tells Hamlet that they saw the Ghost 'upon the platform where we watched' (1.2.213), and 5.1 is spent exploring the old and new residents of the graveyard. These spaces fit their actions well – the graveyard, the most carefully realized exterior location, provides a focus for the performance of *memento mori* and the platform on which the ghost appears has liminal qualities which give it a sense of uncertainty and perhaps threat. Inside, Hamlet tells Osric in 5.2 as they prepare for the duel, 'Sir, I will walk here in the hall' (5.2.134), and in the second quarto's extended version of the passage a Lord tells him 'My lord, his majesty commended him to you by young Osric, who brings back to him that you attend him in the hall.' This location does shape the action which takes place there in the audience's mind, and of course it is the action which constructs the room itself: a duel needs the logic of a large room, and its significance is given an especially pointed quality by it taking place in the most public and impressive room of an elite house, as a showpiece of court entertainment analogous to the play-within-the-play. Hall and Graveyard are both spaces with a visual focus – the latter on the trap used as a grave, around which most of the action revolves, and the former a table necessary to hold the cups and weapons. The closet scene, similarly focused upon its chair, is the epitome of the play's development of the mutually constituting relationship between space and action.

In many cases, however, these spaces are identified long after the action first begins in them – Marcellus reports that they saw the Ghost on the platform in the following scene, he does not say this while they are actually there. Spatial identification is also often precisely targeted at a particular effect. Over 160 lines into 2.2 Polonius, searching for a way to 'try further' his theory that Hamlet's problems are caused by love for Ophelia, lights upon the idea of overhearing them. Only at this point do the audience need to know where the characters are: 'You know sometimes he walks four hours together/Here in the lobby' (2.2.162–3). The location is significant only when a particular kind of space is needed. In contrast, the closet as a location is very carefully built up in advance: both Polonius and

Rosencrantz identify it by name, and discussion of and preparation for the proposed meeting permeate the majority of act 3.

A significant aspect of space which the play sets up in advance of the closet scene is its susceptibility to control. Ophelia tells Polonius that 'as you did command/I did repel his letters and denied/His access to me' (2.1.109–11) – she is capable of managing space in a way effective enough to keep Hamlet out. Claudius' request to 'good Laertes' that he should 'keep close within your chamber' (4.6 101–2) suggests that all the characters possessed private rooms within this open court, and we are told that 'The King and Queen are all coming down', in the Q2 version of 5.2, underlining the relationship between the public, open space of the hall and the private apartments of the castle. Indeed, also in Q2 Ophelia is said to have her own closet, meaning that both of the play's women have a relatively personal and private space to which they can retire, but one whose controllability is contested by Hamlet.

And there are a couple of moments when the audience is given a sense of the political significance of being able to prevent access. In 4.5 Claudius says 'The doors are broke'(109) and Laertes enters with his followers, threatening the King's rule with the power of mob feeling which cannot be kept out. Later on there is *A noise within*. Coming so soon after the danger posed by an uncontrollable political space, the noise offstage has the effect of reintroducing the idea of external threat, but this time the trope is inverted as Ophelia enters, mad (155) – the danger is a domestic one now, of the emotional kind. When Hamlet shouts, as he discovers he is dying, 'O villainy! Ho! Let the door be locked!' (5.2.264), his words recall that connection between political and domestic danger established in the earlier scene. The way the physical controllability of space is set against the exercise of power to exclude and include lies behind the closet's physical qualities.

It is around the closet scene that the most sustained sequence of spaces is generated. In 3.2, Rosencrantz tells Hamlet that his mother 'desires to speak with you in her closet ere you go to bed (318–19); in the following scene Polonius tells Claudius that 'he's going to his mother's closet' (3.3.27); after the scene itself the opening stage direction to 4.1 is *Enter King Claudius to Queen Gertrude*, showing that this scene takes place in the same conceptual space. And in the course of it, Claudius tells Rosencrantz and Guildenstern that Hamlet has murdered Polonius 'And from his mother's closet hath he dragged him./Go seek him out, speak fair, and bring the body/Into the chapel. I pray you haste in this' (34–6). Having refused to tell them, Hamlet finally confesses to Claudius that 'if you find him not this month, you shall nose him as you go up the stairs into the lobby' (4.3.35–6). This relationship between closet, lobby and chapel is the clearest, most palpable geography of Elsinore which the play offers, but it is still a primarily metaphorical set of locations which plots the relationship between spaces within which things might be hidden, those in which they become public, and those through which the wider spiritual implications of actions can be explored. More than any other location within the play, Gertrude's closet is bound into Elsinore's spaces in a way which gives it a deeper texture of significance than *Hamlet*'s other settings.

In the way the space for action is set up, the closet scene is most closely linked to 3.1 in which Hamlet and Ophelia's meeting is overheard by Polonius and Claudius. The two scenes have in common the arras behind which Polonius suggests he and the king hide in the first, and behind which he 'silences' himself in the Folio text, or 'shrouds' himself in the first quarto, in Gertrude's closet. 3.1 too is set up for the audience in advance, when Polonius suggests to Claudius in 2.2, 'I'll loose my daughter to him./Be you and I behind an arras then./Mark the encounter' (164–6). But the scene itself opens with the entry of Claudius, Gertrude, Polonius, Ophelia, Rosencrantz, Guildenstern and some lords: in other words it looks, at the outset, like a scene of state, but the lords have no purpose whatsoever in it, Rosencrantz and Guildenstern exit after revealing that they have been unable to find out the cause of Hamlet's madness (perhaps the lords go with them?), and Gertrude is told by Claudius:

> Sweet Gertrude, leave us too,
> For we have closely sent for Hamlet hither,
> That he, as 'twere by accident, may here
> Affront Ophelia.
> Her father and myself, lawful espials,
> Will so bestow ourselves that, seeing unseen,
> We may of their encounter frankly judge
>
> (30–6).

His speech makes it clear that those present can now be trusted: it is almost defensive about the level of its policy – Hamlet has been 'closely', i.e. privately, sent for, and his identification of his own and Polonius' role as '*lawful* espials' or spies only serves to raise a question mark over just how lawful such actions may or may not be. The neat wordplay on their status – 'seeing unseen' – gets to the heart of the compromising physical and political position in which king and an 'assistant for a state' (2.2.168) find themselves. The final piece of stage management involves Polonius instructing his daughter: 'walk you here . . . Read on this book,/That show of such an exercise may colour/ Your loneliness' (45–8). Ophelia is to pretend, both to be at her devotions and to be alone, and this level of artifice is perhaps the key element of the scene – it makes what appears to be an intimate conversation between past, present or potential lovers into an event of political espionage.

Act 3 scene 4, coming only two scenes after this overhearing, both replicates and alters the model of a qualified and undermined privacy. It is set up in such a way that there is considerable ambiguity about what kind of event will take place within – encouraging the audience to question the extent to which the meeting in 3.4 will be one between monarch and courtier or between mother and son. The action which leads to the scene begins at the play-within-the-play in 3.2, when Claudius rises in anger. 'How fares my lord?' (255) Gertrude asks; 'Give me some light. Away' (257) is his indirect answer to her. Hamlet is left on stage with Horatio, joined by Rozencrantz and Guildenstern, and then later by Polonius who tells him 'My lord, the Queen would speak with you, and presently' (364). The inference is that she has told him so offstage, as a result of the uproar caused by the play. After the fruitlessly comic discussion of the shape of the cloud, and apparently decided by it, Hamlet replies 'Then will I come to my mother by and by' (371). The closet scene is therefore linked to the 'Murder of Gonzago', generated by a command given indirectly whose rationale the audience are left to guess at, in action which is to be taken to have run its course while they were watching something else. When the meeting is discussed again in 3.3, there is the suggestion that it may have been the subject of more extensive planning. Polonius' 'My lord, he's going to his mother's closet' and the subsequent 'And, as you said – and wisely was it said –'Tis meet that some more audience than a mother . . . should o'erhear' (30–2) indicate that the idea has in fact been generated in discussion either by the two men or by them in conversation with Gertrude. In any case, the reasons for this meeting in the closet are shady, shrouded in a foreknown and therefore unspoken set of confidences to which the audience are not party, and closely linked to the security of Claudius' rule.

Gertrude's role is unclear as the scene opens then – is she acting politically on behalf of her husband or personally in relation to her son? Will this be a public or a private scene? It appears to be developing along just the same lines as 3.1: Polonius is told by Gertrude to 'withdraw' as she hears Hamlet coming, and he once more hides himself behind the arras. This cloth, presumably hung across one of the doors of entry to the stage, locates 3.4 as it did 3.1, giving the stage-space a sense of a defined interior. In this scene, however, it connects to the chair on which Gertrude later sits to make an identifiable room rather than a passageway: recognizable elements in an elite interior when brought into configuration with one another. It is these two props which create the physical sense of Gertrude's closet as the play's most concentrated space. And in this play of political and emotional isolation, in which rule is uncertain, love tokens are displayed only as they are handed back, old friends turn out to be current spies, and revenge must be worked out alone, bounded space has a particular kind of resonance.

The connections between 3.1 and 3.4 tie the latter into the dynamics of spying. It is Polonius who appears to control how the space of the closet will be used. His presence is justified by Claudius' assertion which he repeats in the previous scene: ''Tis meet that some more audience than a mother,/Since nature makes them partial, should o'erhear/The speech of vantage' (3.3.31–3). His presence, then, is explicitly as an outsider, and one hidden from the view of one of the parties again. And his words are very close to commands to his queen, striking in a play which makes considerable use of the language of deference:

> Look you lay home to him.
> Tell him that his pranks have been too broad to bear with,
> And that your grace hath screened and stood between
> Much heat and him

(1–4).

And then at the end finally a more civil request: 'Pray you be round with him' (5). The fact that he speaks first, that he does so in such a directive way, and that the matter he raises is entirely political rather than domestic in the quotidian sense, plays against the sense of privacy and controllability suggested by the location's interior qualities, making Gertrude's closet seem an extension of her husband's court rather than her own private quarters.

The connections between the two scenes of espionage also show how important the discourses of sight, revelation and spying are to the construction of space. The action in 3.1 takes place, of course, as a way of bringing to light Hamlet's hidden emotions – Polonius says Ophelia's dealings with him 'must be known' rather than 'being kept close' (2.1.119), and that he will 'find/Where truth is hid, though it were hid indeed/Within the centre' (2.2.159–61). As these dynamics feed into the closet scene, they palpably alter the quality of the stage space within which the encounter takes place. Patricia Parker points out 'how closely bound up both the plot of *Hamlet* and its obsessive language of "seeing" are with the visual preoccupations of the world of informer and spy', and suggests that the play comes at a crucial historical juncture; 'the point where an older language of divine or angelic intelligence was being converted into the new lexicon of espial and the "privy intelligences" provided by a progressively more organized network of informers and spies'.[6] These languages have their material manifestations: the lobby is brought into being by the arras – by the audience's sense that they are not the only ones watching Hamlet and Ophelia – as a particular kind of space which permits characters to be simultaneously physically present and visually absent. The arras is the material signifier of a curiously liminal type of presence which is intended to unsettle the audience's sense of the relationship between public and private spaces and scenes.

But the differences between the two scenes are as important as their similarities. The audience is asked to construct in their imaginations the two very distinct domestic areas of 'lobby' and 'closet', and to bring the logic of such spaces to bear on their understanding of the events which take place there. The lobby is an open space with a particular set of semi-political meanings. The *Oxford English Dictionary* gives a primary meaning of 'A passage or corridor connected with one or more apartments in a building, or attached to a large hall, theatre, or the like', and this coincides with its use in *Hamlet*, where people pass through it on their way from chambers or closets to a hall which may also have been used for the performance of a play. In other words, it is a connecting space, not a location so much as a place which facilitates motion between locations – a space in which to be moving, not stopping. But the definition continues, 'often used as a waiting-place or ante-room', and this seems to pick up on aspects of a later meaning, given as dating from the 1640s: 'In the House of Commons, and other houses of legislature, a large entrance-hall or apartment open to the public, and chiefly serving for interviews between members and persons not belonging to the House'. The earlier meaning also has some of this sense of a place where one waits for political favours – for instance this example from *2 Henry VI*, 'How in our voiding lobby has thou stood/And duly waited for my comming forth?' (4.1.62–3), or *Timon*, 'All those which were his fellows but of late,/ . . . Follow his strides, his lobbies fill with tendance' (1.1.79–81).[7] In addition to the sense of movement which the space gives then, there is an impression of its position on the fringes of political power, a space whose habitation is controlled by the influence of the authority which lies beyond.

On the other hand, the royal closet in this period 'was situated increasingly at the heart of a succession of public rooms', following in succession from the gallery, presence chamber, privy chamber and finally royal bedchamber.[8] It was movement through these spaces in sequence which created the relative sense of the size and quality of experience of the innermost room, and which made palpable for those entertained within the awareness of their own superiority and their proximity to power in ways which used spatial closeness as a metaphor for political influence. The closet was the 'private apartment of a monarch or potentate; the private council-chamber' or 'a room in a palace used by the sovereign for private or household devotions' (*Oxford English Dictionary*). These three related definitions suggest the overlap between monarchical domestic and religious space (those activities usually limited to individuals and their families) and rooms used for discussions of state matters amongst a small group of advisors – the 'privy council' is a pertinent concept here.

But the closet also had meaning outside this royal context, and it is some version of these significances which *Hamlet*'s audience is likely to have brought to the theatre. In an article on the diversity of early modern meanings, Lena Orlin demonstrates that there was no single definition for the word, but rather the kind of 'considerable slippage in contemporary usage' shown by Ophelia's reference to sewing in her 'closet' in the second quarto or 'chamber' in the Folio. Orlin traces nine different types of early modern room referred to as closets: the prayer closet, study, counting-house, storehouse, private pantry, jewel house, pharmaceutical closet, parlour and bedchamber. Of course, these meanings have several things in common – Orlin points to the fact that 'the closet was that which could be closed; it could be locked', we might also want to add that these meanings underline the preservation of things which are reserved, and not for all the house-hold – they materialize domestic hierarchies by keeping servants, for example, out. And crucially, of course, these various rooms have their small size in common and their relatively private nature. They all facilitate the intensification of experience – they are smaller than those spaces through which their occupants have recently passed and potentially more controllable. In several of the meanings there is a further suggestion of a kind of honesty or truthfulness linked to the type of behaviour which was possible within them: 'In 1625, Lady Katherine Paston advised her son to pray "in thy Closet privately by thy own self, when none may hear or see thee, but He alone who searcheth the heart" '.[9] The layers of social identity seem here to be stripped away to produce something more sincere and honest.

Orlin reads her disparate evidence as offering a series of largely separate possibilities: the 'absence of other reference points in *Hamlet*', she says, 'only keeps all these meanings alive: nine different closets and, in consequence, nine different Gertrudes as well as nine different Hamlets and nine different notions about what Shakespeare was up to in setting this scene in a closet'.[10] But this is the skill of the way the scene is put together – the chair around which the space is brought into being is generic enough to hold some or all of these meanings in place at the same time like spokes around the hub of a wheel; unlike a bed, for instance, it does not prioritize some meanings over others. The simplicity of the staging allows meanings to crowd in upon the stage space, picking up echoes thrown out by the language: Hamlet's prayer when his father's ghost enters might, for example, draw out the notion of a closet for devotions.[11] The fact that the word 'closet' has currency in the direct experience of those from the middling sort upwards and their servants suggests that this is a relatively open and inclusive kind of scene, one which permits many of its audience to think through its meanings from their direct experience. Minimal staging brings disparate meanings and dissimilar audience experiences together.

And these intersecting meanings of the word closet suggest the complexities of the confrontations which the audience witness in Gertrude's room. As explored above, the scene is comparatively closely tied into the play's other spaces, and it is also possible to see the action in similar terms: 3.4 can be conceptually tied to 3.3 in which Claudius tries to pray, in the sense that he may well be doing so in his own closet, and although it is not explicitly named, such connections can be brought out in performance. It is also firmly linked to the scene which follows it in spatial terms, as 4.1 begins with the stage direction *Enter King Claudius to Queen Gertrude* – which makes it clear that the action takes place once more within the same room. The dramatic sequence of revelation and encounter can, in other words, be extended beyond the closet scene, but in emotional terms 3.1 possesses its own significant integrity and distinctive shape. In terms of the way the characters and action inflect the general meanings of the word closet, 3.4 is divided into three distinct sections. In the first one which we have been considering here, Polonius enters, discusses his plan for the meeting with Gertrude, hides and is killed; in the second, Hamlet and Gertrude discuss her new and old husbands; in the third the Ghost appears and disappears and Hamlet and his mother reach a conclusion. Each of these sections is differently focused, and the qualities of the space altered as a result of the characters on stage, their actions and their position in relation to one another. By exploring the rather different feel of each section and thinking about how they cohere into one scene, we can investigate the way Shakespeare makes stage space.

Some context is useful here. Shakespeare's plays contain several intense interior scenes which bear comparison with the closet scene. They are explicitly set within bedchambers, however, and their dynamics are interestingly different as a result. In both *Othello* and *Cymbeline*, the chambers contain and develop female identity. Both begin with a discussion between an elite woman and a servant: Innogen tells her maid Helen to 'Fold down the leaf where I have left' reading her book and 'Take not away the taper; leave it burning' (2.2. 4–5). Similarly, Desdemona asks Emilia to, 'Prithee tonight/Lay on my bed my wedding sheets, remember' (4.2.107–8), and when Emilia mentions the sheets again in 4.3, saying that she has laid them upon the bed, Desdemona asks her '[i]f I do die before thee, prithee shroud me/In one of these same sheets' (23–4). In the later scene, Desdemona asks to be unpinned, and in doing so she makes clear that this is a space where women might expect to be uninter-rupted, where they might find a physical privacy. The distinctive intimacy of tending to a woman's needs as she goes to and rises from her bed, explored in the previous chapter, gives the bedchambers an initial sense of being set away from the public spaces where one's image is read by strangers. Here, those public identities are both made and unmade daily. And the way both scenes use the pragmatism of domestic detail is striking. The small processes of household main-tenance, the quotidian activities of daily life such as the tending of candles and the making of beds, create a space which is familial and as such secure and protective, nurturing. It is ripe to be violated as a result.

This impression is given through the use of small props in relation to large ones. The presence of a book and a candle, sheets and clothing on stage with a bed creates an almost mimetic sense of a bedchamber, acting more as scenery than as a series of props. The beds which fill the stage in both plays create a room in and of themselves in the sense that they do not only focus the audience's attention but also permit action within them. And they bring with their physical form a range of themes about marriage, procreation and lineage which therefore become the ground of the action which takes place there.[12] Bedchambers give a very different and more compact set of meanings to closets through their distinct dynamics between props and actions.

Considering the way the chambers in *Cymbeline* and *Othello* are set up makes us realize just how different Gertrude's closet is. The distinction comes partly from the order in which events take place. Desdemona's and Innogen's activities open the scenes, and they set out a baseline of domestic normality, underwrite their own control of the space and define its purpose as one of feminine nurture and rest. These peaceful openings can then contrast sharply with the violations which follow. But we first see Gertrude's closet as a place of tension and haste: 'A will come straight' Polonius says of Hamlet, opening the scene with the insistence that the conversation must be concluded quickly so that he can conceal himself. As he ends his brief speech Hamlet can be heard within calling 'Mother, mother, mother!', a line which both adds immeasurably to the sense of the onstage space as interior and domestic and builds the pressure upon Polonius' concealment. Whereas the furnishings of the room in *Othello* and *Cymbeline* work with the quotidian, female language spoken within to create a sense of an interior, in *Hamlet* the more limited props and the contention over control of the space work against one another, stressing just how rich but conflicted a space this is.

This lack of a sense of Gertrude's closet as a still space from the start has the potential to increase the authenticity of her encounter with Hamlet which is at the centre of the scene. The murder of Polonius calls a halt to the production of a scene of potential intrigue with its shocking, almost casual speed – 'How now, a rat? Dead for a ducat, dead. *He thrusts his sword through the arras*' (23). It is almost comic in the way it undermines the parallels between *Hamlet*'s two scenes of spying, and disempowers the all-seeing court. It reshapes the room as a conceptual space, altering it from a semi-open one of overlooking to a closed one of intimacy, and it permits the action within it to change in its turn from the dynamic of espionage – spying as a way of getting at the truth of emotion – to the domestic dynamic of dialogue – talking as a way of achieving sincerity. The chair and the arras come to symbolize two very different modes of acquiring knowledge, one operated by the state and one generated by dynamics within the family. Dramaturgically, they also offer two distinct styles of staging discovery, only one of which gives the emotional satisfaction which marks this scene out. When he stabs Polonius, Hamlet also stabs the arras, symbolically removing its operative power perhaps, but leaving body and prop to point up visually the change of focus of the scene.

Polonius' murder is the turning point of the closet scene, the moment when it tips from a public to a private and a household to a strictly familial space in a way which mirrors in action the distinctions which offstage closets set up within domestic spaces. When the second section of the scene starts, after Polonius' murder, it becomes clear that a meeting orchestrated by subtle policy is to be overtaken by a scene of intimate passion, and the huge satisfaction here is the directness of Hamlet and Gertrude's communication after all the oblique and invidious interactions which have come before it – its face-to-face qualities are extremely powerful. But in contrast to Shakespeare's other concentrated female spaces, it is clear that there is a significant tension here, between this section of the scene as the physically calmer and more focused passage, and the emotional violence which is nevertheless perpetrated within it.

Gertrude's chair stands testament to the changes in the quality of the closet which the scene develops between its first two sections. In the first, Gertrude sits because Hamlet's gender and his anger enforce her sitting; in the second, she sits because she is looking in detail at something, and an important part of the conjuring of these intimate and intense rooms in tragedies is the focused activities which take place within them around small props. The 'glass' which Hamlet offers to set up to enable his mother to see her inner self turns out to be, of course, not a mirror but two pictures: 'Look here upon this picture, and on this' he says, 'The counterfeit presentment of two brothers' (52–3). He then describes the image of his father in terms which resemble the formal description of the image of a loved one:

> See what a grace was seated on this brow –
> Hyperion's curls, the front of Jove himself,
> An eye like Mars, to threaten or command,
> A station like the herald Mercury
> New lighted on a heaven-kissing hill;
> A combination and a form indeed
> Where every god did seem to set his seal
>
> (54–60)

Hamlet's description is, in narrative terms, an explication of the image for his mother, a reading which explains its significance through description. For the audience it outlines a figure which they probably could not see – describing whilst hierarchizing, showing his partiality rather than replicating the image. Mother and son's joined, rapt attention closes off the space, makes this an interior in the sense of a space where the audience are excluded by the united direction of their gaze. 'Have you eyes?' he asks her, and then, later 'Ha, have you eyes?'. His interest in her looking, in her interpretation of what she sees, suggests the raptness of unified concentration.

The insistence on Gertrude's seated position and the element of comparison which Hamlet subsequently introduces are suggestive in terms of potential staging – 'This *was* your husband. Look you now what follows. Here *is* your husband, like a mildewed ear/Blasting his wholesome brother. . . . and what judgement/Would step from this, to this?' (62–70). His description is relentlessly physical, fully engaged with the materiality of the dynastically similar but morally different images. Gertrude expresses the change which the experience of look-ing has wrought in her in language reminiscent of the sonnets: 'Thou turn'st mine eyes into my very soul' (79) she says, employing a conceit which follows her eyes from the pictures of her past and present loves into the soul which should mirror their image – a complex and illegitimate twinning in which two resemble one.

It is considerably easier to produce the effect of comparison of two pictures by using portrait miniatures than paintings on panels, and this would also give a totally different effect. Patricia Fumerton suggests that 'Viewers could not stand back disinterestedly from a miniature as with a large-scale painting. They had to "press" together . . . getting intimately close to the limning and each other.' Rather than a formal portrait which showed the sitter in their official, public role, the miniature represented 'a lover, a mistress, a wife, an intimate friend'. The scene is therefore totally altered, depending on which kind of likeness we imagine – Old Hamlet the soldier in 'complete steel' perhaps, or Old Hamlet the husband and father pictured '*in his night gowne*' as Q1 has it later on in the scene. The miniature brings back into play the private meanings of the closet and perhaps its associations with sexuality because the image viewed is such a personal one. And the closet was an often-used space for such viewings: 'The Elizabethan aristocracy commonly sought out the most private room of the house – the bedchamber, or its attached closet or cabinet room – to view between intimates their miniatures.'[13] If we imagine other props on stage, then perhaps the two images were kept in a box or casket, but if we picture a more pragmatic type of theatre then it would be perfectly possible to pull such a prop from an actor's pocket or from their bosom – indeed it would be feasible to mime a miniature, as an object which fits into the palm of the hand. We might then suppose that it is Hamlet who produces the image of his father, kept close about his person as a token of his remembrance and his grief, and that he finds the image of Claudius on his mother, perhaps around her neck. If this was the case, then looking at one another's images would bring the actors physically even closer and it would underline visually the complex connections of kinship, love and sexuality which bind all four individuals together. The sense of a resonant interior which we associate with this scene is generated largely by this central section, then, in which mother and son explore close and personal familial issues through props which bring them physically close together. It is this section, in contrast to the opening with Polonius, which makes us consider the closet a private space – which moves its meanings from the political to the domestic sphere.

In doing so, it brings questions of sexuality into play within this bounded space. Gertrude's sins are what contemporaries might have called 'closet sins' as opposed to 'stage sins', the former being 'secret, hidden in a private personal space'.[14] Unlike her new husband's crimes, they are intimate activities undertaken and then brought to light in small rooms. And Hamlet's discussion of her actions in 'the rank sweat of an enseamèd bed,/Stewed in corruption, honeying and making love/Over the nasty sty –' (83–5) draws our attention to the connections between women's bodies and small interior spaces.[15] It is at this point that the specifically gendered meanings of the closet as a metaphorical space come into play most strongly. The connection which Patricia Parker makes between rhetorical and judicial ideas of secrecy and openness and female sexuality are very pertinent to the connections suggested here between the first two sections of the scene: 'Like informing or espial', she says, 'the vogue for anatomy in the early modern period involved a fascination with the ocular, with exposing what lay hid to the scrutiny of the gaze.' The 'lap of women', for instance, 'like a "doore" might be "opened" or "shut"'.[16] Through language, privacy and sexuality are directly linked here, and the moral landscape of interiors is closely explored as a result. But here again, setting the scene within a closet as opposed to a chamber is crucial. The use of the chamber in *Cymbeline* taps very explicitly into just the dynamic which Parker outlines: Giacomo asks Innogen to 'take in protection' the 'plate of rare device and jewels/Of rich and exquisite form' (1.6.190–4), which she agrees to do 'Willingly,/And pawn mine honour for their safety; since/My lord hath interest in them, I will keep them/In my bedchamber'. The connection between the rareness of the objects, her honour, and the bedchamber as their fitting location is, of course, developed at length in the 'inventory' which Giacomo takes of the room: 'Such and such pictures, there the window, such/Th'adornment of her bed, the arras' (2.2.25–6), and then 'some natural notes about her body/Above ten thousand meaner movables/Would testify t'enrich mine inventory' (28–30). He explicitly connects this small room with the body which is its greatest treasure. At this point in *Hamlet* the connections are subtler: this is not a bedchamber, it is a space within associated with an individual woman, Gertrude. As such the readings of this space are not unproblematically or solely ones which equate small rooms with women's bodies. The subtlety of the links between personal spaces and sexuality at this point in *Hamlet* permits a much broader exploration of the comparison between public and private actions and consequences.

Although these interior scenes produce the impression of a close encounter which reveals character, the knowledge the audience gain is rarely if ever equal. Gertrude is fundamental to the closet scene – it is she who is its 'anchor character' – there throughout to point up the contrasts and connections between the characters who join her for a part of it. The scene's most explicit investigation is of her sexuality and her private domestic life with her husband. And yet we learn comparatively little about her thoughts about Claudius here, only that Hamlet's words wound her. Unlike her son, about whose thought processes we know an excessive amount, this woman tells us nothing – she is the least visible major character in the play because, even in a scene such as this, her emotions remain largely unexplored.[17] The closet scene, then, pairs an inscrutable blank against a tell-all, but it is nevertheless the best source of an experiential sense of Gertrude's emotions. We are told that 'The Queen his mother/Lives almost by [Hamlet's] looks' (4.7.11–2) in Claudius' discussion with Laertes later on, and Polonius' description of the partial, biased mother, which he appears also to have heard from Claudius, reinforces this aspect of emotive relationships in advance of the closet scene itself. Gertrude's anguish at the sins Hamlet has shown her and her pained anger that he does not stop showing her even when she has seen – 'No more, sweet Hamlet' (86) and then just 'No more' (92) – makes her more vulnerable, subjugated and humiliated here than at any other point in the play. Gertrude's lack of control over space is echoed by her lack of control over the things which are brought to light within it. But when she hears her son speak to the ghost her language changes: 'Alas, how is't with you,/That you do bend your eye on vacancy,/And with th'incorporal air do hold discourse?...O gentle son,/Upon the heat and flame of thy distemper/Sprinkle cool patience!'(107–115). Responding to Hamlet's 'How is it with you, lady?', which is in itself a response to the Ghost's instruction to speak to her, she joins the three of them in tenderness in her longest speech in the scene. The quality of the space which is produced in 3.4 enables this kind of heightened emotion – it is the only kind of location in which it is possible in *Hamlet*.

That relationship of mutual tenderness which the third section of the scene ushers into the pain of the second alters the space of the closet once again, and this time in a very different direction. Hamlet is part way through his raging on the contrast between the two portraits and their subjects when the Ghost enters, an even more palpable *aide memoir*. For the second time, there are now three people in the closet, and just as Polonius brought the affairs of state into the room and sharpened the audience's perception of the quality of its space with his spying, so the ghost too alters the properties of the closet, adding to the richness of its atmosphere with the allusions which he brings with him.

Stephen Greenblatt talks of the 'topographical implausibility' of purgatory, getting to the heart of the curiousness of the ghost's presence in the room. Purgatory was a kind of anti-location, somewhere defined largely by where it was not – heaven, hell or earth – and yet given a palpable reality by its ability to hold souls, to keep them there until they could gain release. It is made very clear that the ghost of Old Hamlet is only able to leave occasionally, that his presence in Denmark is circumscribed. His statement that 'My hour is almost come/When I to sulph'rous and tormenting flames/Must render myself up' (2–4) gives urgency to his dialogue with his son in 1.5, and his assertion that he is 'Doomed for a certain term to walk the night,/ And for the day confined to fast in fires/Till the foul crimes done in my days of nature/Are burnt and purged away' (10–3) gives a pathos and gravity to the information he relates: it is as though a part of him was still there, pulling him to return. The emotional connections between worlds make the ghost appear – his own inability to rest as a result of his murder and his son's inability to let go of his memory – and these emotions of anger and of grief and loss forge their own route from purgatory to the closet. The effect of death upon the living, as became clear in Chapter 2 in the context of the troubled histories of *Merchant*'s rings, generates physical longings, yearnings for sensory presence.

Greenblatt traces an early conception of purgatory in which 'souls are compelled to return for their purgatorial suffering to places where they had most sinned'. In other words there are associations not only between a ghost and the people to whom he appears, but also between a ghost and the space in which he appears – it is one with which he was familiar in life, a place with meaning for him. In the stories of 'miserable ghosts [who] are forced to witness the pleasures, including sexual pleasures, of their widows' we see a different kind of surveillance – a need to be proximate to the emotional and physical intimacies of this world even though presence causes pain.[18] The striking Q1 stage direction is pertinent here: *Enter the Ghost in his nightgown*. His change of clothing from act 1 to act 3, from full armour to an informal gown (not a nightshirt) worn in the house after the formal public attire of the day is removed, makes it clear that these are familiar human surroundings for him, ones in which he feels governed by the proprieties of human action. In this switch between armour and nightgown the ghost seems to respect the logic of the space he enters, appears to inhabit it more fully than a Ghost should and not to seem out of place. Reginald Foakes has argued that 'It seems we can have materiality or the supernatural, but not both convincingly at the same time, whereas Shakespeare could, I believe, assume that his audience would find both plausible in the staging of the play.'[19] This is a crucial distinction – for early modern men and women it was material culture, as opposed to the spiritual or the ethereal, that was the stuff of memories. It endured long enough to pass through many hands and acquire histories, and was resonant enough to bring discourses, narratives and recollections into play. The ghost's materiality is a guarantee of his real presence, as both Hamlet and the audience can see him, but also a challenge to the logic of his bodily absence.

Old Hamlet's material presence on the stage – he is played by an actor just as Hamlet and Gertrude are – does not convey his other location explicitly, in fact quite the opposite. When Othello enters Desdemona's chamber, he brings the elevated language of tragedy into a space which has previously been characterized by domestic concerns. 'It is the cause, it is the cause, my soul./Let me not name it to you, you chaste stars' (5.2.1–2), he says, appealing to the heavens in a way which suddenly opens the room out to a wider imaginative scheme. But in *Hamlet* something rather different happens. The language does not explode the feeling of a bounded household space: 'But look, amazement on thy mother sits' the Ghost says, 'O, step between her and her fighting soul... Speak to her Hamlet' (102–5). His words are perhaps tender, certainly concentrated on the scene in front of him, and it is only that fracturing of the focused dialogue of mother and son into this curious three-way conversation in which father and son watch a mother who cannot hear both sides which marks the moment out as something extra-domestic. If we do imagine the ghost in his nightgown, in that informal garment which signals relaxation and intimacy of a domestic kind, then we have a scene which would not be at all unusual if one of the characters was not dead. That fact, conversely, makes it almost incredible, and material culture is the centre of these contradictions. As a result, this is by far the Ghost's most shocking appearance, exactly because of his almost-normality. Unlike other tragic interiors then, this closet gains its power from oddness, from the simultaneous quotidian manner of its staging and insistence upon a character's radical otherness. In the most bounded space in the play, one of the characters knows no physical boundaries. The incredible juxtaposition of purgatory and the household puts different worlds and world views within a small space which therefore becomes crowded with meaning. The Ghost, whose material presence is the epitome of both closeness and distance, colours the room in which the most intimate family discussion takes place, giving it a timescale (from before to after his death) which includes conflicting intimacies.

The presence of the Ghost brings material memory into the closet scene and makes this a space with time-depth then. In doing so, it connects the two pictures of Gertrude's husbands, the chair and the arras to the kind of resonant props explored in Chapter 2. They relate the present to the past and they bring personal history into the room. Like the skull of Yorick, the image of Old Hamlet is a material object which stands for the deceased and which can be compared to memories of them to show the change which death brings about or perhaps, in this case, doesn't. The play's wider project, that of not forgetting, is dependent upon just such material traces. In a culture steeped in things which guided the thoughts of men and women towards their end and kept the memories of those who had gone before on fingers, backs and in pockets, an early modern audience might be expected to recognize the significance of such objects instantly. And they might connect all these things about Hamlet together – his 'father's signet' which he happened to have on his sea voyage 'in my purse', which was the 'model of that Danish seal' (5.2.50–1), or the 'remembrances' of his which Ophelia delivers back to him in 3.1, given with 'words of so sweet breath composed/As made the things more rich' (100–1). These collections of things suggest for Hamlet the character a past tinctured by his material relationships with other people. And these goods are powerful – they have efficacy within the narrative, in the case of the ring a deadly efficacy, in the case of the image of his father the capacity to effect moral change – and they stress the way their owner, so often soliloquizing alone, is tied to the community of Elsinore through the objects which provoke memories of his past there.

And memory and rooms were, of course, closely linked through the practice of the Arts of Memory. Classical authors in particular recommended the house as a site which might be easily and profitably impressed with the elements of remembrance: for example 'Quintilian suggests imprinting in orderly progression a spacious house with many rooms, and then marking items to be remembered by a *nota*'.[20] The narrative could be reclaimed by reanimating the connections between space and objects through the power of the mind. As Giulio Camillo, the creator of a 'memory theatre' said, 'all the things that the human mind conceives but that cannot be seen with the eyes of the body can ... be expressed with some bodily signs, so that everyone can see directly with his own eyes all that which otherwise is submerged in the depths of the human mind'.[21] Signs bring to light the emotional core of thought by making it material; things which are brought to light are rediscovered in material form. Memory needs to be materialized, and rooms offer an ideal spatial schema for such clarification. In return, memories might transfer onto rooms, might load them with a sense of their narrative potential.

There are other kinds of space in *Hamlet* which I did not consider above, and they are in some ways the most clearly imagined in the play. They are vignettes – concentrated descriptions of events which have taken place in the past which are described in detailed spatial terms.[22] In 2.1 Ophelia tells her father the following tale:

> My lord, as I was sewing in my chamber [in F, or 'closet' in Q2],
> Lord Hamlet, with his doublet all unbraced,
> No hat upon his head, his stockings fouled,
> Ungartered, and down-gyved to his ankle,
> Pale as his shirt, his knees knocking each other,
> And with a look so piteous in purport
> As if he had been loosed out of hell
> To speak of horrors, he comes before me
>
> (78–85)

The intensity of the relationship between event and location, the fullness of the description of what took place, is a feature of the power of memory. It is a force which, by sorting the confusingly over-detailed quality of experience into the clarity of a visual image, makes the past clearer than the present, makes it also, perhaps, more real, more clearly seen because static in two-dimensional terms and therefore able to be viewed in its entirety at once. Like Ophelia's tale, Gertrude's closet tends to leave a mental image which stays with readers and audiences alike, and Shakespeare's concentrated scenes of heightened emotions in domestic interiors come closest to the focus and sharpness, the attention to detail and the visceral clarity of memory.

The closet, then, magnifies the significance of physical presence, and in doing so it draws on that thread which connects Hamlet's discussion of his mother's sexuality to his other musings on physicality in the play. The status of materiality both disgusts and fascinates Hamlet throughout, and here its most positive and most negative elements come into contact with one another: his father's presence and his obsessive imagination of his mother's sexuality. Greenblatt characterizes Hamlet's repeated mentions of putrefaction as 'an obsession with a corporeality that reduces everything to appetite and excretion'.[23] Things which in other contexts within the play turn out to be the material remnants of memory, Hamlet repeatedly sees as the degraded materiality of a worldly nature. He has an obsessive mind which cannot help imagining material connections: 'Why may not imagination trace the noble dust of Alexander till a find it stopping a bung-hole?' he asks in 5.1. 'Twere to consider too curiously to consider so' (198–201), Horatio replies. The closet is a space susceptible to producing and receiving such intense and over-wrought ideas, and its bounded space magnifies them as it is produced by them.

In this play of secrets and hidden truths then, an intimate encounter between mother and son must signify very strongly. Domestic space in this context is inherently revelatory – it effects the theatrical trick of showing the audience something real by getting inside, underneath the veneers of public identity. The organization of this scene in particular, with its third person present at intervals, works to make the central emotional crux of Gertrude's realization appear inherently honest and truthful. Perhaps there are useful comparisons to be drawn between the relationship between public and intimate scenes and the relationship between dialogue and soliloquy: both produce the illusion of interiority; the audience feel as though they are getting to the heart of the matter as they 'go inside'. In the same way that the play-within-the-play in *Hamlet* guarantees the reality of the fiction which surrounds it, unlocated or public scenes create the reality effect of Gertrude's closet. To an extent, *Hamlet* is about a desire to penetrate beneath the surface in order to get to the inner truths of both this life and the next, and the room represented in 3.4 is central to that endeavour. This scene is the closest the play gets to those 'things which pass show', because of the painful honesty its space permits.

Rooms on the stage, this chapter has argued, are created in relation to the whole play's uses of space – they are drawn as a series of comparisons. But they are also carefully built up through the relationship between props, actions, gestures, and linguistic webs of materialistic language. And there is, of course, a reciprocal relationship between language, action and space – discourses are deepened by their performance inside, and the intensity of their performance simultaneously helps to create that sense of an interior. Focused on the relationship between key props, Gertrude's closet brings the play's interests, obsessions, pasts and presents into itself.

# 5

## *Banquet and celebration*

Silver basin and ewer, London, 1610-11, Victoria and Albert Museum.

This chapter takes up the question of Shakespeare's representation of domestic interiors and family dynamics explored in the previous chapter by examining the way they play out in a range of practices around marriage and the forging of new familial connections. It looks at stage banquets as another example of the materially organized units of social meaning discussed in Chapter 4, analysing how they bring into play notions of hospitality and reciprocity. It starts with an image of a pair of objects which we can be fairly sure were never seen on stage: a silver ewer and basin made in London just as *The Tempest* was being performed. The basin would be offered to elite guests during and after a meal, filled with sweetly scented warm rose water, in a European tradition which dated back to the medieval period. And from the thirteenth century a design which evoked the sea was thought most appropriate to the action of washing the hands. Its ritual status is perhaps indicated by the depth of the bowl – at only 9cm the washing provided would be a partial and symbolic refreshing.[1]

The style was particularly popular at the Jacobean court – this set allowed those familiar with monarchical practices to emulate them in their own homes. The modelling of fantastical and complex forms in silver was a style of craftsmanship which had originated in the previous century in the mainland European courts, and its prevalence therefore linked the aristocracy of the Old World together in a common aesthetic appreciation. These crucial ceremonial objects were often exchanged as gifts of state or courtly presents, and their size and the complexity of their decoration made them amongst the most impressive, and expensive, pieces of household silverware. Such figurative and fantastical pieces fire the imagination – they are self-consciously wonderful and connected to subjects well known not from life but from literature. In other words they insist upon a shared context of elite education which generates a capacity to imagine a world outside the everyday. As such, their visual and physical form is linked to the imaginative world of the entertainments which also accompanied banquets, most obviously the fey and allusive masque.

The mermaid ewer is especially magical – the scales of her tail and her fins are extremely detailed, the sheen of their polished metal making them appear to gleam with an exotic roughness. The scales are chased and engraved to give them a textured relief, and the fins are set into the seam of the two halves of the tail, both covering and drawing attention to the method of construction. In contrast, her sensuously smooth torso is covered in the falling curls of the hair which she combs with her right hand. The fully realized detail of her moulding makes her seem hyper-real, and yet the comb and the mirror (which has since been lost) invite her to be read allegorically, as a type of vanity.

The mermaid's poise is stately and suggests the skill of the maker, who has calculated how to balance her when she is full. Her stomach swells fruitfully and provocatively to form the front of the cavity for the water – other versions of these fanciful ewers exaggerated the prow of a ship or the curve of a shell in a similar fashion. These connections between the mermaid's fertility and the provision of plenty which is the key element of elite hospitality are epitomized by the way in which the ewer is actually used. The tip of the tail unscrews so that it can be filled before the meal and its method of opening and closing concealed again. The tail is then, presumably, used as a handle and the mermaid tipped forwards so that the perfumed water can spill from her over the hands of the diners and into the shell-shaped bowl underneath. The bowl is chased up from a single sheet – hammered from the flat metal until it forms the undulations of a scallop shell. It can be held on the very edge, so that the whole form of the fluted shell radiates outwards towards the guest in a shape which suggests bounty – the open hand and the unstinting giving of the true elite. It is from the mermaid's nipples that the warmed water pours in two streams, and this conceit, combined with the inviting gesture of the bowl (you can see this more clearly if you turn this book upside down and look at it as it would be offered to you at the table) are intimate gestures of inclusion. The initial surprise and the intricacy and playfulness of the design make the piece ideally suited to the showiness of banqueting, as ewer and basin extend and play punningly upon those ideas of female bounty and fertility.

Down the mermaid's chest from neck to stomach falls the chain of a large jewel which covers the upper part of her abdomen, the lower compartment of which contains the coat of arms of the owner of the basin and ewer. The thrust of her pose, then, causes the light to catch the proof of his elite identity as the ewer is in use. Interrupting the play of light along the ridges of the fluting and therefore the movement of the eye of the guest along the basin is a larger version of this coat of arms. As the mermaid pours, so her shield moves towards the one on the bowl underneath, underlining the fact that the connections between the two pieces, with their echoed shell shapes, their sensuous curves, and their shared theme, are a part of the coherent aesthetic conception of one man. The Victoria and Albert Museum suggests that ewer and basin belonged to Sir Thomas Wilson (d.1629), whom the *Oxford Dictionary of National Biography* describes as 'record keeper and author'. Wilson was a man on the edge of several of the circles which are pertinent to a book on Shakespeare and material culture. He travelled a good deal, working as a 'foreign intelligencer' for Sir Robert Cecil in the later years of Elizabeth's reign, employed in diplomatic negotiations with the Italian states and on the lookout for Catholic conspiracies. These trips were not entirely spent in political negotiation, however. 'While staying in Italy and Germany in 1596', for instance, 'he translated from the Spanish Gorge de Montemayor's *Diana*, a romance later used as a source by William Shakespeare for *Two Gentlemen of Verona*,' which he originally dedicated to the earl of Southampton, and he may also have been involved in publishing some of Philip Sidney's works.[2]

It is of additional interest, in relation to the ocean-inspired silverware which is reputed to have belonged to him, that Wilson was one of the original subscribers to the Virginia Company, and 'kept a keen watch on discoveries in the East Indies, maintaining a correspondence with persons in most quarters of the globe'. His interests in colonial power also lay closer to home, where in 1618 he petitioned for a grant of 2,000 acres in Ulster, and 'drew up a scheme for the military government of Ireland'. If the arms on the ewer and bowl are indeed his, then his choice would reflect interestingly on the form hospitality took for a man who saw the allure of the ocean as a place of wonder and discovery, and was closely linked with the colonization of the New World and the administration of England's dominions over the waters. It might suggest that the old connections between ritual washing and sea themes which such pieces reflected took on a new twist in an age of voyaging and exploration.

I wanted to start this chapter with this extraordinary piece of craftsmanship because it gives us an insight into the splendour of banquets in the period in which Shakespeare was writing. The complexities of the food consumed at a banquet were equal to the intricacies of the plate on which it was served. As the ewer and basin shown above were extraordinary versions of the bowls and jugs in regular use around a house, so the banquet was an exceptional kind of meal. It was therefore related to the reserves of domestic objects stored for use on special occasions which belonged to those of higher status. The term banquet refers either to a sumptuous feast or, more usually in this period, to a 'course of sweetmeats, fruit, and wine, served either as a separate entertainment, or as a continuation of the principal meal, but in the latter case usually in a different room' (*Oxford English Dictionary*). It was a spectacular display of uncommon foods, positioned as the culmination of various kinds of entertainment, culinary and theatrical. In other words banquets were structurally linked to the varied kinds of performance to which elite domestic space played host. Gervase Markham, in his *The English Housewife* (1615), describes the variety of dishes which might be offered, and the importance of a kind of 'narrative of food' in which the visual and flavoursome effects of each course took shape in relation to the ones which came before and afterwards: 'you shall first send forth a dish made for show only, as beast, bird, fish or fowl . . . then your marchpane [marzipan], then preserved fruit, then a paste, then a wet sucket, then a dry sucket, marmalade, comfits, apples, pears, wardens, oranges, and lemons sliced; and then wafers, and another dish of preserved fruits'. As there were 'no two dishes of one kind going or standing together', the whole would appear 'delicate to the eye' whilst also inviting 'the appetite with the much variety thereof'.[3] Beginning with inedible dishes made only for show, Markham's list makes clear the intention to whet the appetite, and to pattern its sharpening and satisfaction in ways which give point to Katherine's comment to Grumio during her taming by Petruccio in *The Taming of the Shrew* that he 'feed'st [her] with the very name of meat' (4.3.32), as the list of dishes with which he tempts her stimulates rather than satisfies her hunger.

In addition to the extensive parade of courses, banquets were a fitting display of elite status because they used very expensive raw materials. The foods were rich in flavour, heavily spiced or sweetened with the objects of overseas trade. Fruit, pepper and sugar were imported into London in significant quantities: from the 1560s to the 1630s, the percentage of London's import trade which all three formed roughly doubled, fruit increasing in real terms from £17,000 to £114,000, pepper from £9,000 to £38,000 and sugar from £15,000 to £86,000.[4] Purchased in London either in person or through a third party, these goods were bought and shipped back to the provinces by the elite for use at their banquets. The historian Joan Thirsk describes entries in the household accounts of the elite Willoughby family of Wollaton which record purchases of 'spices and foodstuffs, including five hundred oranges and three hundred lemons in one delivery', in addition to other things not readily available in the provinces such as 'books, paper, pictures, and musical instruments'.[5] Thomas Puckering of Warwick bought sugar, spice and fruit in large quantities from his London grocer Thomas Shipton – at over £14 in money and 400lbs in weight (admittedly including other goods) the scale of such purchases is obvious.[6] And such celebrations altered household finances considerably: the increase in Sir Nathaniel Bacon's weekly expenditure at Christmas from somewhere between £7 and £9 to £28 3s 11d shows how expensive such entertaining could be.[7]

The other noteworthy feature of the banquet was its aesthetic quality. The marchpane in particular was intended to be a thing of wonder, formed into 'letters, knots, arms, escutcheons, beasts, birds and other fancies', or 'castles, towers, horses, bears and apes'. More elaborate designs could be constructed out of plaster or wood with sugar paste painted onto them, or poured into wax moulds.[8] In other words, these dishes leaned so far in the direction of artistic creations that they were no longer food at all. Returning to the posies with which this book began, which were written on 'banqueting dishes of sugar plate' or 'march panes', shows that poetry, banquets and the theatrical entertainments which often accompanied them were more closely linked than we might at first expect – aphorisms written on food, intended to be spoken, to be performed by the guests. William Harrison describes them as being 'wrought with no small curiosity',[9] a word whose contemporary meanings refer to 'elegance; artistic character' – to the artistic merits of the finished thing – and to 'careful accuracy of construction' with a sense of the time and care with which the thing is put together. Like many other words used to describe elite practices, however, the meanings of 'curiosity' shade into the pejorative: 'A matter upon which undue care is bestowed; a vanity, nicety, refinement' (*Oxford English Dictionary*). As an end in itself with no real purpose in assuaging hunger, the banquet's relationship to art objects and performance made it, in the contemporary moral terms surrounding consumption explored in the Introduction, a thing which might be 'clean spared'.

On the stage, these scenes of feasting were amongst the most visually spectacular. They usually called for a large table surrounded by a good deal of seating which must have filled a substantial proportion of the acting area, and the guests would invariably be wearing their finest apparel as befitted such a formal occasion. In terms of costumes and properties, then, such scenes represented a substantial investment of time, energy and theatrical resources. But the level of artistic sophistication of the offstage banquet and the complexity and value of works like the basin and ewer above make a particularly strong contrast with the stage directions for banqueting scenes, which suggest that a fairly limited selection of vessels was used to represent the elaborate rituals around the elite plate collection. Offstage, in a noble household, a table known as the 'ewery board' housed the array of plate under the charge of the Yeoman of the Ewery – mainly basins, ewers and candlesticks – and the wide variety of specially shaped and named towels for which he was responsible. It was here that the servants themselves washed and were 'armed' with the accoutrements needed for serving and then 'unarmed' when they returned from each duty.[10] Onstage, there might have been plates, trenchers (platters), covered serving dishes and smaller dishes to contain food, larger and smaller bowls or cups for ceremonial drinking with the pots, flagons or bottles from which they were filled and the impressive and symbolic container for salt. With a carpet covering the table, tapers to light the meal and napkins for the guests, the stage banquet was complete.

We can be fairly sure, in other words, that theatre companies would not own items such as the ones with which this chapter began, and that they would therefore be unable to stage them in the nearly 100 plays from this period which contained banqueting scenes. Unlike clothing, it is improbable that there was a ready supply of cast-off elite silverware, inherited pieces sold on, or uncollected pawns.[11] The literary critic Chris Meads plausibly suggests that large set pieces of marchpane might have been transferred to the London stages by actors who mixed in the kind of circles where banquets were served – by virtue of their art, as they went there to perform, if not their social status. But the intricacy of the objects shown above calls into question his further assertion that 'Polished pewter would be indistinguishable from silver on stage, and gilded or painted wood would be indistinguishable from gold.'[12] The level of decoration possible in wood would give it a ponderous, lumpen and prosaic effect; the difference between pewter and silver dining equipment was, of course, one of the key articulations of the distinctions between social groups in this period as was shown in the Introduction. No one was likely to mistake the one for the other, although they might be lured into using their imaginations.

Despite the fact that the complex list of food and equipment needed for offstage banquets exceeded the resources and the requirements of its staged equivalent, the qualities of the objects themselves came into play through the intricate behaviours associated with them. In her work on hospitality Felicity Heal shows that 'the social ritual of the great household, at its most effective when presented for a large audience, was a coded language, designed to articulate both power and magnanimity'. A wide range of ritualized behaviours clustered around these objects, whose elaboration demonstrated the householder's status and whose subtle discriminations articulated the guests' relative standing. These processes began with the reception of visitors, when an usher would observe the 'extraordinarily fine gradation of order' which characterized lists that placed 'wives in relation to husbands, prelates in comparison with one another, former office-holders below the current occupants', thereby determining the sequence in which they were served.[13] A key element of this performance was, of course, the ceremonial washing, for instance of a member of the nobility's hands after a meal: when the table had been cleared, the Sewer carried a long folded towel with a surnape, or long table cloth, beneath it from the ewery table (where the vessels and towels were kept) to the dining table. The Marshal drew the cloths along the length of the table. He then laid an estate, or pleated fold, measuring exactly nine inches, in the cloths in front of the lord, on which the ewer and basin were placed after grace had been said. 'Two of the senior table-servants then raised each end of the estates so that the inner edge of the towel held the lord's sleeves back from his extended hands,' to prevent his fur cuffs being damaged, and he dried his hands on the towel when they had been washed.[14] This richly allusive language, complex and hedged about with customs of precedence, was read very carefully: an entertainment in itself, it was watched in close visual and behavioural detail by all present. Such self-conscious codes were relatively easily assimilable to the stage version of the banqueting scene, giving a gravitas to the sham properties on the table.

And audiences watching a banquet within a play, then, might also be expected to bring some of the absent material splendour to the event in their knowledge of the connections it made between an extraordinary occasion, the impressive space within which it took place, and the unusual foods which were offered to guests there. As Felicity Heal explains, 'The household is sometimes described as an arena, in which the host can dramatize his generosity, and thereby reveal his hegemony.' It was within the substantial spaces of palaces, castles and prodigy houses that magnificence could be expressed to an appropriately large audience. And this was thought to be the sole location for the proof of status: 'While individual members of the community of honour could demonstrate their standing in isolation – the quest would be the obvious moment here – in normal circumstances a full display of honour required a suitable domestic establishment to personate the qualities of the knight.'[15] Crucially for the audience's understanding of these kinds of artistic and behavioural complexities, however, such occasions were not limited to the elite. London's livery companies and the guilds of provincial towns also used symbolic meals as a way of exploring their hierarchies and their sense of brotherhood. They did so in what were often the largest rooms in a town – housed in properties which had sometimes previously been parts of monastic complexes and which might subsequently be inhabited by elite families.[16] They used a significant range of plate owned or employed by the town rather than an individual.[17] In other words, spaces of this size and the use of extraordinary silverware were crucial to the materialization of urban power and authority, and experience of them linked the practice of townsmen and women to the conduct of the elite. The connections between institutional and aristocratic plenty were central to the theatre's making of meaning in such scenes.

Like the deathbed scenes explored above, these stage representations of banqueting use a conjunction of key props, the physical bodies of actors, and a socially prescribed set of gestures to replicate offstage events. They bring onto the stage, as a result, a very distinct social meaning with a complex set of attendant moral discourses that can therefore both interrogate the construction of community within the play, and itself be examined through the way it operates within that community.

Several of Shakespeare's plays explore the festive nature of banqueting by focusing on the preparations which go into such an occasion. In *Romeo and Juliet*, for instance, small vignettes of provisioning build the audience's anticipation of the 'old-accustomed feast' which Capulet is to hold, '[t]his night' as he tells Paris, and to which he has invited 'many a guest/Such as I love, and you among the store/ One more most welcome, makes my number more' (1.2.18–21). The feast comes hot on the heels of the passionate feuding, and Capulet's insistence that it is for those he loves reminds the audience of the significance of feasting with friends as a way of cementing the loyalty of faction. Paris, the prospective son-in-law, has not so far been invited, and his apparent status as an afterthought shows his liminal position on the edge of Capulet's group of trusted family and friends.

Act 1 scene 3 introduces Juliet, exploring her own position within the Capulet family through her mother and her nurse's discussion of her childhood – ''Tis since the earthquake now eleven years,/And she was weaned – I never shall forget it –/ Of all the days of the year upon that day,/For I had then laid wormwood to my dug,/Sitting in the sun under the dovehouse wall' (25–9). The wanderings of the nurse's mind generate the comedy here, as she moves from one thought to another backwards through time to Juliet's weaning. As a result, when Peter the servant appears, the haste of his preparations is a sharp contrast to the indulgences of memory and the less contracted time of the past. The concentrated speed of his in many ways equally gallimaufrical speech bursts in upon their recollections of the past and dreams for the future with thoughts entirely immersed in the present: 'Madam, the guests are come, supper served up, you called, my young lady asked for, the Nurse cursed in the pantry, and everything in extremity. I must hence to wait. I beseech you follow straight' (1.3.102–5). The breadth of Peter's concerns covers the public spaces of the house in which the supper is served to the newly arrived guests and the preparations of the pantry in which the Nurse is cursed, and his intimate knowledge of both demonstrates the fact that he has been coming and going between the two and indeed returns to 'wait' upon host and guests alike. The energy of his presentism and his focus on process, on the making of the event which takes place behind the scenes, shows the feast from the inside and contrasts lower-status preparation with high-status consumption.

Peter appears again with his fellows at the start of 1.5, after Mercutio's Queen Mab speech: *[Peter] and other Servingmen come forth with napkins*. In fifteen lines they introduce the feast and keep up the energy of this opening act in preparation for Romeo's arrival: 'Where's Potpan, that he helps not to take away? He shift a trencher, he scrape a trencher!' (1–2), and then 'Away with the joint-stools, remove the court-cupboard, look to the plate. Good thou, save me a piece of marzipan, and, as thou loves me, let the porter let in Susan Grindstone and Nell. Anthony, and Potpan!' (6–9). It is the specificity of this interchange, its focus on the material basis for a feast in trenchers and joint stools, court cupboards and plate which must be brought to their right places, and in the marzipan which is to form the centrepiece of the banquet, which gives the rest of the scene its particular quality. This kind of lower-status discussion of manufacture and of component parts rather than the overall effect of a completed elite display is essential to the definition of Capulet's power and authority – his ability to produce display through the loyalty and energy of his servants. The representation of preparation is important to the way banquets explore elite identity – the extent to which organization is shown on the stage, who does it and how it is planned and executed, points to a productive household of social integration such as the one pictured here, or the isolation of the elite and their unstable authority as pictured elsewhere in Shakespeare. In this play, the detail of preparation underlines both the optimistic mood of the event and the coherence of the domestic unit whose hospitality Romeo abuses by falling in love with Juliet.

And this question of preparation is also an important element of the banqueting scene's contribution to the generic development of the plays in which it occurs. It is central to comedy's interests in the confusions and energies of those below the elite: the insistence on the use of such scenes at this point in *Romeo and Juliet* provides an intense burst of comedy in this opening act which is gradually undone and parodied in the latter stages of the play.[18] Chris Meads argues for a very different function for banqueting scenes in comedies and tragedies, largely based on the way they draw around themselves the contrasting metaphorical languages of the craving for revenge and for love. The hunger for sustenance can operate as a metaphor for the appetites for both revenge and sexual fulfilment, symbolized by extravagant or 'rich (often tacitly aphrodisiac) food'.[19] In both cases, eating is patterned with other types of consummation, and the fantastic strangeness of what is consumed permits the plays to explore the extremities of emotion in a mannered and heightened setting. Investigating the way these dynamics play out in two generically straightforward cases, *Titus Andronicus* and *As You Like It*, suggests a route through the complexities of generic negotiation in *The Tempest*, to which this chapter then turns.

*Titus Andronicus* is Shakespeare's epitome of the relationship between feasting and revenge. The play contains two banqueting scenes, the finale in which Tamora is tricked into eating a pie containing the bodies of her sons in 5.3, and an earlier scene in which Titus, Marcus, Lavinia and Young Lucius enter to eat together. This earlier banquet comes at the point at which the family believe that they have sunk to the nadir of their fortunes,[20] and the effects of their fate are made palpable in the gross mutilations which those at the table have suffered – Titus lacks one hand, Lavinia two and her tongue. Shakespeare chooses to stage this scene as a banquet then, in order to explore the mutilation suffered by the family in material terms – as a series of losses which, whatever else they may affect, make their social interaction almost farcically clumsy. Watching two characters banqueting without hands shows the audience the awkwardness of the simplest physical processes. But such indignities are magnified for an elite family, who are thus unable to eat in a way which reflects their status and are instead forced into the kind of practices which would mark them as at best at the bottom of the social hierarchy, at worst bestial. Imagining now the elite rituals associated with cleanliness and the hands, picturing the ewer and basin at the head of this chapter, makes it clear that this both is and is not a banquet, as half of those present are unable to perform in a way capable of bringing such a rarefied occasion into being.

Setting these facts against the stage direction which insists upon *A Banquet*, we might want to push this question of what *makes* the scene a banquet further. The 'guests', for instance, number only Titus' daughter, brother and grandson, so it is an intimate family occasion.

Critics offer two main models of staged banquets, the large hospitable feast with honoured guests, which this clearly is not, and the intimate meal of lovers which occurs most often in comedies, which again this does not resemble. Felicity Heal suggests that rites of passage off-stage, such as weddings and christenings, might be marked by such intimate family feasts, and this seems the most promising light in which to see Titus' meal.[21] However, it is of course a grotesque parody of such a celebration, serving instead merely to mark the emptiness of family honour and the damage done to the group. If it is a celebration of anything, it is of revenge – Titus opens the meal with a speech which would normally proffer the bounty of the house as a kind of mutual blessing, but which instead invites his guests to 'sit, and look you eat no more/Than will preserve just so much strength in us/As will revenge these bitter woes of ours.' (1–3). Eating together, supposed to nourish the body and make it strong, is here offered merely as a way of prolonging it to the point of revenge and no further. With no guests, no elite gestures, and no appetite for food, the contrast between the staged table with its vessels and the social processes which go on around it could not be stronger.

There is little to no narrative information in 3.2 – it does not advance the plot – and its clearest purpose is to foreshadow the larger banquet at the play's end. And 5.3 can be seen to develop many of the themes presented within it. Titus' invitation to the table this time is fulsome if conventionally self-depreciating: 'Welcome...Although the cheer be poor,/'Twill fill your stomachs. Please you, eat of it' (26–9). But already here, of course, the ironies are rich as the 'poor cheer' is the very stuff of his revenge, his identification of its deficiencies a further insult to his guests. The scene has been elaborately prepared for, and the audience have even witnessed the provision of the meat for the pies as a kind of perversion of servants' practice: the stage direction reads *Enter Titus Andronicus with a knife, and Lavinia with a basin* (5.2) and they proceed to cut the throats of Chiron and Demetrius, doing their own work of preparation for the feast both to make the meal 'personal' and to demonstrate their social isolation as they must labour alone. In the end, however, the banquet itself is swift and compressed in its achievement of its goals. Rather than the usual entertainment offered at dinner, Titus performs for his guests the murder of his daughter while they eat, the revelation of the thing they feed on as he lifts the lid of one of the banqueting dishes, and then the murder of Tamora. With Titus himself and Saturninus also dead, Lucius expresses the symmetry of these events: 'There's meed for meed, death for a deadly deed' (65), and in 40 lines the banquet is at an end. The banquet, of course, provides the perfect context in which to explore the fracturing of society because it offers a contrasting moment of great social formality and order.[22] And the material consequences of such a shattering show very clearly the tensions inherent in revenge – the stage picture remains largely the same, its material arrangement of chairs in a close and regulated proximity evocative of social harmony and connection intact, as the structures of justice and the hierarchies of social life disintegrate. Indeed, many plays show a marked increase in the staging of scenes of domestic order leading up to the moment of social collapse, their repeated focus on hospitality and domestic provision providing a richly ironic context for deceit, betrayal and death.[23] Generically, it is also possible to see the comic scenes of preparation in *Romeo and Juliet* in this light, as contrasts with the impending tragedy.

It is a very long way, generically and in terms of atmosphere, from the near-anarchy incited by Titus' feast to the song which accompanies the preparation of Duke Senior's banquet in the forest in *As You Like It*. The lords 'cover the while' (2.5.28), readying the banquet for their master, as they sing 'Who does ambition shun,/And loves to live I'th' sun,/Seeking the food he eats/And pleased with what he gets'/ Come hither' (35–9). The mood is contemplative and calm. In the following scene, in contrast, Orlando's desperation builds as Adam tells him 'I die for food' (2.6.1), and he bursts in on the banquet *with sword drawn* in 2.7 in *As You Like It*'s more muted display of generic juxtaposition. These short scenes set up contrasts around the banquet then, but food to sustain life and food to sustain courtly identity come together when Orlando enters in 2.7, threatening both the complex formal ceremonies and the reaffirmation of group identity which the jeopardized meal stands for. He brings a different set of criteria into play, insisting that they 'Forbear, and eat no more!' until 'necessity be served' (88–9). In doing so, he points to the distinctions between hunger as an essential need and the kind of titillation of the palate which banquets were designed to offer.

The lords who prepare the banquet do so as the type of gentry-status servants who would perform the key tasks of food service with its complex ritual elements in a noble household, including the washing of hands. And Orlando, whose search for food offers a parallel process of the hunt for sustenance, says he does so through his own 'labour' (2.6.11), a word suggestive of a low status kind of work: 'If this uncouth forest yield anything savage I will either be food for it or bring it for food to thee' (4–5) he promises Adam. The contrast in the methods by which food is provided shows what a low ebb Orlando's fortunes have reached, but also demonstrates his resourcefulness and willingness to perform the lowly role of service for a higher purpose. Duke Senior's banquet is a proof of his continuing authority in his woodland court – he is able to produce food appropriate for courtiers because his followers are sufficiently loyal to him to fulfil the role of servants.

The meal functions to reveal the ideological underpinnings of the Duke's alternative woodland community, and work on the wider cultural history of food shows how crucial such connections could be. Ken Albala points out the significance of the practices around food consumption for the maintenance of elite identity – 'one becomes a courtier only by eating like one' – and he explores the political significance of meals shared by the rulers of European states; Robert Applebaum shows how particular patterns of consumption could evince 'membership in an aesthetic community'.[24] In other words, partaking of a banquet both produces elite identity – confirms it in the complexity and status of banqueting practices – and binds its participants to one another each time such a meal is performed. The fact that the Duke opens his banquet up to Orlando and Adam, in the face of some very uncourtly behaviour, demonstrates his moral superiority in the strongest possible terms – assuring Orlando that 'Your gentleness shall force/More than your force move us to gentleness' he bids them 'welcome to our table' (105), the crucial gesture of hospitality.

The tensions of Orlando's raised sword serve to highlight the terms in which resolution is reached. The Duke initially offers Orlando two opposing motivations for the behaviour which 'in civility... seem'st so empty': 'Art thou thus boldened, man, by thy distress?/Or else a rude despiser of good manners' (91–3). It is central to the comic mode of this banquet that both men share a similar concept of civility, one which allows Orlando to explain that it is 'the thorny point/Of bare distress' which has 'ta'en from me the show/Of smooth civility' (94–6). Civility is smooth in contrast to both the rudeness of his current behaviour and the thorniness of his distress, and its smoothness is a feature of its polished etiquette. Orlando, expecting 'all things' to be 'savage here' (107) is wrong footed, and instead makes a plea to their memories of the society from which all are banished:

> If ever you have looked on better days,
> If ever been where bells have knolled to church,
> If ever sat at any good man's feast,
> If ever from your eyelids wiped a tear,
> And know what 'tis to pity, and be pitied
>
> (113–17)

Their response to him, he assumes, will be conditioned by their experience of life in the community to which they have belonged outside the forest, a community based on religious practice, the feasting of honest neighbours and the empathetic social relations which spring naturally from Christian charity and its accompanying concept of neighbourliness. And it is because they have indeed been a part of such a society with its 'sacred pity' (123), as Duke Senior assures him, that he is once more bid welcome – invited to 'sit you down', this time explicitly 'in gentleness' (124). Shared concepts of society underpin the comic mode of banqueting.

Duke Senior's banquet offers Shakespeare the opportunity to connect the gentle behaviour which is the mark of true social status to the ritual forms of social life in a situation removed from the structuring and supportive context of the elite household. And he does something very similar around a decade later in *The Tempest*, where another Duke's methods of entertaining the men with whom he shares an alien landscape are put under scrutiny through scenes of banquet and masque. Banquet scenes are especially effective for such purposes because they allude so directly to the complex conventions of early modern hospitality – as George Wheler, writing later in the seventeenth century, described it 'a liberal entertainment of all sorts of men, at ones house, whether neighbours or strangers, with kindness, especially with meat, drink and lodgings'.[25] It is a part of the dynamic of Christian charity which Orlando searches for and finds in the forest, stretching from the feeding of the hungry which is one of the seven corporal acts of mercy which all Christians are morally compelled to perform, to the aristocratic responsibility to offer 'entertainment' both edible and aesthetic to a houseful of people. Like so many medieval notions of appropriate behaviour, the idea of an open hospitality through which the rich man's gate was perpetually ajar to provide alms for the poor was fading in Elizabeth's reign, however. As poor laws were enacted, which removed the direct material contact between the top and bottom of the social scale by translating the physical gift of the food left over from the banquet table into the collection of a regular monetary payment, so the banquet of equals became increasingly central to the articulation of elite identity. Social mobility and the growth of London, the ills blamed for so many shifts in communal behaviour towards the end of the sixteenth century, speeded up such changes.[26] These tensions around the question of inclusivity of provision were the subject of contemporary concern, and the ideal of hospitality itself remained of great rhetorical significance, especially in the lower orders' conception of the responsibilities of their betters.

In all cases then, hospitality was a material expression of a facet of identity – the gift of alms which demonstrated the giver's piety or the offering of a masque which exhibited his bounty. Whilst Duke Senior's sharing of his banquet with the hungry shows the former, Prospero's banquet and masque deal with the latter, with the 'peculiar quality of the nobleman able to deploy large resources' known in the Renaissance as 'magnificence: that contempt for moderation and any form of meanness which revealed itself in elaborate display and conspicuous consumption'.[27] When Hamlet jokes hollowly that 'The funeral baked meats/Did coldly furnishe forth the marriage tables' (1.2.179–80) he is accusing Claudius of 'thrift', a shameful tight-fistedness which is at odds with just this ethos of courtly show. On the island, Prospero uses his magic to perform such ennobling displays, and in doing so he makes up for the want of his Ducal household.

But Prospero's island presented a more complex set of problems for a Duke wishing to demonstrate hospitality than Senior's wood – in the latter the courtly party were largely self-contained, able to minister unto themselves and kept apart from the various wandering bucolic characters with Touchstone to mediate between the forest's usual and extraordinary inhabitants. Colonization of foreign lands, by contrast, offered a unique set of problems of integration. Hospitality has been identified as 'a recurring theme in contemporary accounts of what happens when the white man comes to a new land'.[28] As it was a concept generated in response to the social structures of Western societies, it was not immediately obvious how it might be applied to the very different communities of the New World. The often truncated social hierarchies of settler communities made it hard to find either the poor to feed or a sufficiently wide circle of fellow elites to impress. On the other hand, the maintenance of a policy of hospitable provision for all was also problematic when territory was shared with an 'other' who occupied such an ambivalent place in relation to the hierarchies which structured the settlers' accustomed societies. Indigenous peoples were seen as being of the lowest status in the sense that they 'lacked' basic necessities such as Western clothing and domestic goods, and yet the provision of alms for them was neither desired nor desirable. These very different communities, existing within the same place, make plain the significance of that shared notion of social priorities which Orlando and Duke Senior exhibit, and point up the problems of establishing a parity between two radically different social and cultural systems. It is only within a shared architecture of meanings that objects like the basin and ewer above achieve their considerable cultural power. And the absence of unification also points up the extent to which hospitality connected and integrated communities in a mutual engagement, a giving and a receiving on both sides in which the gift of charity is matched by the gift of prayer and the gift of entertainment is repaid by the granting of respect.

It should be no surprise, then, that hospitality in *The Tempest*, a play steeped in colonial discourses, is a radically compromised business. Prospero appears to offer it but then takes it away in spectacular form at the banquet scene in 3.3, replacing it with a kind of revenge. Later, however, he is able to fulfil his qualified promise of entertainment, saying to Alonso,

> I invite your highness and your train
> To my poor cell, where you shall take your rest

For this one night…
And in the morn
I'll bring our ship, and so to Naples,
Where I have hope to see the nuptial
Of these our dear-beloved solemnized

(5.1.304–13)

The play is punctuated by a linked series of entertainments, from banquet, through masque, to the invitation to share a cell to, finally, the solemnization of Ferdinand and Miranda's marriage, in which the related processes of reconciliation and repatriation will be completed. These entertainments accent the narrative and make their meaning by the way they build upon one another. Like the closet scene in *Hamlet*, the wedding celebrations in *Taming of the Shrew*, or the appearance of Banquo's ghost at the feast in *Macbeth*, banqueting scenes often offer a climax of the play's themes and discourses, and provoke a turning point in the plot. And they are therefore, also like the closet scene, carefully built up as events, often foreshadowed in earlier scenes and prior practices, and have their preparation threaded through plots and subplots in a way which ties them firmly into the development of the narrative.

Act 3 scene 3 opens with Gonzalo's statement that he 'can go no further…My old bones ache…I needs must rest me'(1–3), and Alonso's entertainment of the certainty of his son's death. In other words it is a significant echo of *As You Like It*'s scene between Orlando and Adam, although with the discordant addition of Antonio and Sebastian's subversive plotting. The dialogue which has led into the banquet suggests how open the scene is, balanced at the start between the equal possibilities of a restitutive comic, or a revengeful tragic, meal. The stage direction calls for *Solemn and strange music. Enter Prospero on the top, invisible*, and then *Enter spirits, in several strange shapes, bringing in a table and a banquet, and dance about it with gentle actions of salutations, and, inviting the King and his companions to eat, they depart*. There is then a space of some thirty lines during which the onstage audience for the banquet try to establish the nature of the entertainment and whether they are its intended guests. Instead of a host's welcome, Prospero offers an aside, spoken from the highest point in the theatre from whence he looks down on them: 'Praise in departing', he says, a proverbial expression advising guests to 'reserve their praise for the host's entertainment until they depart, lest they prematurely praise something that will prove unsatisfactory'.[29] It sets the banquet squarely within the terms of the offer of hospitality and emphasizes the significance of the recipients' response.

And the responses which follow fall into two very distinct groups. Hearing the music which is the banquet's prelude, Alonso asks 'What harmony is this?', to which Gonzalo replies 'Marvellous sweet music' (18–19). The two men note its concord and the way it pleases the ear, and they are also well disposed towards the spirits who bring in the feast: 'though they are of monstrous shape, yet note/Their manners are more gentle-kind than of/Our human generation you shall find/Many, nay, almost any' (31–4), Gonzalo generously points out when they have left, and Alonso concentrates on their ability to communicate, to show the 'gentle[ness]' of their 'salutations' without words. So these two characters mirror back the banquet's implied hospitality in a language which shows both their moral probity and their courtly manners.

Sebastian, on the other hand, characterizes the spirits as 'A living drollery' – in other words a comic show, or a puppet show. The association of the banquet with 'drolleries' connects it to Trinculo's response to Caliban: 'Were I in England now, as once I was, and had but this fish painted, not a holiday-fool there but would give a piece of silver. There would this monster make a man . . .' (2.2.27–30). These are cheap and fairly explicitly lower-status forms of entertainment. And Sebastian and Antonio take as their context of interpretation not the elite discourses of hospitality but the improbable fantasies of travellers' tales: 'Now will I believe/That there are unicorns' (21–2). They fail to perceive the episode as offering a kind of hospitality – as a comic mode of harmony and integration – seeing it rather as a jest, to be laughed at harshly rather than responded to with generosity. And the distinctions between these two modes of response to the banquet are characterizing: they shape the audience's understanding of the differences between the two pairs of lords in ways which feed into their appreciation of those lords' relative capacities for repentance.

At the end of this dramatic space of response to the spectacle, left open as a pause for wonder and then partly filled with scorn, Sebastian proceeds to invite his fellows to the banquet as though it was his own. He dismisses Fransisco's observation that the creatures 'vanished strangely': 'No matter', he says, 'since/They have left their viands behind, for we have stomachs'. Usurping the role of host, he invites them, 'Will't please you taste of what is here?' (40–2). But as they approach the table they are greeted by, *Thunder and lightning. Ariel [descends] like a harpy, claps his wings upon the table, and, with a quaint device, the banquet vanishes.* The image of the banquet, set up by the spirits on its table to signify hospitality, is cracked apart loudly, spectacularly, and threateningly. The 'quaintness' of the device lies in its ability to juxtapose the magnificence of plenty with the shock of nothing: the stage direction in *The Wasp*, an anonymous play about Roman Britain which explains the substitution of a table of roses and violets with one of snakes and toads with the words, 'the table turns', seems to catch just that sense of reversal.[30]

Act 3 scene 3 is generically very interesting, then, as it moves from the potential for a comic mode of banqueting to the certainty of a tragic one in which Ariel's speech on revenge identifies three of the guests as 'men of sin' (53) whom he has made mad, 'And even with suchlike valour men hang and drown/Their proper selves' (59–60). He pronounces 'Ling'ring perdition – worse than any death/Can be' (76–8), harsh words which change the tone of the play. But the possibility of return to comedy is offered as a way out of perdition, through 'heart's sorrow/And a clear life ensuing' (81–2). Crucially, Ariel tells the spectators to 'remember', to recall from the past the fact that they 'From Milan did supplant good Prospero' (70) and to hold it in their minds in the future. This scene governs the connections between past, present and future in the play, and therefore the relations between the two groups of characters on the island.

The removal of the banquet and Ariel's explanation of its meaning are cathartic in other words: the play offers an unusual instance of 'revenge by banquet'. This swift dealing with past wrongs through the ritual performance of hospitality proffered and then removed works because it offers a connection to those wrongs in its form. Meads argues that 'What Antonio stole from Prospero, fired by his appetite for the dukedom and the advantages it would bring, Prospero presents in a quintessential form as a banquet and all it had come to signify, and denies it to the wanderers.'[31] In performance and in earnest, as a kind of moralizing entertainment, Prospero executes his own metaphorical usurpation by taking his banquet away again. It is these themes of revenge tragedy which cause the banquet to be replaced by a different kind of show, one which fulfils Sebastian and Antonio's earlier reading of the scene: a true drollery of spirits which this time lacks any kind of harmony or elite splendour: *enter the spirits again, and dance with mocks and mows, and they depart, carrying out the table*. They literally get what they deserve, a show which reflects back the limits of their empathy with spectacle.

It has been argued that the banquet offers a metaphor for the lifestyle of the court,[32] that it is an epitomizing event because it is the most prominent cultural form which the court as personnel bring with them from the court as location – the central thing which these elite men are able to salvage, to reconstruct outside the appropriate physical context of the noble buildings within which their lives are normally played out. But this raises the question of how it fits in with the rest of social life on the island which is distinctly uncourtly, and what and how it signifies there. As it is Prospero who controls the social relations and orchestrates the social encounters on the island, then this is in the first instance a question of the dynamics which govern his characterization. It has been suggested that Prospero, 'Like Gonzalo . . . exhibits a marked aversion to manual labor,' and that he 'functions more like a colonial administrator than an actual planter'.[33] But this is too schematic: Prospero as a character in some ways stands apart from the play's engagement with colonial discourses – he is presented first and foremost as a member of the ruling elite uprooted and transplanted on the island, rather than as a colonist engaged with its social or physical geography. He does not labour because having no necessity to undertake physical work is the mark of elite identity, and the ways in which such men measure the success of their identity-making is different: although the entertainments which Prospero stages are the epitome of his exercise of his elite status, its more quotidian manifestation is the way he exercises his command over his inferiors. It is this which reveals the social organization which he imposes on the island. As was the case in *Romeo and Juliet*, the methods by which authority is exercised in the construction of spectacle through third parties is crucial to establishing the nature of power.

The distinctions between Prospero's servants are instructive. They have, of course, a very different attitude to and language of authority and subjection. On his entry, Ariel confirms Prospero's status with 'All hail, great master, grave sir, hail' (1.2.190); he later calls him 'my commander' (4.1.167) and, between banquet and masque, the two profess love for one another: 'Do you love me, master? No?', asks Ariel, 'Dearly, my delicate Ariel' (4.1.48–9) is Prospero's reply. These mystical, mystified forms of service are contrasted against Caliban's ready worship of a new master: 'How does thy honour?', he asks Stefano, 'Let me lick thy shoe' (3.2.23), and then later he pledges himself 'For aye thy foot-licker' (4.1.219). The physicality of his service is both obscene and absurd and it epitomizes his perpetual state of subjection. These differences between loving spirit and shoe-licking slave are symptomatic of and contributory to the distinct roles which they perform for their master. Caliban's tasks are domestic ones. As Prospero says to Miranda, 'We cannot miss him. He does make our fire,/Fetch in our wood, and serves in offices/That profit us' (1.2.313–5). His domestic status is reinforced later in the play when Prospero tells him to, 'Go, sirrah, to my cell ... trim it handsomely' (5.1.295–7). As Caliban scents 'freedom' under a new master, he sings himself a song of the employment he hopes to leave behind:

> No more dams I'll make for fish,
> Nor fetch in firing
> At requiring,
> Nor scrape trenchering, nor wash dish.

> (2.2.179–82)

These lists of Caliban's tasks lay out the quotidian existence which a household servant is expected to facilitate. It is a daily routine which Ferdinand joins in Act 3 as he is ignobled by his prospective father-in-law. But this routine is, it seems, separate from the magnificent entertainments which are produced by Prospero's other set of other-worldly servants, and the division comments interestingly on the banquet – although Caliban catches, cooks and washes up after their food, the special fare of the banquet has to be produced (and indeed removed) by magic. So, the two servants divide our sense of Prospero's rule into the everyday and the extraordinary – split between dealing with the island and dealing with forms which come from elsewhere – and they equate the special vessels and foodstuffs of the latter kind of occasion with a magical process. The magic, interestingly, supports what is for Prospero the most 'normal' – recognizable but not prosaic – part of his island life, the aspect most strongly reminiscent of home.

It is Prospero's old life, then, which controls the shape of island society. Perhaps this seems so natural that we do not pause to think about it – how else would he conduct himself except through the social forms with which he was familiar? But the play does, of course, entertain thoughts of other ways of creating society on a desert island. Gonzalo imagines a utopia which is the opposite of his current culture, an ideal world cast in the negative which lacks every familiar feature of Milanese society:

> Had I plantation of this isle, my lord...
> And were the king on't, what would I do?...
> I'th' commonwealth I would by contraries
> Execute all things. For no kind of traffic
> Would I admit, no name of magistrate;
> Letters should not be known; riches, poverty,
> And use of service, none; contract, succession,
> Bourn, bound of land, tilth, vineyard, none;
> No use of metal, corn, or wine, or oil;
> No occupation, all men idle, all
>
> (2.1.149–60)

Prospero's island, however, is explicitly not a utopian dream, but rather a place of work where all activity moves towards return. Against this idle idyll is set the hard labour of Prospero's entertainments. Coming directly after the maimed rites of the banquet, the wedding masque is, as many critics have noted, its antithesis – where the presentation of the banquet pursues those revengeful connections between feast and tragedy, the masque explores the celebratory associations between hospitality and comedy. And the preparations for the masque itself show Prospero's understanding of the need to pull out all the stops of elite entertainment in order to demonstrate his status. The bounty of his presentation is stressed, the magnitude of investment in it, in terms of the multiplication of magic: 'Bring a corollary', Prospero insists – something beyond the ordinary measure, a surplus – 'Rather than want a spirit.' And the attention which Ariel is to pay to the detail of the work is underlined. Throughout the play, he performs tasks 'to point; to every article'; he does exactly 'All points of' Prospero's command, following them 'To th' syllable' (1.2.2–4). After the banquet Prospero congratulates him that 'Bravely the figure of this harpy hast thou/Performed, my Ariel; a grace it had devouring' (3.3.83–4) and he and the 'meaner ministers', 'nothing bated' (85) of his master's instructions. The precision with which the spirits carry out their tasks sets them apart from Caliban's grudging performance of domesticity, but it also underlines the complex detail which the audience is to take to go into the making of such entertainments and, by implication, the fertile, sophisticated and cultured mind which has created them. When Ferdinand asks whether the actors are spirits, Prospero agrees that he has 'from their confines called [them] to enact/My present fancies'. In other words the spirits body forth his imagination. This entertainment, then, demonstrates Prospero's taste and his power.[34]

Like the banquet, the masque is a complex contract between host and guest, between creator and viewer, offered and received within the context of hospitality: the notion of largesse, which 'implies the giving of rewards without immediate return'.[35] But whereas both masque and banquet would normally be offered to the same audience, Prospero's second entertainment is for a much more intimate group of spectators. This change in the group of onstage viewers picks up on the questions of reception which the banquet raised, sharpening the theatre audience's awareness of the nature of responses to such show. The six men from whom the banquet is snatched are, as we have seen, not uniform in their responses to what they see, but their reactions are nevertheless all shaped, in a complex and indirect way, by their attitude towards the host whom they cannot see. The masque, by contrast, is performed for a select audience of two, both of them allies whose allegiances are assured (in Ferdinand's case by a regime of hard labour which proves his sincerity). Ferdinand's response to the masque shows that Prospero's faith in him was not misplaced. He calls it 'a most majestic vision, and/Harmonious charmingly', echoing Gonzalo's and Alonso's reaction to the banquet. The harmonies, presumably, come from the perfect combination of word and image, and the vision is majestic, betokening majesty – of the highest possible solemnity and eminence. This spectacle has a different function then: it is intended to bind maker, actors and audience together in shared loyalty and in common purpose for a space of time – until 'All sanctimonious ceremonies may/With full and holy rite be ministered' (16–17). That latter moment must necessarily be deferred because it needs resources that are not available on the island, and that it would be blasphemous to suggest could be replaced by magic. This masque keeps the couple bound to one another until that point and, in its production of a shared perspective, it is the closest *The Tempest* comes to a marriage. It is in that sense transformative – it palpably strengthens social relations and ensures that they progress to the next stage.

The way Prospero guides the couple's response to his art in the masque ('No tongue, all eyes! Be silent' (59)) connects this performance to other moments in the play when he shapes his daughter's emotions through her aesthetic reactions. His art has to influence the capacity for intense emotion which she reveals in her response to the cry she hears from the shipwreck, for instance, (which 'did knock/ Against my very heart!' (8–9)). It has to form these passions and fashion them towards the production of a new family, one which will guarantee his salvation. Miranda's responses to Ferdinand himself are therefore conditioned by and hedged about with her father's magic: Prospero has Ariel sing Ferdinand onwards to his initial meeting with Miranda, and her first glance at him is in the aural context of the richly imagistic and curious 'Full fathom five thy father lies./Of his bones are coral made . . . ' (1.2.399–400). Prospero asks her to look at Ferdinand in terms reminiscent of Olivia's injunction to Cesario as she lifts her veil: 'The fringèd curtains of thine eye advance,/And say what thou seest yon' (411–12). In an age before curtains were common at windows, he likens the image of Ferdinand most obviously to a portrait whose curtain both protects it and adds to the dignity of its image. Ariel and Prospero provide the context in which Miranda's response is conditioned, given the best chance, and they stage it as something spectacular. Even before the masque, then, elite spectacle is seen as productive, as giving a context in which love can grow, and these examples have a common aim. Their controlling and shaping effects upon emotion are very clear – rather than binding groups of friends and allies together in ways which are at heart political, these entertainments are closer to home, more personal. They shape his daughter's emotional engagements.

The masque might bind Ferdinand and Miranda together socially but it holds them apart physically, by controlling the heat of their passion. Iris, Ceres and Juno enter, 'A contract of true love to celebrate,/And some donation freely to estate/On the blest lovers' (84–6). Their discourse of natural growth explores sexuality and fertility in a series of poised and studied classical speeches whose form refines what is natural into what is cultured. The qualities of the landscape which it celebrates are pointedly those of agriculture, not wilderness, as many critics have commented: Iris celebrates the 'pole-clipped vineyard' and Ceres promises 'Barns and garners never empty...' Stephen Orgel, for instance, points out that Ceres was said by mythographers to have 'brought civilization to human society'. In a contemporary account she, 'first found and taught the use of corn and grain, and thereby brought men from that wild and savage wandering in woods and eating of acorns to a civil conversing and more orderly diet, and caused them to inhabit towns, to live sociably, to observe certain laws and institutions'.[36]

These discourses of the culture of control speak to that temporal gap between masque and marriage then; they are about holding emotion in check. The connections are complex: 'temperance leads to fertility'[37] as a type of productive restraint, and masque is a form of entertainment which produces its beauty through aesthetic control; it is the refinement of base matter into ethereal, the resolution of elemental tensions into harmony and wonder. The masque performs the sense of order, of control and self-control, which sets the elite themselves apart from their less sophisticated peers. But it also provides an analogy for Prospero's rule over the island. As the island itself is imagined largely in Caliban's descriptions of it – his 'clust'ring filberts' and 'young seamews' for instance (2.2.169–70) – so, analogously, Caliban's nature is altered, worked upon and moulded by Prospero's culture, and the imposition of the entertainments which he stages performs that action most clearly. The 'culture' of agriculture is central to these notions of the imposition of social forms upon the island – the civilizing process involved in the formation of taste, and the social production involved in inculcating that taste in the next generation. Prospero's colonization of the island is his imprinting of elite authority on the failed projects of rule which had previously been exercised there, in order to reshape wild nature into the controlled expression of courtly hospitality.

And these social forms therefore bring back ideas of home – their performance ushers in the habitual places in which they used to be staged, connecting two locations as Hamlet's Ghost did purgatory and Gertrude's closet. It is through the performance of banquet and masque that Prospero intends to effect his return. Their politics of display are partly a feature of his control over the spirits and the shows they put on, and partly an element of his ability to wield aesthetic authority – to reproduce the dominant cultural forms of the courts of Europe. Prospero's display enables him to demonstrate his continuing authority, to retain his ducal status outside his Duchy, by proving that he has imposed European hierarchies on this island rather than permitting its uncultured life to seep into his own social practice. Unlike those Englishmen who occasionally 'turned native' abroad, for instance, Prospero retains a recognizably elite set of rituals by which to assert his status – he remains fit to rule.[38]

To lay on a banquet, however temporarily, and to stage a masque on a deserted island is quite a striking assertion of power. Ferdinand's total engrossment with the masque shows this power – it causes in him a sense of absolute satisfaction that, as a result of the masque's vision, nothing can be lacking on the island: 'Let me live here ever!/So rare a wondered father and a wise/Makes this place paradise.' The wonder of the masque is partly generated by the improbability of such an entertainment in such a place: the psalmist was, after all, even moved to ask, 'Can God furnish a table in the wilderness?' (Psalms 78, 19, *King James Bible*). The supremacy which such a feat would body forth in Europe was that of money, education and influence. On the island such hierarchical determining factors are irrelevant – the problem here is clearly larger than whether one has the funds or the circle of acquaintances to stage such entertainment. Prospero and Miranda's quotidian food is the product of the island – its ingredients are the fish, and no doubt the crabs and nuts of which Caliban has a special knowledge – but Prospero's elite shows of hospitality use different servants and, we presume, altogether different fare. His banquet does not directly re-make the stuff of the island in other words, it is imported from elsewhere – the problem becomes rather how one brings a banquet into being without the supply chains from major ports, without the skilled retainers, and without, of course, the material accoutrements of house and household such as a silver bowl and ewer, on which such shows would usually depend. Banquet and masque lend themselves to a translation into magic. These elite forms supersede their material components – are more than the sum of their parts – and seek to mystify the workmanship which has gone into them in favour of an illusion of magical process, of both being and not being the thing represented. In other words, they seek to obscure their origins in the things and labour which go into their construction. Seen from this angle, Prospero's whole system of magic becomes a way of dealing with material lack, of surrounding himself with those things which his usurping brother had taken from him.

Despite the force of Prospero's magic, however, there are of course material connections between Milan and the island. He recounts a narrative of origins in 1.1 in order to re-create his erstwhile public identity for his daughter – she knows him only as a father he points out, and therefore herself only partially: 'Art ignorant of what thou art, naught knowing/Of whence I am, nor that I am more better/Than Prospero, master of a full poor cell/And thy no greater father' (1.1.18–21). The things which connect this story of the past to their experience of the present are those which they brought with them from Milan: Gonzalo, Prospero tells his daughter, made sure that the two left with objects which would sustain and define them. And he did so 'of his gentleness', both because he was gentle in kindness and because he was a gentleman – someone with an understanding of the requirements of a peer cut off from ways of demonstrating that status. Like the supposed corpse of the eponymous Pericles' wife which is cast adrift freighted with 'cloth of state, and crowned,/Balmed and entreasured with full bags of spices' (*Pericles*, 12.62–3) as both tribute and identification, Prospero and Miranda arrive on the island supplied with 'Rich garments, linens, stuffs, and necessaries/Which since have steaded much', along with the 'volumes that/I prize above my dukedom' (1.2.165–69), which have provided a way of furnishing more.

The rich garments, linens and fabrics, staples of elite appearance, materialize at the end of the play and are apparently seldom if ever used; the necessaries must therefore be the things which have 'steaded' them, which have in some way sustained them. Perhaps the audience are to connect these with the banqueting things offered to and then withdrawn from the same nobles who would have seen and used them at Prospero's palace in the past? Or perhaps the silverware was a memorial reconstruction of those Milanese vessels, one which formed a part of Prospero the artist's vision of elite entertainments remembered. Either way, these objects link the offenders to their victims just as they link Milan to the island. They offer connections back to the Old World, transmitting cultural and social practice each time they are looked upon and used, and they carry with them power dynamics encoded in those practices, the hierarchies of making and using, of cleaning and washing, which find their form in the objects' material shape. For this reason, they are the stuff of revenge and restitution.

Prospero's clothing, on the other hand, is less culturally homogenizing: it appears at the end of the play as a way of bringing two value systems into relation with one another. Leaving the masque to deal with the threat from the insubordinate men, Prospero instructs Ariel to 'go bring it hither/For stale to catch these thieves' (5.1.186–7). These objects, which are of course of tremendous value – when he reenters he does so *laden with glistening apparel* – will here provide a trap for those who only understand value in financial terms. Trinculo bows in mock admiration of his fellow, 'O King Stefano, O peer! O worthy Stefano, look what a wardrobe here is for thee!' (4.1.221–2). The clothes, however, show once again the irredeemable inferiority of this group of characters.

Prospero, in contrast, refers to it as 'The trumpery in my house', and Caliban advises Trinculo to: 'Let it alone, thou fool, it is but trash' (4.1.223). Trumpery is a word familiar from probate inventories for those things which are left over – not important enough to be accounted – and trash of course follows similar lines. These clothes are seen as worthless in both monetary and moral terms, and as such they become a key point of contest between Old and New World, cultural and natural value systems. Caliban's use of such terms also, rather strikingly, sides him with both Prospero and the Old World moralists, those who can see through earthly show to the more lasting finery of the soul. 'What do you mean/To dote thus on such luggage?' Caliban asks sarcastically, suggesting they murder first and play later.

And he offers a different kind of fabric to explain the stakes: 'If he awake,/From toe to crown he'll fill our skins with pinches,/Make us strange stuff.' Strange stuff is foreign, unfamiliar and exceptional – it is the stuff of cultural alienation and wonder, and it links back to the 'rich and strange' bodies which suffer a 'sea change' in Ariel's song and forward to the 'strange maze' through which he leads Alonso – it gets to the heart, in other words, of the nature of life on the island. And strange stuff is foreign and exotic fabric, pinched meaning pleated or perhaps pinked – covered in the kind of decorative small holes which would give that all-over spotted appearance. This different kind of 'finery' characterizes Caliban's experience of Old World materiality. Attitudes to clothing bring into play competing colonial discourses, where natives are either valorized for a nakedness which avoids the competitions of status, or condemned for their immoral and lust-provoking nudity.[39] Like *Merchant*'s rings, these items of dress focus often contradictory discourses and the characters' opposed moral outlooks around themselves. Attitudes to material culture explore the nature of a life outside society.

There is a point, then, just before the play tips into its final restitutions, when these crucial objects of his old life seem to hold Prospero back, and it is the only moment in the play where he and Caliban see eye to eye, where their values are the same. It seems to provide a second's hesitation, a backward glance at the simplicities of island life which surfaces only implicitly, through his response to dress. But the moment passes, and the clothing which Prospero takes with him is finally central to the recapitulation of his identity as Milan. It is part of a focus on dress throughout the play. 'I remember', says Sebastian, 'You did supplant your brother,' to which Antonio replies 'True;/And look how well my garments sit upon me,/Much feater than before.' Feater suggests a better fit, a more fitting fit, one to which he is well suited. Antonio is talking metaphorically, of course, about being suited to the role of Duke and its considerable material accompaniments. But there is also something curiously metatheatrical about the moment, the character played by an actor equally unfitting to wear the still-fresh garments of a Duke. And if the actor who plays Antonio is dressed as a Duke at this point then he is probably wearing very similar clothes to the ones his brother used to wear, and which he will wear again – his usurpation is material and visual, as an aspect of its political impact. At the end, as the drama of forgiveness and repatriation reaches its climax, Prospero instructs Ariel to 'Fetch me the hat and rapier in my cell./I will discase me, and myself present/As I was sometime Milan.' His identity was ready and waiting in his cell to be put on when it should be needed. Standing on the stage at that point there might be two men appropriately and hence fairly similarly dressed as Dukes, visual symbols of the kind of disparities between outer clothing and inner state on which Hamlet commented so bitterly.

When Prospero puts his Ducal dress back on again it must transform him, because when Caliban sees him he is amazed: 'O Setebos, these be brave spirits indeed!/How fine my master is! I am afraid/He will chastise me.' The pairing of Caliban's and Miranda's amazement suggests that both her 'O wonder!/How many goodly creatures are there here!/How beauteous mankind is! O brave new world/That has such people in't!' and her father's rather world-weary ''Tis new to thee' are associated as much with the beauty of the clothing which is suddenly visible to eyes unused to the impact of luxurious fabric as with the men who fill it. Apart from its more metaphorical meanings, the insistence that the elite characters come through the shipwreck materially unscathed seems designed to add to the wonder of this moment, to ensure that they are able to create a sense of courtliness and retain their authority: 'our garments are now as fresh as when we put them on first in Afric, at the marriage of the King's fair daughter Claribel to the King of Tunis' says Gonzalo, and then 'Is not, sir, my doublet as fresh as the first day I wore it?' Like the banquet and the masque, these garments have survived the sea journey intact.

These complex material journeys from Milan to the island and back are clearly centrally involved with colonial projects and discourses then, but as a kind of cultural transmission which narrows the focus of elite identity to its epitome in masque and banquet. And as the audience imagine the stuff of elite entertainment, as they translate wooden stage props into silver ewers and basins, so the transfer of material culture from Old to New worlds happens over again in the magic of every performance. These versions of elite objects bring units of social meaning onto the stage – pieces of action in which objects, actors and gestures cohere. And they have a particular, forceful utility in the play as they give access through their complex social forms to concepts of inclusion and exclusion which make it possible to explore the relationship between Prospero and Miranda's island life and the social structures of Milan. Within such an isolated setting, the material splendour which lies at the heart of banquets' operation and appeal is also interrogated. By staging a banquet outside the elite society which generates such forms, its cultural meanings become resonantly clear – a rich description of Milanese and by implication European elite society more generally.

6

## *Words and things*

Wool winder, pearwood, English, possibly East Anglian, 1580.[1]

This chapter draws together and extends the book's previous discussions of the many different ways that objects and language interact. It begins by examining the kind of discourses which 'produce' things in the minds of the audience by appealing to their imagination, and it goes on to draw some conclusions about the different ways in which material culture functioned on the stage in Shakespeare's plays – how it interacted with language and action.

I start with this piece of pearwood, shaped and then incised with text. This non-elite thing is a striking contrast to the elite lace and silverware of previous chapters, and offers a way into a discussion of material culture and status. After spinning, wool was wound into hanks for washing and then dyeing, either for domestic use or as part of a growing 'putting out' system of by-employment. Spinning and winding were, generally speaking, women's work. They were tasks which could be undertaken in between, in odd moments, whilst caring for children for instance. They could be put down and picked up again. Both were repetitive tasks, and it is that sense of repetition and reiteration which seems to have led to the presence of writing on this object. On the side pictured here and the reverse it says: LEAD ME FORTHE IN THY TRUETH AND LEARNE ME FOR THOU ART THE GOD OF MY SALVACION IN THE [E] HATH BEEN MY HOPE AL THE DAY LONGE O LORD HAVE MERCI UPON O LORD. These verses about being taught throughout the day by a God who is the believer's hope were constantly present with the owner as they turned the object back and forth in their hands during the rhythmical task of winding. It would be held around the words 'truth' on the front and 'hope' on the back, and just above the date which occupies the narrowest part of both sides, perhaps reminding of a marriage. Carved into the winder, the inscription becomes a part of its form – wood and text combined to make the object. In her writing on early modern graffiti, Juliet Fleming reminds us that 'the posy – a piece of writing with physical extension – cannot exist as text in the abstract'.[2] Like the words on the ring with which the book began, this text becomes posy, becomes meaningful and chosen material, as it takes its form on the winder.

And as it does so, it becomes a part of the usefulness of the object. Working and praying both use the object which speaks as it moves; the words are an imperative to action and a castigation of sloth – they work either with or against a woman's labour and give it a moral guidance. Speaking a prayer at work provided a moral alternative to the thing for which women were famed, the kind of "flim-flam tale, as women tell when they shell peas', or 'old wives tales as they tell when they spin', which had 'neither head nor foot, nor time nor reason'.[3] This object provides its user with the shape and the pace of her prayer, giving her thoughts and her speech a direction – a 'head and a foot' as she turns it back and forth. Turning it makes the words flow – it completes the verse which is broken at a place which makes one want to read on towards salvation.

The text is largely from psalm 25, so the words that this winder spoke were perhaps the most familiar kind of early modern poetry, sung to music as part of a reformed theology. As poetry they kept their form in the memory – Philip Sidney, who translated many of the psalms, said in his *Apologie for Poetry* that 'verse far exceedeth prose in the knitting up of the memory... the words... being so set as one word cannot be lost but the whole work fails'.[4] Like the rhythmic processes which turned wool into cloth, measure and sequence guaranteed completeness.

I hope that image of a woman winding wool and speaking or singing the verses of her faith gives a sense of the vibrancy of the links between words, things and actions – the way they depended on one another and worked together. It reminds us how much more direct lower-status engagement with material culture could be. Comparing this set of processes to the aristocratic 'use' of the ewer and basin in the previous chapter, for instance, reveals the latter to be an engagement with the properties of things which is at one remove, mediated by servants and therefore lacking the kind of tactile involvement which comes from working with things. This type of lower-status use of objects seems to me to be much closer to the way we should imagine the connections between words and things on the stage – an immediacy and a visceral bond between thinking, speaking and touching which tends to evaporate in the lengthy discourses of critical analysis which are necessary to tease out the finer meanings of objects across the plays. I will return to the issues which the wool winder raises of objects' interaction with words later in this chapter, as part of a concluding discussion of the various relationships between language and materiality. But I want to work back to that point by starting with some of the least material (as in physical) aspects of Shakespeare's plays – the way he uses words to make the audience imagine objects, locations and events.

There has been a tendency in recent criticism to call all things material, and it is one which has made Marxist critics testy: Terry Eagleton, for example, asks 'what, once you have demonstrated that language, culture or even consciousness is "material," do you then do? If *everything* is "material," can the term logically retain any force? From what does it differentiate itself? . . . When one comes to speak of "the materiality of the poem's feeling," has the term not merely reverted to its alternative meaning of "important" or "of some substance," dwindled to sheer emphasis or gesture? . . . For there is an important sense in which, in redescribing all or most phenomena as "material," one leaves everything just as it was.'[5] He has a point, but what he puts his finger on is critics' desire to get to grips with the palpable, to account for both the physicality inherent in writing and the way that writing attempts to render physical experience.

Several of Shakespeare's plays, for example, contain a particular kind of highly visualizing speech. In 2.1 of *A Midsummer Night's Dream*, for instance, Oberon and Titania have their first tense and uneasy meeting. The disturbances of the natural world which Titania describes at length come, she says, 'From our debate, from our dissension./We are their parents and original' (116–17). And the cause of this monstrous progeny is, of course, 'a little changeling boy' (120) which Oberon does 'but beg' to be his henchman. The short speech of only four lines in which he begs the boy is the hub of this section of the scene. It stands between Titania's two long speeches, one about the bad weather and the other about why he cannot have the boy, breaking them up physically as it connects them causally.

And Titania's second speech begins by addressing him: 'Set your heart at rest', she says, 'The fairyland buys not the child of me' (121–2). This opening seems to move her address from her husband ('your heart') to the other characters on the stage ('the fairyland' of their respective courtly trains of followers) and to alter the original proposition significantly from Oberon's begging of the boy to her own extreme of purchase – even if Oberon was prepared to buy the child with the currency of his whole kingdom, he would not be for sale.

These questions of audience and of the nature of the proposed exchange set the context for the rest of her speech, fifteen lines which explain the position which she takes:

> His mother was a vot'ress of my order,
> And, in the spicèd Indian air by night
> Full often hath she gossiped by my side,
> And sat with me on Neptune's yellow sands,
> Marking th'embarkèd traders on the flood,
> When we have laughed to see the sails conceive
> And grow big-bellied with the wanton wind,
> Which she, with pretty and with swimming gait
> Following, her womb then rich with my young squire,
> Would imitate, and sail upon the land
> To fetch me trifles, and return again
> As from a voyage, rich with merchandise.
> But she, being mortal, of that boy did die;
> And for her sake do I rear up her boy;
> And for her sake I will not part with him.

> > (123–37)

In these few lines, Titania constructs a palpable and forcefully visual picture. It is a powerful image of an event which is in every way foreign. It is actually the third mention of India in the scene – Puck has already explained to the fairy that she has 'A lovely boy stol'n from an Indian king' (22) and Titania herself maps an exotic journey for Oberon, describing him as having 'Come from the farthest step of India' (69). But in these earlier incarnations India is only a name. Here it is the location for action, and it is present as a heady and intoxicating environment in which one can sit on the sand at night because it is warm, and where the air is 'spiced' – perfumed with the substances which gave banquet foods their strange glamour and whose colours were sandy ochres and reds. And this richness is, of course, a fertile one. A series of images of a large curve give the passage its imagistic unity in growth and creation's plenty: the traders rest on the flood – on the fullness of the sea, the sails conceive with wind and the woman, her gait swimming like the ships, follows with her womb before her in a perfect visual echo of their sails, 'rich' with the child as both opulent fertility and the wealth of lineage and regency. Sea, sail and female body make a shape which denotes the moment of total fullness – a completeness in which things are stretched to their limits and in which they have reached the totality of their potential – it is an image familiar from the shape and meanings of the mermaid ewer with which the previous chapter began. Sitting on the margins of land and sea, Titania's votaress watches a tide which will turn and the inevitable point of change in her own fullness, the moment of birth which turns this carefree tale of shared laughter into a tragedy.

Like, for instance, Shylock's identification of his ring, this image has a power much greater than its size, greater perhaps than the sum of its parts. That power comes partly from its alterity – from the way its balmy spiced air, warm colours and moment of common abundance contrasts with the 'crows fatted with the murrain flock' or the rotted 'green corn' in the 'drownèd field' (94–7) of the present situation which Titania sets out in such shockingly withered detail. The two forms of excess – the satiety of plenty and the putrid decay of too much of the wrong thing – are clearly patterned.

Everything about the image is in harmony, governed as it is by the shared shape of all its elements, and that shape is explicitly female because of its links to female sexuality and fecundity. Literary critics have seen it as providing a vignette of a female world of consonance and cooperation which is opposed in every way to the opposition between Titania and Oberon, a 'world in which the relationship between women has displaced the relationship between wife and husband', in which 'an experience of female fecundity' offers 'a lyrical counterstatement to paternal and patriarchal claims'. C. L. Barber has also seen a rejection of patriarchy: 'women who gossip alone, apart from men and feeling now no need of them, rejoicing in their own special part of life's power'.[6] The emotive power of female friendship developed through shared activities is picked up again by Helena in 3.2:

> We, Hermia, like two artificial gods,
> Have with our needles created both one flower,
> Both on one sampler, sitting on one cushion,
> Both warbling of one song, both in one key,
> As if our hands, our sides, voices, and minds,
> Had been incorporate. So we grew together,
> Like to a double cherry: seeming parted,

But yet an union in partition,
Two lovely berries moulded on one stem.

(204–12)

In both of these images the female space of shared cooperation is transitory and called to mind precisely because it has ended. It has been punctured by the world of men to which it has, apparently necessarily, given way, and patriarchy has intervened. In both cases this intervention is a rite of passage, or a liminal stage in the women's lives: Helena's and Hermia's painful and tortuous affections for potential husbands, the votaress's childbirth which is also her death and, at stake in Titania and Oberon's argument, the transfer of her son's care from the surrogate mother under whose protection he would spend his childhood to the father figure who would be expected to mould him into a man.

Writing about racial identity, Margo Hendricks tries to account for the changeling's repeated identification as Indian. She studies Shakespeare's 'use of the lexicon engendered by early modern English mercantile activity in India'. Because Titania's words 'vividly reproduce the idealized imagery in the writings of travelers to India' and her speech is '"rich" with the language of English mercantilism', so India 'becomes the commodified space of a racialized feminine eroticism'.[7] The Indian sands are not just a female space of mutuality and harmony then, they are a space where the visual patterning of sail and womb signifies a consonance of female sexuality and mercantile activity, of the economic and sexual meanings of richness, which invites the audience to read its sensuality as erotic.

But Hendricks also argues for the significance of the Indian vignette in terms of its introduction of another place into a play pulled taut between two locations – a town and a fantasy land – as a way of bridging the gap: 'Like Athens, India is an actual geographic place, and, like fairyland, it is still figured as a place of the imagination.' And as a result of the characteristics it shares with both, she sees it functioning as 'the center of linguistic and ideological exchanges between Athens and fairyland.'[8] It is the third point in a triangle which explores continuities and discontinuities between reality and fantasy, the domestic and the exotic.

Through these arguments about the essential juxtaposition of Titania's Indian memory and the fairyland into which she brings it we can begin to sketch out the function of such compact, highly visualized speeches. They act as linguistic bubbles which contain something desired and yet complex, keeping the fact and value of the difference of the scene they represent apart from the rest of the action – as an 'otherwhere' – but also keeping it contiguous, its meanings always in play within the very different imagery and concerns of the rest of the drama which is, as a result, brought into comparison with it. Such speaking pictures show how contingent the meaning of the image is on the field which the surrounding narrative determines for it. In a book on literary figures, Gérard Genette argues that 'there are no descriptive genres', and that description is 'a mere auxiliary of narrative' – description is never an end in itself.[9] We can see that Titania's thick description plays temporally and metaphorically against the narratives into which it is set. Its detached nature, in other words, is a formal matter – it is a function of the way its words work to make images, rather than a question of their significance within the play.

These speeches gain their visualizing power from their rhetorical style then: they are forms of *copia*, the opposites of brevity. Desiderius Erasmus, in his sixteenth-century rhetorical textbook *De Copia*, characterizes this style as speaking most fully, enriching 'its matter with as varied an ornamentation as possible, expanding the subject until nothing can be added to it'.[10] More specifically, they are linked with *dilatio* or divergence from the course of the narrative. As Patricia Parker argues in relation to Titania's speech, the 'pregnant votaress is almost literally an image of dilation or swelling... And the "grand" style associated with rhetorical dilation or "swelling" is described by Quintilian in precisely the image used here of swelling sails.'[11] So *copia* involves ornamentation and expansion – more words – and *dilatio* is a grand style which elevates its subject, both honouring and magnifying it at the same time and therefore making its significance clear. That formal insistence upon significance is one of the charms of this particular image of the nights on the Indian sands – it is in fact a casual scene of women laughing, sharing both the joke and the joy of pregnant female bodies which makes them consonant with sails in their richness if not their size. It is, in other words, presented as though it was a singularly *un*important moment at the time, but one which has gained its significance because it cannot now be repeated – it was ephemeral in its mirth and made more so by the votaress's death.

Unusually, in *A Midsummer Night's Dream* this pictorial speech is followed fairly swiftly by another one. On Titania's exit, Oberon states his decision to 'torment' her for 'this injury' and, with only Puck and his own train now on the stage, shares another memory. 'Thou rememb'rest', he asks Puck,

> Since once I sat upon a promontory
> And heard a mermaid on a dolphin's back
> Uttering such dulcet and harmonious breath
> That the rude sea grew civil at her song
> And certain stars shot madly from their spheres
> To hear the sea-maid's music?
>
> (149–54)

The power of this opening to the image-speech comes partly from the insistent use of alliteration which gives to the ear of the audience exactly the kind of inspirational calm which the mermaid is said to have given to the waters. But it is also compelling in the audacity of the picture it presents – Oberon looking out over an extraordinary scene, something rarely glimpsed and therefore offering an exclusive show. This is the second commanding perspective which the audience have been asked to imagine him taking up – first the 'farthest step of India' and now a promontory apparently overlooking the sea. As a pair, Oberon's and Titania's speeches insist upon the king's and queen's ability to travel and their contact with exotic lands, but also their engagement in entertainment – their ability to be captivated and delighted by spectacle and their expectation of grand performances. That this is a particularly elite show is clarified here at the start – the sea is 'rude', it is rough and unmannerly, but it becomes 'civil' when overcome by the harmony of the song. This moral change, signified through an alteration of behaviours with a clear status inflection, is familiar from court masques.

Oberon's entertainment has nothing of the casual poignancy of his wife's. It might be that it happened by chance, but it is a finely crafted show set on a huge scale:

That very time I saw, but thou couldst not,
Flying between the cold moon and the earth
Cupid, all armed. A certain aim he took
At a fair vestal thronèd in the west,
And loosed his love-shaft smartly from his bow
As it should pierce a hundred thousand hearts.
But I might see young Cupid's fiery shaft
Quenched in the chaste beams of the wat'ry moon,
And the imperial vot'ress passèd on,
In maiden meditation, fancy-free.

(155–64)

The scene as a whole has been associated repeatedly with the entertainments offered to Queen Elizabeth whilst on progress: for instance the mythological pageants on the lake and the firework displays which greeted her at Kenilworth, or at Elvetham in the 1590s. Whether or not it has a literal historical referent, however, there is no doubt that in sharing the imagery and scale of a courtly entertainment it ennobles Oberon, combining with the presence of his retinue and his no-doubt majestic costume to create a hierarchy in fairyland.

Puck's recollection of this scene is crucial in generating a time-depth for his relationship with Oberon – it gives the audience a sense of their shared past. His one line within his master's narrative is the succinct, confirmatory but distinctly uncopious 'I remember' (154). Bringing the past to mind gives those who remember 'an increasingly precise orientation in the dramatic present', literary critic Lina Perkins Wilder argues.[12] It sharpens the audience's understanding of their relationship, giving it an important inflection in terms of authority because Puck's memory is in an interesting tension with Oberon's recounting of the scene. He is asked to recall how 'once *I* sat upon a promontory' – required to confirm what exactly – Oberon's presence on the promontory on his own? And then, from an imprecise vantage point somewhere near the promontory, he is further removed from the scene: 'That very time I saw, but thou couldst not . . .' This exclusion underlines the exclusiveness of the image for his master, but it also offers a perfect encapsulation of the visual dynamics of service – Puck is present at the show, but it is not for his eyes. In the magic of a view which only the King of the Fairies can see is encoded a multitude of less mysterious lower-status blindnesses – of masques played out behind those who served food; of music performed but not for their ears, of songs addressed to others. The wool winder above is owned and used by the same person; those who touch the ewer and the basin do so on another's behalf.

This elite viewing is static observation – both Oberon and Titania stay still while their entertainments take place. And because they do so, their way of allowing both on- and offstage audiences to share their privileged visions is to recount them as events for which they were the central audience around which all the action moved. Comparison to Titania's earlier speech on the decay of the seasons shows just how intense and specific the vision of these events is. Although it is enormously detailed and often concentrated in specific images and objects, the range of her earlier discourse is great – that is its function, to describe the palpable ripples of contention throughout the natural world:

> And never, since the middle summer's spring
> Met we on hill, in dale, forest, or mead,
> By pavèd fountain or by rushy brook,
> Or in the beachèd margent of the sea
> To dance our ringlets to the whistling wind,
> But with thy brawls thou hast disturbed our sport.
> Therefore the winds, piping to us in vain,
> As in revenge have sucked up from the sea
> Contagious fogs which, falling in the land,
> Hath every pelting river made so proud
> That they have overborne their continents.
> The ox hath therefore stretched his yoke in vain,
> The ploughman lost his sweat, and the green corn
> Hath rotted ere his youth attained a beard.
> The fold stands empty in the drownèd field,
> And crows are fatted with the murrain flock.
> The nine men's morris is filled up with mud,
> And the quaint mazes in the wanton green
> For lack of tread are undistinguishable ...

> (82–100)

Unlike the ranging imaginative sweep across times and places of this earlier speech, the later pair of images have a clear shape which gives them a sense of completeness. They describe a scene in a logical order, noting those elements which tie it together as an image, which connect its various parts. Their power derives from this shaping focus borrowed from the visual arts, a focus which controls the dynamics of their interpretation. Because as coherent, organized images within their own frame or border of opening and concluding passages, they come very close to ekphrasis.

Ekphrasis is properly the description of a work of art in such a way that it makes the reader or listener imagine it to be physically present, to imagine that they are seeing it. But classical examples in particular aim to exceed the description of those elements of the object which it might actually be possible to see, and rather attempt to bring the thing to life. Homer's description of Achilles' shield in *The Iliad*, for instance, combines material and physical description with details of the vital and sensory scenes on which its decoration was based: there were pictured, for example, 'two cities of mortal men exceeding fair. In the one there were marriages and feastings, and by the light of the blazing torches they were leading the brides from their bowers through the city, and loud rose the bridal song. And young men were whirling in the dance, and in their midst flutes and lyres sounded continually; and there the women stood each before her door and marvelled' (18.490). Here representation fights with experience in the reader's mind as they see two-dimensional young men 'whirling in the dance' but are then asked to hear the flutes and lyres, or are they only being asked to see a representation which suggests they are being played? In *Cymbeline* Giacomo plays on this conceit as he describes a scene for the audience which exceeds what they are actually witnessing: ''Tis her breathing that/Perfumes the chamber thus' he suggests of Innogen, and tells them how 'The flame o'th' taper/Bows toward her, and would underpeep her lids' (2.2.19–20). He makes the scene much more animated, in other words, than it could ever be in its material presence before the audience, thus literally altering their sight. The tensions between inanimate objects and the deceitfully animating language which describes them are what give this form its power, as part of an ongoing debate about the potential of written words. Such images are simultaneously passive and active. In the plays, the speeches' association with ekphrasis makes them self-conscious about the relations between description and material form, interested in presenting things of aesthetic value through words, in a manner which then inevitably bestows aesthetic value back on the things it represents.

Such ekphractic qualities also put the speeches in a peculiar spectatorial relationship with their audiences: watching action is very different to listening to this kind of call to the imagination. They slow down the pace of the scenes in which they occur and induce an interiorizing process of thinking about things which are absent. But they also potentially induce a sense of voyeurism – these very private shows are suddenly opened up for on- and offstage audiences to share, even if that sharing is only partial, a skewed vision.

Such speeches have the potential to function rather differently in tragedies. In *Hamlet*, Gertrude enters bringing the news that 'One woe doth tread upon another's heel,/So fast they follow. Your sister's drowned, Laertes' (4.7.135–6). In response to his 'Drowned? O, where?', she expands this terse report with a much longer description:

> There is a willow grows aslant a brook
> That shows his hoar leaves in the glassy stream.
> Therewith fantastic garlands did she make
> Of crow-flowers, nettles, daisies, and long purples,
> That liberal shepherds give a grosser name,
> But our cold maids do dead men's fingers call them.
> There, on the pendent boughs her crownet weeds
> Clamb'ring to hang, an envious sliver broke,
> When down her weedy trophies and herself
> Fell in the weeping brook. Her clothes spread wide,
> And mermaid-like awhile they bore her up;
> Which time she chanted snatches of old tunes,
> As one incapable of her own distress,
> Or like a creature native and endued
> Unto that element. But long it could not be
> Till that her garments, heavy with their drink,
> Pulled the poor wretch from her melodious lay
> To muddy death.

(138–55)

This speech shares many of the formal features of Oberon's description of his view of the mermaid, as well as allusions to its subject matter.

It provides a contrast with Gertrude's assertion that woes come fast upon one another by describing Ophelia's death in a detail which slows it down almost to the static image of a painting. This is partly because of the time given to her period in the water 'mermaid-like', borne up by her clothes, and the idea that she chanted a few bars of several songs in a way lacking the urgency suggested by distress. But it is also because Gertrude begins her description obliquely – Ophelia is not in this scene at the start, it does not begin with her actions, but rather with the comforting timelessness of a willow growing over a brook. It then moves to her making of garlands and, a digression within a digression, to the gendered etymology of 'long purples'.

In Gertrude's tale of Ophelia and the water, then, the two only meet half way through, and their encounter is dilated almost to the point identified by Erasmus and quoted above, where nothing could be added. The effect is to slow a scene of fevered plotting generated by forceful grief and anger to a point where appropriate courtly respect can be paid to Ophelia's passing. Gertrude's image is the rhetorical opposite of Laertes' assertion to Claudius earlier on in the scene that 'It warms the very sickness in my heart/That I shall live and tell him [Hamlet] to his teeth,/"Thus diddest thou' (4.7.54–6), and the emotional opposite of his statement that he would 'cut his throat i'th' church' (99) to revenge his father's death. Instead it is elevated and stately. Its pace holds it out of time, sets it outside the temporal scheme of narrative which is at this point particularly energized as the play begins to pick up speed towards its finale.

The description shares some of the qualities of Marcus' speech about Lavinia's ravished and mutilated body in *Titus Andronicus* – it is a poetic rendering of what, were one to engage with it as it happened, might be a nightmarish scene of bodily anguish: Gertrude's description of Ophelia's death seeks, instead, to cover experience with language, to use it like clothing – the way in which rhetoric was often described. It is strongly decorative both in its use of individual adjectives ('hoar leaves', 'fantastic garlands', 'pendent boughs' etc.) and in the overall image it presents. It patterns and aestheticizes the physical and thereby rises above it through language. The copious addition of language becomes a process analogous to that of the waves in *The Tempest* which, in Ariel's song, turn the bones of Ferdinand's father into 'something rich and strange'. As Philip Sidney puts it, quoting Aristotle, 'those things which in themselves are horrible, as cruel battles, unnatural monsters, are made in poetical imagination delightful'.[13] But what exactly might delightful mean? Perhaps that their aesthetic quality overrides their unpleasantness in reality? Perhaps that they bring other images to bear on top of the actual event described, or perhaps that they put the frightening at one remove, making it merely curious? Writing in 1551 about the value of encyclopaedias, the Swiss naturalist Conrad Gessner suggested that, rather than risking an encounter with a real sea monster, they offer the possibility of viewing a drawing of one in a controlled environment – the encyclopaedia's images, he says, 'offer themselves to be viewed . . . for any length of time, even perpetually, and apart from labour and danger'.[14] Perhaps the production of delight, then, is partly a process of holding events out of time by recreating them in an artistic form.

Gertrude's speech and others like it engage the audience in a curious kind of way – the fullness of the description makes the scene feel richly present, and yet the exclusivity of the view makes it seem distant. In Gertrude's case, the proportion and regularity of language which gives the description its dignity can also make it feel utterly lacking in emotional engagement. And the dispassionateness of her story is troubling. Not so many lines previously, Claudius had asked Laertes whether his father was dear to him, 'Or are you like the painting of a sorrow,/A face without a heart?' (91–2). The relationship between this kind of sorrow and the measured, controlled courtly regret which Gertrude voices is complex in a play centrally concerned with appropriate responses to death and its accompanying grief. Visual engagement and human response pull away from one another, leading the audience in different directions. Whereas Titania's image of India offered a 'third place' for the comedy against which tensions could be worked through, Gertrude's image in the tragedy holds the corporeal at bay. In comedy, these images are a part of the plays' puzzling out, an element of their processes of resolution in dramas where emotions and motivations are on show; in tragedy they contain information of uncertain status which has the potential to alter the close dynamics of competition in plots whose passions and purposes often remain hidden.

All these questions about such speeches cluster around their 'separateness' from the actions and feelings of their audiences, and that discreteness gives them a very oblique function in the play as a whole. Gertrude's image of the willow and the brook is at best an indirect answer to Laertes' question, certainly one which we might imagine would frustrate Ophelia's easily aggravated brother, were it not for his shock. Instead of being told 'at the brook' he is offered an image just as Oberon was – 'where did my sister die?', 'why can't I have the boy?'; both questions are answered by pictures of scenes whose implications, not themselves, give an indirect reply. And neither 'reply' is commented upon. Perhaps it is not surprising that none of the other characters onstage either in *Midsummer Night's Dream* or in *Hamlet* engage with the image offered – Laertes has the rather redundant line 'Alas, then she is drowned' (156); Oberon moves on with 'How long within this wood intend you stay?' (138); and Puck replies 'I'll put a girdle round about the earth/In forty minutes' (175–6), responding to the command to fetch the flower rather than the scene which lay behind that order. The images are hard to engage with partly because they are so complete: it is difficult to find a way in. As a result, they are left to ripple through the rest of the play in the audience's imagination.

It is perhaps significant that each of the images I have considered here is a picture of a woman which deals more or less explicitly with her sexuality. Patricia Parker links the ekphrasis of Giacomo description of Innogen's bedchamber in *Cymbeline* to the blazon – the literary description of virtue or beauty. She draws on an analysis of this form's 'structurally triangulated nature, in which the speaker describing the body of woman... speaks not directly to that woman, but rather of her, to others'.[15] In this formulation, a space set apart, separated off from speaker and audience as a self-contained aesthetic object, becomes a location of desire. But it is a particular kind of removed, contemplative desire – the longing of a viewing rather than a participating subject. These images, then, are complex in the way they both share and hold off the audience's participation – in their method of offering the representation of a woman as guarantee of the argument the image makes, and yet aestheticizing that image in ways which hold back emotional engagement. Making such an image means offering something up, giving the scene to an audience to be evaluated – making a 'closed' scene public.

This process of offering up is efficacious in *A Midsummer Night's Dream* as a kind of proof – it is testimony of the strength of Titania and her votaress's bond, and of the power of Oberon's potion. In tragedy, again it is more problematic. Because the other way in which Gertrude's story seems so unconnected from the emotions is in that central ekphractic question of audience, and in this way her speech offers similar qualifications of the scene to those which Puck's absent-presence gave to Oberon's description: how does she know how Ophelia died? The decorous copiousness of the image gives a level of expansive detail which, in legal terms, would offer proof of the teller's presence – it would guarantee that their tale was heard as experience rather than report. The conceit of ekphrasis – that it shows more than could be seen by the eye – here sounds rather discordantly, rather worryingly, within *Hamlet*'s hyper-real investigation of emotion and action. If Gertrude or someone else had seen so much, watched so long and carefully, so filled with the strange slow beauty of Ophelia's drowning, why did they not intervene? Or, if this is not really how the event took place, then what is the role of the speech? Is it merely another aspect of policy; a way of calming Laertes' potentially deposing energies?

This capacity of words to create such realistic images in the mind's eye that they become the narrative form of truth carries potential dangers. It is part-cause of the tragedy of Othello, and it brings *Cymbeline* close to that genre too. When Giacomo returns in 2.4, he brings with him a description of Innogen's chamber:

> it was hanged
> With tapestry of silk and silver; the story
> Proud Cleopatra when she met her Roman,
> And Cydnus swelled above the banks, or for
> The press of boats or pride: a piece of work
> So bravely done, so rich, that it did strive
> In workmanship and value; which I wondered
> Could be so rarely and exactly wrought,
> Such the true life on't was.

(68–76)

He goes on to describe the chimney piece of 'Chaste Dian bathing'(82), the roof and the andirons in the fire: 'two winking Cupids/ Of silver, each on one foot standing' (89–90). The liveliness of the description – the interpretation of the tapestry; the Cupids winking in the light of the fire – is intended to guarantee to his audience that what he presents is a memory and his visualizing scene is also, therefore, offered as an answer to a question, as proof that an act of seduction has taken place. Talking about a material environment, then, gives the audience a different kind of mimesis in 2.4 of *Cymbeline* to the one they actually see on stage in 2.2: rather than seeing the room in front of them, symbolized by the bed in which Innogen lies and the chest from which Giacomo emerges, they see the light glinting off the metalwork and bring to life in their minds the complex narratives of the tapestry. The scene is an extended version of that offered by Ophelia as a representation of her own chamber in *Hamlet*. By encouraging a material imagination in the audience, such an image invites them to follow the thought process of Posthumus, whose imagination is encouraged to run away with him.

These distinctions and connections between showing and telling have implications for our understanding of the mimetic project of the early modern stage – its interest in representing things realistically, as though they were really happening – and for our appreciation of the role of material culture within that project. Sidney states that 'The poet never maketh any circles about your imagination, to conjure you to believe for true what he writes.' He assures his readers that the very shape of poetry is, in fact, outside those notions of counterfeiting. But then he does claim truth for poetry in a more essential sense: the poet, he says, 'painteth not Lucretia whom he never saw, but painteth the outward beauty of such a virtue'.[16] He offers not an image painted in such a life-like manner that it would fool its viewers into believing it to be a material thing, and to respond to it like the child who bites into plastic fruit. Rather, it is a sense of moral truth which defines and delimits the form which representation takes. The physical form is dictated by what are for Sidney a clear set of metaphorical equivalents between outer material qualities and their inner moral states: beauty equals goodness and ugliness denotes sin.

For Sidney then, representations are true in this deep, Platonic, anti-material sense, rather than in the particular one which he attributes to the work of Historians – a mimesis governed by the real world, of things as they really are, which comes a poor second to his ideally ordered imagery. This is the abstracted form of moral drama, rather than the early modern depiction of specific individuals. But even within his own treatise, Sidney runs into problems with such a clear definition. 'Poesy' he says, 'is an art of imitation, for so Aristotle termeth it in his word *mimesis*, that is to say, a representing, counterfeiting, or figuring forth – to speak metaphorically, a speaking picture – with this end, to teach and delight.'[17] Imitation might refer to the replication of those essential moral truths, but 'counterfeiting' sounds less simply disentangled from the material qualities of their worldly expression. The techniques of perfecting nature, of making it as it should be, which for Sidney set the poet above and beyond the historian in his skill and social value, are less easily accommodated into the exactness of representation suggested by the kind of 'counterfeiting' which takes place on Shakespeare's stage.

Bringing this discussion of the difference between the speaking picture and the counterfeit image back to the tragic potential of Shakespeare's visualizing speeches shows the extent to which they fall short of Sidney's general truths. This kind of spectacle of words is tied to its speaking subject – it affords a scene which describes an event, and through it a narrator. The audience is presented with an image which is much richer in detail, but whose detail is not disinterested – rather twisted into the likeness of the event which its speaker wants us to believe has taken place. The elements of that scene which the speaker presents to their audience are selected, the logic of characterization leads us to assume, to portray it as they remember it; those elements are therefore replete with information about the processes of choice involved – which elements and objects of the scene would catch the eye of such a person. Image-making speeches characterize the speaker, and they intervene in the political environment of which that speaker is a part – they are very much in their possession. The guarantee of authenticity which their full description gives appears a kind of material proof, but it could just as easily be a fabrication. It is this tricky moral judgement which is played upon in tragedies, as a space for doubting the most materially convincing thing.

These images are so compelling because of the way they use individual details to build up a scene. They produce their impressive effects by moving the mind's eye from the part to the whole: Titania's speech gains energy and makes meaning from its movement from the large and distant sails to the smaller and closer votaress on the sand; Oberon's description follows 'certain stars' and Cupid's arrow across a spacious and imposing landscape; Gertrude's speech pieces together the place of Ophelia's death through the 'crow-flowers, nettles, daisies, and long purples' with which she constructs her 'weedy trophies'. As a result of their construction from individual parts, these speeches alter focus, sometimes sharply, from the micro to the macro and back again. The scale of Oberon's speech in particular is hugely impressive – from an arrow whose trajectory stretches right across the night sky, to a tiny flower.

And there are interesting parallels to be drawn between Titania's and Oberon's speeches in *A Midsummer Night's Dream* and the imagery through which the rest of the play constructs the material nature of fairies. Act 2 scene 1, in which the king and queen speak their image speeches, is also the scene in which fairyland first appears. It opens with the Fairy's conversation with Puck, discussing a series of activities generated by the requirements of service:

> And I serve the Fairy Queen
> To dew her orbs upon the green.
> The cowslips tall her pensioners be.
> In their gold coats spots you see;
> Those be rubies, fairy favours;
> In those freckles live their savours.
> I must go seek some dewdrops here,
> And hang a pearl in every cowslip's ear.

(8–15)

The Fairy's language plays with ideas of perspective in a way interestingly similar to and different from his mistress's and master's speeches. The size of the things mentioned here aims to affect the audience's sense of the actor's height as they try to imagine him collecting dewdrops to hang on cowslips. Titania's arrival is anticipated through the description of her 'tall' cowslip pensioners (the gentlemen attendant on the monarch in her palace) with gold coats spotted with rubies, which gives the audience a sense of the scale of fairyland. The tiny rubies and pearls make a kind of gemmology of natural things which miniaturizes and ennobles this court simultaneously. There is an echo here, as there is with ekphrasis, of intervention in the *paragone* – the argument between art and literature over who can represent nature more effectively – as words actively work against what the audience sees to create a different world from that of Athens. Delight in the cunningness of this verbal dexterity comes from the demands it makes on the audience's imagination, which it plays with in a less painterly and more theatrical way than the ekphractic speeches.

So far so charming a conceit. Mercutio's Queen Mab speech performs a similar trick in *Romeo and Juliet* of course, in a form which is reminiscent of the ekphractic speeches in *Midsummer Night's Dream*. He too minimizes his images, suggesting that Mab comes 'In shape no bigger than an agate stone/On the forefinger of an alderman' (1.4.56–7). It is not so much the mention of the stone here, but rather the stone as ring on an alderman's finger – in other words the visual shift which is involved in imagining fairies in relation to aldermen's fingers – which causes the imagination to warp. It happens again when Mercutio asks his audience to see her race over men's noses with her 'team of little atomies' in her hazelnut coach.

But Mercutio's minuscule inventions twist away from the charming diminutiveness of the coach towards slightly tawdry imaginings of the intimate parts of the human beings across which it travels – from courtier's knees and lawyer's fingers to the ladies' lips which Mab blisters. Similarly, Puck and the Fairy's discussion of his identity becomes closely physical: 'Are not you he/That frights the maidens of the villag'ry,/Skim milk, and sometimes labour in the quern... Mislead night wanderers...' (34–9), Puck is asked. And he agrees: 'sometimes lurk I in a gossip's bowl/In very likeness of a roasted crab,/And when she drinks, against her lips I bob,/And on her withered dewlap pour the ale' (47–50). These images share the startling intimacies of Mercutio's Mab – Puck comes objectionably close, bobbing against the gossip's lips and, later, slipping from the bum of the old aunt. It is the focus on his shifting shape – becoming the quotidian objects of everyday life – not just impersonating them in a theatrical sense but turning into them, that insists upon an other-worldly nature imagined through words, set against the resolutely corporeal nature of the actor.

Mary Ellen Lamb's investigation of the identity of Puck as a character in other contemporary writings turns up fascinating evidence of his interaction with the material world, such as his ability to transform himself 'into a bear in order to have a large posset [drink] all to himself' and the way he 'saves a young maiden from rape by transforming himself into a horse to carry away a lecherous gallant', or 'becomes a raven and then a ghost to terrify a wicked usurer into liberality'. As Lamb points out, 'his traditional activities – misleading travelers, shapeshifting, grinding malt, and spinning hemp' are ones which 'fulfill bodily pleasures in sex and food' – they are earthy and basic and tied into the routines of consumption and reproduction. They are, like the winder with which this chapter began, linked to work, incorporated into the practices and performances of everyday life. Lamb suggests that Shakespeare's play 'popularizes a tradition that literally takes away the fleshliness of [the fairies'] bodies, rendering them the ethereal figures of later centuries',[18] but in this context we can see that the forms Puck is said to take on rather make him wholly material in his invisibility: he becomes the things around one, and he could, therefore, be anywhere.

Shakespeare's fairies construct the environment of the wood through a similar focus on its material environment. The Fairy's opening speech, in answer to Puck's question 'whither wander you?', introduces a dramatically different language to the rustic prose which the audience have just heard in the mechanicals' distribution of parts:

> Over hill, over dale,
> Thorough bush, thorough brier,
> Over park, over pale,
> Thorough flood, thorough fire:
> I do wander everywhere
> Swifter than the moonës sphere
>
> (2–7)

These short lines, broken half way by the repetition of phrases which identify different kinds of landscape, are tightly rhymed and full of rhythm. They almost bounce, sparkling with the energy of the Fairy's constant movement, and they do so partly because their emphasis falls emphatically on eight nouns.

We know that on Shakespeare's stage there might have been a mossy bank (because the list of the Admiral's Men's properties includes two),[19] but the illusion of the natural world is mainly built up through such noun-textured poetry. Oberon's description of Titania's bower is filled with scent which flows from the many flowers which it lists:

> I know a bank where the wild thyme blows,
> Where oxlips and the nodding violet grows,
> Quite overcanopied with luscious woodbine,
> With sweet musk-roses, and with eglantine.
> There sleeps Titania sometime of the night,
> Lulled in these flowers with dances and delight;
> And there the snake throws her enamelled skin,
> Weed wide enough to wrap a fairy in
>
> (2.1.249–56)

In both of these speeches, it is the insistent cataloguing of nouns which builds up our image of fairyland in language which is a kind of patchwork of things – a collage which defines the space.

This type of language, in which things crowd thick and fast, is familiar from other plays. After the entertainment has been disrupted by Claudius' departure, for instance, the language of Hamlet's supposed madness leads Polonius a merry dance as it morphs its way through several animals:

> HAMLET: Do you see yonder cloud that's almost in shape of a camel?
> POLONIUS: By th' mass, and 'tis: like a camel, indeed.
> HAMLET: Methinks it is like a weasel.
> POLONIUS: It is backed like a weasel.
> HAMLET: Or like a whale.
> POLONIUS. Very like a whale
>
> (3.2.364–70)

Such language signifies madness because as far as Polonius is concerned it has no structure, and because it is irrelevant to the issue at hand – Hamlet's visit to his mother in her closet. Similarly, Ophelia's language of madness is plagued with the random specificity of nouns: 'God 'ield you' she says to Claudius, 'They say the owl was a baker's daughter' (4.5.41–2). And of course she gives flowers which she names very precisely – rosemary, pansies, fennel, columbine, rue and daisy. The songs which Ophelia sings at this point in the play have their fair share of this kind of potentially irrelevant detail: for instance 'By his cockle hat and staff,/And his sandal shoon' (25–6). Her words are allusive – they appear to relate to events within the play with their mentions of fathers, daughters, death and sexuality, but they stop short of a precise meaning, failing to offer the answers the audience seek. So the language of madness is characterized by a misplaced confidence in the concreteness of things, which things in fact assemble a strange selection of images in the audience's imagination – it is the clashing and irrelevant pictures which this kind of speech draws for its audience that indicate the mental state of the speaker. Things make pause for the uneven movement from the image of one object to the next, and as a result they produce the opposite of the kind of harmonious visualizing which ekphractic pictures bring into being.

This type of hodgepodge speech is a sign of diminished status – either temporarily through the loss of mental faculty or as a result of low birth. As used by the fairies in *Dream* it creates a coherent otherworldly hierarchy which matches that of Athens: high and low are linked by their different but connected identification of a very material nature. There is in many of Puck's speeches what one might call a kind of 'old English' listing of the names of plants and animals which is not a million miles from the language of Ophelia's madness, and Bottom's seductive song for Titania uses a similar technique to comic ends:

> The ousel cock so black of hue,
> With orange-tawny bill;
> The throstle, with his note so true,
> The wren with little quill . . .
> The finch, the sparrow, and the lark,
> The plainsong cuckoo grey

(3.1.118–24)

These lists are very folksy; they come out of an ancient tradition of careful observation of nature for the information it gives about the weather and the growth of crops. As such material engagements with a distinctive environment, they are a prominent aspect of the Englishness which balances the Latinate names of the characters and the setting of the opening and closing scenes in and around Athens. It is the attention to detail in these speeches which ties them together into a coherent view of the play's settings, but it is also that detail which politicizes them. In a period in which manner of speech was beginning to distinguish the different status groups from one another, these uses of material language are especially significant. Historian Adam Fox points out that elite and non-elite speech were becoming recognizably different: 'problems of communication existed not only between people from the various regions of England, but between those of different social classes living in close proximity'.[20] The way the natural material world is called to mind in the characters' imagery, then, suggests the governing aesthetics of upper and lower status speech which offer, respectively, a language of polished and refined consonance of material detail or of the coarse and uneven texture of too many things.

Lower-status speech is, of course, the stuff of comedy. In *The Merry Wives of Windsor* in particular we can begin to see one distinctively comic connection between props on the stage and the language of nouns. It is this kind of 'working' relationship with objects, just the sort of atmosphere which the wool winder suggests, which is at the heart of *Merry Wives'* connection between things and words. Ford causes dirty clothes to be pulled out of the buck basket, scattering objects across the stage, but he also thinks through things: 'There's a hole made in your best coat, Master Ford. This 'tis to be married; this 'tis to have linen and buck baskets!' (3.5.130)'. And Falstaff's relaying of the tale of his escape to Ford as Brook exploits the thingness of experience evoked in language: 'By the Lord, a buck-basket! Rammed me in with foul shirts and smocks, socks, foul stockings, greasy napkins, that, Master Brook, there was the rankest compound of villainous smell that ever offended nostril' (3.5.81–5). The Host's absurdly copious language has a particular tendency to proliferate things: directing Simple to Falstaff he says, 'There's his chamber, his house, his castle, his standing-bed and truckle-bed.'Tis painted about with the story of the Prodigal, fresh and new' (4.5.5). In the scenes of searching Ford's house, hiding places are repeatedly listed, bringing them into being on the stage: 'If there be anypody in the house, and in the chambers, and in the coffers, and in the presses, heaven forgive my sins at the day of judgement' (3.3.198–200), says Sir Hugh.

*The Merry Wives of Windsor* makes a great deal of its comedy from things then – they are central to the physicality of a humour which creates a strong sense of a tangible context for action. Objects on the stage and in language form a material environment which is a version of Gertrude's closet based on toil and industry – a space which comes into being through both physical and linguistic attention to things. A language freighted with objects is appropriate to the lower concerns of comedy – things tie it to the quotidian matter of daily life and stop it soaring to the poetic heights of tragedy. Mistress Ford's rebuke of her husband, 'You were best meddle with buck-washing' (3.3.146–7) gets to the heart of the characters' relation to the domestic – the notion of meddling as a kind of physical involvement. In comedy, then, things and thing language are much more closely connected to one another.

Connections between material language and material objects also have implications for the nature of theatrical representation more broadly – like the opening Chorus in *Henry V* ('O for a muse of fire . . .') they get to the heart of what it is possible to represent in such a theatre. The elite rhetorical shows of image-making speeches are designed to push the boundaries of material possibility, and to advance an argument in favour of words as the medium of greatest spectacle as well as greatest power. The difference between presenting a masque on stage and describing a masque-like scene is, of course, that between the material and the immaterial. But it goes further than that obvious point about the presence or absence of properties, and about the appeal made to the eyes or to the mind's eye through the ears. A good deal of the humour of the workers' version of Pyramus and Thisbe in *A Midsummer Night's Dream* springs from the fact that they misunderstand which things should be seen and which unseen in their attempts at translation, and the 'point' of the play they put on is to mark that crucial border between the form of narrative poetry in which blood can spray the mulberry red and hunters can be turned into stags, and the stage, on which if men are to become asses then the transformation must either take place offstage or flirt with the inherent comedy of disguising, rather than the incipient wonder and mystery of becoming. William Hazlitt's infamous 1818 review of *A Midsummer Night's Dream* shows the pain this transition caused him: 'All that is fine in the play, was lost in the representation . . . Poetry and the stage do not agree together…That which is merely an airy shape, a dream, a passing thought, immediately becomes an unmanageable reality… Thus Bottom's head in the play is a fantastic illusion, produced by magic spells: on the stage it is an ass's head, and nothing more.'[21] For Hazlitt, words should be kept separate from things – the latter bring the former too palpably down to earth – and elite poetry should be shielded from the taint of low materiality.

When Giacomo has produced his fake image of Innogen's chamber, Posthumus contends 'this you might have heard of here, by me/ Or by some other' (77–8). In other words he is not fooled by the mimetic qualities of words – Giacomo might be retelling a tale rather than remembering the context of an event. Description does not, as he insists, save the wager. In the end, it is the production of Innogen's bracelet which convinces him of her infidelity – object rather than narrative. But the context which the description of the room has provided for the object gives it a much firmer significance than it would otherwise have had: 'She stripped it from her arm' Giacomo says, 'I see her yet' (101), thereby putting the bracelet and the woman's body from which it was taken within the linguistic environment which he had constructed. This is one important way in which word pictures relate to material properties: the object becomes a relic, a part of that imagined scene, and it makes a strong connection between current stage space and the imagined past created from words alone. They are melded together in forceful ways which provide mutual contexts for interpretation. Critic Lina Perkins Wilder, however, sees only divergence, arguing that seeing an action and having it described are separate processes for an audience. In a discussion of *Hamlet* she says 'we see Yorick's skull, not the lips that Hamlet remembers kissing'.[22] But surely we 'see' both; the material object in a productive and meaningful tension with the imaginative presence of the memory which Hamlet speaks and which the audience consequently see in their mind's eye? Objects cannot be removed from the contexts of their production.

These ideas about words, detailed specificity, and objects move a little uneasily between several different concepts of authenticity. And in plays like *Hamlet* we can see various mimetic drives working against one another to create meaning. Hamlet's soliloquies are 'real' in the sense that they appear to give access to a character, to a personality thinking independently; Gertrude's speech about Ophelia is 'real' in the sense that it forces its audience to picture a scene which is visually fuller and more detailed in the context which it offers for action than anything else they see before them in the performance; and then Hamlet holds the skull of Yorick which is 'real' in the sense that it is a tangible material presence, one which prompts him to think about the nature of human existence – it moves him from 'very now' to an intangible concept. Things have, if you like, more physical presence, they are undeniably real in the present of the audience's *experience*; words have a greater capacity to create illusion, they are undeniably real in the present of the play's *fiction*. It is these connections which make theatre different to poetry, and it is only by attending to the relationship between words and things that we can, therefore, begin fully to write about plays.

Finally then, by way of a conclusion to this book, it is necessary to draw some of the threads of previous discussions together in order to try to define exactly how Shakespeare's material culture operates within the textures of his poetry. I suggested at the head of this chapter, in relation to the wool winder, that words and objects could alter one another's nature, and that both were influenced by the way in which things were used. I want to suggest now that an understanding of objects which generate narratives might help us to reconstruct early modern responses to things in plays. Adam Fox gives several interesting examples of the relationship between stories and things in his discussion of oral culture. He describes visual images as 'an extremely powerful medium of communication, aid to memory, and stimulus to cultural invention', and this notion of cultural invention indicates the powerful creativity which early modern men and women found in the material culture which surrounded them. Legends of 'The Pedlar of Swaffham' in Norfolk, for instance, were generated by a statue of a pedlar in the parish church, 'cut in stone, with his pack at his back, and his dog at his heels'. Actually representations of a local merchant and benefactor, stories of the pedlar who made his fortune from news of buried treasure heard at London Bridge nevertheless clustered about the image. Fox shows that 'much local tradition was kept in mind, or invented, by images and icons around the community, both in homes and in public' – the stories about origins which communities told as a way of exploring their own identity were organized, in other words, around objects, around images and icons.[23] Stories grew out of those things (were 'invented' as he puts it) and the objects acted as prompts for stories (they 'kept [them] in mind'). In other words, materiality focuses narrative, it gives it a firm anchor with a recognized mnemonic facility: stories seep into things which then prompt their retelling.

That connection between objects and narrative is linked to the memory theatres touched on in Chapter 4, because it is part of an architecture of memory in which ideas are spatialized and distributed materially. In the memory theatre those ideas are linked to one another, and the shape of the material to which they are attached in the memory becomes the form of their narrative, of the story which can be retold by moving around them in the right order. Seeing things, within this 'mental topography'[24] is active – it prompts – it suggests responses and interpretations. And the evidence which Fox gives of the currency of these practices in relation to oral tales and ballads and the material spaces of the community suggests that it travels down the social scale. Although the idea of the memory theatre was an elite one, linked to bookish learning, its similarities to provincial, oral practice indicate that narrative and things were part of an early modern mindset which was familiar to the majority of Shakespeare's audience.

On the stage, as we have seen, objects also generated stories – *Merchant*'s rings; Yorick's skull, for instance. But in a play, those things and their tales are set within a wider narrative, and they often do not partake of its linear path: rather like ekphractic speeches, they tend to head off in their own direction. This suggests an alternative focus for our reading of Shakespeare's plays – we might want to see narrative as being directed into properties and generated by them, might see the props as individual foci in a complex relationship with the linear movement of their stories. This means giving other ways of experiencing a performance primacy: it means working out from the part to the whole, rather than inwards from the story as we experience it as critics of these plays, in its completed state.

A certain amount of support is offered for this kind of relationship between part and whole, both by early modern habits of reading and early modern rehearsal practices. Literary critic Kelly Quinn points out that Humanist reading practices encouraged the seeking out of elements of texts which could be 'put to ready use', rather than the summary of overall arguments. Lisa Jardine and Anthony Grafton observe, in relation to early modern scholar and writer Gabriel Harvey's reading of his Livy, that 'scholarly reading ... was always goal-orientated – an active, rather than a passive pursuit'. Because of this kind of directed reading, individual parts of the text were mined for their pertinence to a particular situation. As a result, 'a single text may give rise to a plurality of possible responses, not a tidily univocal interpretation'.[25] As larger architectures of ideas are broken up into their constituent grammars of ornament – into the individual and pithy phrases of the commonplace book – so those groups of words become atomized into parts, into the material fragments of texts, capable of assembly in a variety of different ways.

In a book about a different kind of 'part', Tiffany Stern traces the emphasis which the early modern theatre put on 'private' or 'individual' rehearsal of a role. Because 'an actor might have to learn a new role every two weeks, while keeping thirty or forty others in his head', group rehearsal was a luxury usually reserved for the essentials: 'parts of plays that could not be learnt alone – songs, sword-fights, quick changes etc.' Actors took their parts away with them then, as physical objects which contained a discrete section of the drama. Plays were therefore 'designed to function quite strongly as separable units, each part containing within itself information as to how it should be enacted', and they were, Stern argues, watched in the same way, 'with the emphasis at least as much on parts as on the whole'. She points out that 'it was not unusual for an actor to fall out of character when not speaking – as when [the eighteenth-century actress] Mrs Cibber, while acting Ophelia in the play scene of *Hamlet*, 'rose up three several times, and made as many courtesies, and those very low ones, to some ladies in the boxes'. And it seems that this kind of partial performance, concentrated on interaction and dialogue, can be traced back to the period in which Shakespeare was writing: 'Burbage was singled out for praise for "never falling in his Part when he had done speaking; but with his looks and gesture, maintaining it still"'.[26]

Tiffany Stern writes that 'Playwrights frequently claim in their prefaces that a sense of the play as a whole cannot be formed in performance, and can be gathered only by reading the text,' and she points to 'the early modern distrust of the unity and completion of the playscript' as a strong argument against understanding a play 'as coherent a piece of literature as an epic poem'. Linear narrative is not, in other words, the only way of interacting with staged drama and perhaps not the most obvious one. The sole surviving professional theatre part, that for the actor playing the role of Orlando in Greene's *Orlando Furioso*, shows gestures and props as the orchestrating dynamics of character – the things which hold it together: it contains a few property notes – 'enters w$^{th}$ a mans legg'; some action notes – 'he walketh vp and downe'; '<he> singes', 'he whistles for him'; and notes concerning other people whose actions will affect Orlando – 'A. begins to weepe'.[27] Parts might come together around things as well as dialogue. Like Chapter 3, which focused on dress as a series of substitutes for the body which broke up identity into material things, these arguments about parts seem to suggest an early modern focus on the fragment which is nevertheless coherent in itself, on the thing which epitomizes the whole, or which offers a way of working out towards the whole.[28] As a process of characterization, it extends the argument touched on in Chapter 4, where a reading of the connections between objects related to Hamlet suggested a material mode of characterization, one in which the audience connected their knowledge of things together into an assemblage of ideas about the role, running parallel to the information they received from his speeches. Fragments get early modern spectators' minds working in three dimensions. Focusing on the materiality of the stage offers us a way back into such fragmented ways of responding to plays, a kind of lower-status engagement with parts instead of wholes which relishes the thingness of theatrical experience.

I have been arguing throughout this book, then, for a material logic as one of the governing paradigms of Shakespeare's theatre – the tensions between objects, images and texts which suggests that things might mean just as strongly as words, and not always in the same way – that they might push against the meanings of language. And within such a logic, meaning might run up and around material things like mice across bookshelves, making connections in rather different places to the ones we – less versed in materiality and with weaker memories – are accustomed to looking.

It has been the contention of this book from the start that the different kinds of material experience which a highly stratified society dictated for its social and gendered groups generated distinct forms of engagement with the material culture of plays. The wool winder with which this chapter began epitomized the material qualities of manual work, and such an occupation was the key division between the elite and those below them. In the context of the non-linear, non-narrative connections between things in particular, this might sound like a fundamental instability in the systems of meaning which control early modern theatrical interpretation: if every different social group in the audience responded in a different way to a play, and if responses were not necessarily or entirely reined in by the controlling hand of linear narrative, then on what did meaning depend? The early modern writer George Puttenham, with whom this book began, calls to mind a riddle told to him in his childhood:

> I have a thing and rough it is
> And in the midst a hole Iwis:
> There came a young man with his gin [thing; tool].
> And he put it a handful in.

The object thus described is, of course, a furred glove, although Puttenham does allow that 'some other naughty body would peradventure have construed it not half so mannerly'. As Kelly Quinn points out in relation to the passage, 'An appropriate moral interpretation, then, relies upon the preexisting moral rectitude of the reader, and not the suggestiveness or purity of the text.'[29] The meaning of both objects and texts is in the hands of the reader.

But if meaning is so radically contingent, so malleable as to be strongly inflected by personal inclination, then what is it that finally ties words or images and their meanings together – where is the breaking point between sign and signified? Feste makes a related joke about a glove in *Twelfth Night*: 'You have said, sir. To see this age! – A sentence is but a cheverel glove to a good wit, how quickly the wrong side may be turned outward' (3.1.11–3). Cheverel was noted for its pliability and the ease with which it could be stretched and hence changed – a perfect metaphor for the elasticity of meaning in language. Feste's conversation with Viola turns along the lines of coarser meanings, just as Puttenham's riddle did:

> VIOLA: Nay, that's certain. They that dally nicely with
> words may quickly make them wanton.
> FESTE: I would therefore my sister had had no name, sir.
> VIOLA: Why, man?
> FESTE: Why, sir, her name's a word, and to dally with that
> word might make my sister wanton.
>
> (3.1.14–19)

Stephen Greenblatt traces the possible meanings which hover around the joke about the glove, unpicking 'the relevance of this image of inversion to a contemporary anatomical as well as social construction of gender – in which the female was understood to be a reverse or inverted male, with the outside turned in'.[30] The implication of Greenblatt's reading is that the meanings audiences attribute to objects will follow culturally determined lines, rather than spinning out of control. Gloves have an inside and an outside, and the hand fits tightly within them; they are often given as tokens or love gifts in the negotiations around marriage. The meanings attributed to them in these jokes and analyses, in other words, spring directly from their material form and its connections to contemporary practice and discourse. Meanings start with, and are governed by the physical properties of things, and that is why the chapters of this book have started with things too.

We might want to suggest that some objects will have a more voluminous set of meanings. Everyday objects common across the social scale might make meaning more economically and reliably than those things owned by a rare few. On the other hand, complex elite objects like the banqueting silverware might make a more self-conscious meaning, drawing more of their extra-theatrical context with them onto the stage because they draw attention to themselves. Like the meanings of the glove, the process of putting the parts of plays back together might reveal its own logical set of possibilities – not infinite, but governed and conditioned by the tendencies of audiences distinguished in terms of status and gender.

So we have come full circle, back to the distinct engagements with things outlined in the Introduction. As we come to understand the audience's experience of language and material culture more fully – to hear the subtle gradations of speech which Adam Fox picks up on sounding out in the words and phrases of plays, and see the distinct and qualified engagements with objects produced by ownership and use – so we will know more about how these plays were experienced. But, lest that seem a backward-looking exercise despite the excitement of its revelations, we will also learn more about how those plays worked then, and therefore how they work now – how they engage our own very different attitudes towards material culture.

# Notes

CHAPTER 1

1. George Puttenham, *The Arte of English Poesie*, eds., G. D. Willcock and A Walker (Cambridge: Cambridge University Press, 1970), p. 58.
2. Juliet Fleming, *Graffiti and the Writing Arts of Early Modern England* (London: Reaktion Books, 2001).
3. Fleming, p. 114.
4. The text is available at: *http://www.elizabethan-era.org.uk/enforcing-statutes-of-apparel.htm*
5. Philip Stubbes, *The Anatomie of Abuses*, ed. M. J. Kidnie (Arizona Center for Medieval and Renaissance Studies in conjunction with Renaissance English Text Society, 2002), pp. 64–5.
6. *Certain Homilies Appointed to be Read in Churches in the Time of Queen Elizabeth of Famous Memory* (London: S.P.C.K, 1851).
7. David William Atkinson, *The English ars moriendi*, Renaissance and Baroque Studies and Texts, Vol. 5 (New York: Peter Lang, 1992), p. 97.
8. Prologue to *Midas* (London: Thomas Scarlet for I. B., 1592).
9. Philip Stubbes, p. 99.
10. Philip Stubbes, p. 120.
11. Laura Levine, 'Men in women's clothing: anti-theatricality and effemi-nization from 1579 to 1642', *Criticism* 28 (1986), p. 121, p. 125, p. 130.
12. Peter Stallybrass and Ann Rosalind Jones, *Renaissance Clothing and the Materials of Memory* (Cambridge: Cambridge University Press, 2000), p. 2.
13. Thomas Stoughton, *The Christians Sacrifice* (London, 1622), p. 168.
14. Susan Vincent, *Dressing the Elite* (Oxford and New York: Berg, 2003), p. 162.
15. William Harrison, *Description of England*, ed. Georges Edelen (Ithaca: published for the Folger Shakespeare Library by Cornell University Press, 1968), p. 200.
16. Robert Cleaver, *A Godlie Forme of Hovseholde Government* (London, 1598), Epistle Dedicatorie.
17. Natasha Korda, *Shakespeare's Domestic Economies, gender and property in early modern England* (Philadelphia: University of Pennsylvania Press, 2002), p. 54, p. 8.

18. Catherine Richardson, 'The Meanings of Space in Society and Drama', unpublished PhD thesis, University of Kent, 1999, p.61; Mark Overton et al., *Production and Consumption in English Households 1600–1750* (London: Routledge, 2004).

19. The analysis offered here relies heavily on Jenny Tiramani, 'Pins and Aglets', Hamling and Richardson, eds., *Everyday Objects: medieval and early modern material culture and its meanings* (Aldershot: Ashgate, 2010).

20. See Joan Thirsk, *Economic Policy and Projects, the development of a consumer society in early modern England* (Oxford: Clarendon Press, 1978), pp. 78–83, from which this information comes.

21. Thirsk, p. 6.

22. The narrative offered in these sections is based on the analysis of 1650 inventories made between 1560 and 1630 covering Canterbury and Worcester dioceses and each example given relates to an inventory of the possessions of an inhabitant of one of these dioceses. The research is part of a larger project on domestic interiors. The poor are, of course, very hard to analyse in this kind of data whose rationale is to record property ownership. For details of printed probate inventories see the Further Reading section.

23. Keith Wrightson, *Earthly Necessities, Economic Lives in Early Modern Britain* (Harmondsworth: Penguin, 2002), p. 200. See also Jonathan Barry, C. W. Brooks, *The Middling Sort of People: culture, society, and politics in England, 1550–1800* (Basingstoke: Macmillan, 1994).

24. Thirsk, p.14, quoting Sir Thomas Smith's *Discourse of the Common Weal of this Realm of England.*

25. For more on theatre and consumption see Kathleen E. McLuskie, 'Materiality and the Market: The Lady Elizabeth's Men and the Challenge of Theatre History' in Richard Dutton, ed., *The Oxford Handbook of Early Modern Theatre* (Oxford: Oxford University Press, 2009) pp. 429–40.

26. Wrightson, p. 195, report on the conditions of workers in the Colchester cloth trades. A national poor-relief system was being run by prominent members of societies whose experience of dealing with the poor 'enhanced their sense of social and moral distance' from them and 'excited their prejudices', Wrightson, p. 220.

27. See Robert Miola, *Shakespeare's Reading* (Oxford: Oxford University Press, 2000), and Jonathan Bate, *Shakespeare and Ovid* (Oxford: Clarendon Press, 1994).

28. Harris, 'The New New Historicism's Wunderkammer of Objects', *European Journal of English Studies*, 4:2 (2000), pp. 111–23.

29. Karen Harvey ed., *History and Material Culture* (London: Routledge, 2009), p. 3. On early modern soundscapes see, for instance, Bruce Smith, *The Acoustic World of Early Modern England* (Chicago, London: University of Chicago Press, 1999).

30. Harvey, p. 5. See also Margreta de Grazia, Maureen Quilligan, and Peter Stallybrass eds., *Subject and Object in Renaissance Culture* (Cambridge: Cambridge University Press, 1996).

31. Pennel in Harvey ed., p. 182.

32. Quoted in Natasha Korda, *Shakespeare's Domestic Economies* (Philadelphia: University of Pennsylvania Press, 2002), p. 196.

33. Jonathan Gil Harris and Natasha Korda eds., *Staged Properties* (Cambridge: Cambridge University Press, 2002), p. 15.

34. He argues that 'naming the skull transforms the scene. It is a moment of "unmetaphoring" in which the conventionalized figure of speech has suddenly become humanized.' 'The skull on the Renaissance Stage: Imagination and the Erotic Life of Props', *English Literary Renaissance* 28 (1998), pp. 47–75, quotes at p. 47, p. 50, p. 53.

35. Bruster, in 'The dramatic life of objects in the early modern theatre', in Harris and Korda eds., uses Frances Teague's six categories of lights; weapons or war gear; documents; riches or gifts; tokens of characters; and 'other' statistically to produce 'an average of thirty-four properties per play'. He also suggests that different genres use their props in different ways: 'tragedies tend to have the most props, histories the second greatest number, and comedies the least', p. 79; p. 81, p. 83.

36. Wendy Wall, *Staging Domesticity: Household Work and English Identity in Early Modern Drama* (Cambridge: Cambridge University Press, 2002), p. 94. Douglas Bruster, critiquing Wall's work, adds to this extradramatic context a series of theatrical meanings for sweeping, including a Mummer's play from Gloucestershire in which Beelzebub enters with a broom and sweeps the room as a way of asking for cash: 'If you don't give us some money I will sweep you all to the grave,' *Shakespeare and the Question of Culture* (Basingstoke, New York: Palgrave, 2003), p. 54.

37. Richard Helgerson, 'The Buck Basket, the Witch and the Queen of Fairies: The Women's World of Shakespeare's Windsor.' *Renaissance Culture and the Everyday*, eds. Patricia Fumerton, Simon Hunt (Philadelphia: University of Pennsylvania Press, 1999), pp. 162–82, p. 169, p. 171, p. 172.

38. Natasha Korda, *Shakespeare's Domestic Economies* (Philadelphia: University of Pennsylvania Press, 2002), p. 10.

39. Peter Stallybrass ed., special edition of *Shakespeare Studies*, 28 (2000), p. 124.

40. Stallybrass and Jones, p. 315.

CHAPTER 2

1. Jackson Campbell Boswell, 'Shylock's Turquoise Ring', *Shakespeare Quarterly* 14 (1963), pp. 481–3, p. 482.

2. See Helen Cooper, *The English Romance in Time* (Oxford and New York: Oxford University Press, 2004), p. 147.

3. Peter Holland draws attention to 'love and pain, the two emotions captured together in the 'wilderness', the arid world inhabited only by chattering monkeys, 'those symbols of lust'. Peter Holland, 'The Merchant of Venice and the Value of Money', *Cahiers Élisabéthains* 60 (2001), pp. 13–30, p. 28.

4. Miriam Gilbert, *The Merchant of Venice*, Shakespeare at Stratford (London: Arden Shakespeare, Thompson Learning, 2002), p. 112–13, which also includes the Stewart quote p. 111.

5. Holland, p. 26.

6. Heather Dubrow, *Shakespeare and Domestic Loss, Forms of Deprivation, Mourning, and Recuperation* (Cambridge: Cambridge University Press, 1999), p. 136.

7. Karen Newman, 'Portia's Ring: Unruly Women and Structures of Exchange in The Merchant of Venice', *Shakespeare Quarterly* 38 (1987), pp. 19–33, p. 19.

8. Holland, pp. 16, 25.

9. Craig Muldrew, 'Hard Food for Midas: Cash and Its Social Value in Early Modern England, *Past and Present* 170 (2001), pp. 78–120, p. 80, p. 83.

10. See for example *All's Well* 1.1.213; *Timon* 1.1.295; *Venus and Adonis* 844.

11. Adelman argues that 'Shylock poses a claim to an older nationhood of blood and ancestry: an apparently self-contained nationhood through time that mere dispossession from the land – mere "wandering" ... – is not able to destroy.' Janet Adelman, 'Her Father's Blood: Race, Conversion, and Nation in "The Merchant of Venice"', *Representations* 81 (2003), pp. 4–30, p. 20.

12. Bruce Boehrer, 'Shylock and the Rise of the Household Pet: Thinking Social Exclusion in *The Merchant of Venice*', *Shakespeare Quarterly* 50 (1999), pp. 152–70, 157.

13. Steve Patterson, 'The Bankruptcy of Homoerotic Amity in Shakespeare's *Merchant of Venice*', *Shakespeare Quarterly* 50 (1999), pp. 9–32, p. 19.

14. *Oxford English Dictionary* 3. a. Morocco mentions 'the vasty wilds/Of wide Arabia' as being 'as throughfares now/For princes to come view fair Portia' (2.7.41–3).

15. From *A Short View of Tragedy* (London, 1693), in *The Critical Works of Thomas Rymer*, ed. Curt Zimansky (New Haven: Yale University Press, 1956), p. 160.
16. Patterson, p. 26.
17. Patterson, p. 27, p. 29.


CHAPTER 3

1. R. A. Foakes, ed., *Henslowe's Diary*, Second Edition (Cambridge: Cambridge University Press, 2002), pp. 99–102; Jean MacIntyre, *Costumes and Scripts on the Elizabethan Stage* (Alberta: University of Alberta Press, 1992), p. 87.
2. MacIntyre, p. 31.
3. Peter Stallybrass and Ann Rosalind Jones, *Renaissance Clothing and the Materials of Memory* (Cambridge: Cambridge University Press, 2000), p. 176.
4. See Jenny Tiramani, 'Pins and aglets' in Hamling and Richardson, eds., *Everyday Objects: medieval and early modern material culture and its meanings* (Aldershot: Ashgate, 2010), pp. 85–94.
5. MacIntyre, p.94; see also Stallybrass and Jones, p. 191.
6. Natasha Korda, 'Household Property/Stage Property: Henslowe as Pawnbroker', *Theatre Journal* 48 (1996), pp. 185–95.
7. R. A. Foakes, ed., p. 180.
8. MacIntyre, p. 83.
9. MacIntyre, p. 56.
10. MacIntyre, p. 104, pp. 140–1, p. 319.
11. Foakes, ed., p. 317. Only about 10% of costumes and properties were attached to named plays. Most 'belonged to the years after 1600, when both the Admiral's and Worcester's Men were purchasing more fabrics to be made up by their tailors and rather fewer existing garments'. MacIntyre, p. 96.
12. MacIntyre, pp. 87, 88.
13. See Reginald Foakes's argument about the materiality of the ghost's supernatural nature, 'The ghost in *Hamlet*' *Shakespeare Survey* 58 (2005), pp. 34–47, p. 44. Stallybrass and Jones argue that ghosts 'testify simultaneously to death's undoing of the body and to the materiality of survival', and that their mnemonic qualities are represented by 'what is most visible and tactile', their clothes, p. 249. For more on contemporary uses of armour see Foakes, p. 35.
14. Foakes, p. 44.
15. MacIntypre, p. 39, p. 42.

16. Stallybrass and Jones, p. 3.
17. Jean E. Howard, 'Crossdressing, The Theatre, and Gender Struggle in Early Modern England', *Shakespeare Quarterly* 39 (1988), pp. 418–40, p. 419; Will Fisher, *Materializing Gender in Early Modern English Literature and Culture* (Cambridge: Cambridge University Press, 2006), p. 6, pp. 32–3.
18. Rudolf Dekker and Lotte Van de Pol, *The Tradition of Female Transvestitism in Early Modern Europe* (Basingstoke: Macmillan, 1989), p. 2, p. 3; Natalie Zemon Davis, *Society and Culture in Early Modern France* (Stanford University Press, 1975), p. 136, p. 147; David Cressy, 'Gender Trouble and Cross-Dressing in Early Modern England', *Journal of British Studies* 35 (1996), pp. 438–65, p. 460, p. 449.
19. Laura Levine, 'Men in women's clothing: anti-theatricality and effeminization from 1579 to 1642', *Criticism* 28 (1986), pp. 121–41, p. 125; Susan Vincent, *Dressing the Elite* (Oxford and New York: Berg, 2003), p. 168, p. 174, p. 171.
20. Howard, p. 418.
21. Robert L. A. Clark and Claire Sponsler, 'The Cultural Work of Crossdressing in Medieval Drama', *New Literary History* 28 (1997), pp. 319–44, p. 319–20.
22. Marjorie Garber, *Vested Interests, Cross-dressing and Cultural Anxiety* (London: Routledge, 1997), p. 35.
23. Roy Strong, *The English Icon: Elizabethan and Jacobean Portraiture*, p. 36, quoted in Christopher Breward, *The Culture of Fashion* (Manchester: Manchester University Press, 1995) p. 68.
24. Ellen Chirelstein, 'Lady Elizabeth Pope: The Heraldic Body', in Lucy Gent and Nigel Llewellyn eds., *Renaissance Bodies, The Human Figure in English Culture c.1540–1660* (London: Reaktion Books, 1990), pp. 36–59, p. 39.
25. David Piper, *The English Face* (London: Thames and Hudson, 1957), p. 87; see also Ellis Waterhouse, *Painting in Britain 1530–1790*, fifth edition (New Haven and London: Yale, 1994), chapter 3.
26. Jane Ashelford, *Dress in the Age of Elizabeth I* (London: Batsford, 1988), p. 11, p. 43; Breward, p. 67.
27. See Robert Tittler, *The Face of the City* (Manchester: Manchester University Press, 2008).
28. Yu Jin Ko, 'The Comic Close of *Twelfth Night* and Viola's Noli me Tangere', *Shakespeare Quarterly* 48 (1997), pp. 391–405. In *Twelfth Night*, he sees it as an essential part of the dynamic of delayed completion which guarantees the continuation of desire: 'If we accept the idea that possession of the desired object necessarily brings about

decay of both pleasure and desire, then the sustaining of desire itself becomes the principal pleasure, and the search for substitutes an essential corollary', p. 397.

29. Laura Gowing, *Common Bodies, Women, Touch and Power in Seventeenth Century England* (Newhaven and London: Yale, 2003), p. 2.

30. Gowing, p. 52, p. 106.

31. Quoted in Gowing, p. 105, p. 94.

32. Ford, in *The Merry Wives of Windsor*, discusses his imagined cuckolding in similarly material terms: 'There's a hole made in your best coat, Master Ford', he says to himself (3.5.130).

33. Gowing, p. 81, p. 73, p. 209.

34. Stallybrass and Jones, p. 213. For practical experiments with unpinning actors on the Globe stage, see Carol Rutter's work at *http://www2.warwick.ac.uk/ fac/cross_fac/capital/teaching_and_learning/projects/unpinning/*.

35. Ashelford, p. 45; Breward pp. 46–8.

36. Stallybrass and Jones, p. 211.

37. Chirelstein, p. 59.

38. Vincent, p. 53.

39. Sigmund Freud, 'The Sexual Abberations,' in *Three Essays on the Theory of Sexuality* (1905), quoted in Stallybrass and Jones, p. 219.

CHAPTER 4

1. My sample of 1,650 inventories produced between 1560 and 1630 covers Canterbury and Worcester dioceses, and is part of a larger project on domestic furnishings.

2. For a list of such uses see Dessen and Thompson, *A Dictionary of Stage Directions in English Drama* (Cambridge: Cambridge University Press, 1999), p. 46.

3. Andrew Sofer, *The Stage Life of Props* (University of Michigan Press, 2003), p. 31.

4. For a discussion of significant linguistic units of meaning see Lisa Jardine, ' "Why should he call her whore?": Defamation and Desdemona's Case', in *Reading Shakespeare Historically* (London, Routledge, 1996). The way in which such units might function materially is crucial to the dynamic between play and audience.

5. Stephen Greenblatt, *Hamlet in Purgatory* (Princeton: Princeton University Press, 2001), p. 4.

6. Patricia Parker, '*Othello* and *Hamlet*: Dilation, Spying, and the "Secret Place" of Woman', *Representations* 44 (1993), pp. 60–95, p. 76.

7. The meanings are 2.a. and 3.a., which continues, 'also (more fully division lobby), one of the two corridors to which members retire to vote when the House divides'.

8. Patricia Fumerton, ' "Secret Arts": Elizabethan Miniatures and Sonnets,' *Representations* 15 (1986), pp. 57–97, p. 62.

9. Lena Cowen Orlin, 'Gertrude's Closet.' *Shakespeare Jahrbuch* 134 (1998), pp. 44–67, p. 64, p. 55.

10. Orlin, p. 64.

11. Orlin points out that, if we see the room as a prayer closet, then parallels are set up both 'with Ophelia, who was instructed to attend to her devotions for the first eavesdropping scene' and 'with Claudius' prayer scene, immediately preceding the closet scene', p. 59.

12. For more on this subject, see Sasha Roberts, ' "Let me the curtains draw": the dramatic and symbolic properties of the bed in Shakespearean tragedy', *Staged Properties*, eds. Jonathan Gil Harris, Natasha Korda (Cambridge: Cambridge University Press, 2002), pp. 153–76.

13. All quotations from Fumerton, p. 61.

14. Stewart, 'The early modern closet discovered', *Representations* 50 (1995), pp. 76–100, p. 76.

15. Parker sees 'The association of a female body with a "chamber" ' as finally inseparable from the violation of the chamber to which her sexuality is reduced,' and she sees the inventorying of the room in careful detail as a substitute for the act of rape, *Literary Fat Ladies, Rhetoric, Gender, Property* (London: Methuen, 1987), p. 136.

16. Parker, 'Dilation', pp. 65–6.

17. Parker argues that 'the obsession everywhere in *Hamlet* with spying and being spied upon linked with the secrets of women that can be exposed to "show"', is 'a fascination that makes women, marginalized as *characters* within the play, paradoxically central to it', 'Dilation', p. 75.

18. Greenblatt, p. 114, p. 146.

19. Reginald Foakes, 'The ghost in *Hamlet*' *Shakespeare Survey* 58 (2005), pp. 34–47, p. 44, although he finds the change to the nightgown unconvincing.

20. Mary Carruthers, *The Book of Memory* (Cambridge: Cambridge University Press, 1990), p. 107.

21. Quoted in Lina Perkins Wilder, 'Towards a Shakespearean Memory Theater', *Shakespeare Quarterly* 56 (2005), pp. 156–75, p. 162.

22. For a more extensive formal analysis of such speeches see Chapter 6.

23. Greenblatt, p. 243.

CHAPTER 5

1. Ewer: height 31.7 cm, width 12.5 cm, depth 21 cm, weight, 1,287 g; basin: height 44.5 cm, width: 44.5 cm, depth 9 cm, weight: 1,658 g.

2. All information on his life comes from the *Oxford Dictionary of National Biography* entry, A. F. Pollard, rev. Sean Kelsey. There is some material suggestion that another coat of arms was originally on the set, in which case he may have purchased it second hand, perhaps when he was knighted (at Whitehall in 1618) as a celebration of the pinnacle of his status.

3. Gervase Markham, *The English Housewife*, ed. Michael R. Best (Montreal and Kingston, London, Buffalo: McGill-Queen's University Press, 1986), p. 121.

4. Brian Dietz, 'Overseas Trade and Metropolitan Growth', in A. L. Beier and Roger Findlay, eds., *London 1500–1700, the making of the metropolis* (London and New York: Longman, 1986), pp. 124–5, Table 10: The composition of London's import trade.

5. Joan Thirsk, 'England's Provinces: Did They Serve or Drive Material London?' in Lena Orlin ed., *Material London c.1600* (Manchester: Manchester University Press, 2000), pp. 97–108, p. 236.

6. Mark Merry and Catherine Richardson, eds., *The Account Book and Inventory of Sir Thomas Puckering of Warwick and London* (Dugdale Society, 2011).

7. Felicity Heal, *Hospitality in Early Modern England* (Oxford: Clarendon Press, 1990), pp. 71–2.

8. Quoted in Chris Meads, *Banquets Set forth. Banqueting in English Renaissance Drama* (Manchester and New York: Manchester University Press, 2001), pp. 16–18.

9. Chapter 6, 'Of the Food and Diet of the English', http://www.fordham. edu/halsall/mod/1577harrison-england.html.

10. See *Anthony, Viscount Montague's Book of Orders and Rules*, edited, mapped and modernized at: *http://www.elizabethan.org/book-of-orders-and-rules/ A-Book-of-Orders-and-Rules-by-Anthony-Viscount-Montague-1595.pdf*.

11. Jeremy Boulton, in *Neighbourhood and Society: a London suburb in the seventeenth century* (Cambridge: Cambridge University Press, 1987), estimates the proportion of Henslowe's business at: 62% clothing, 12% household, 11% plate (mainly rings), Table 3.5, pawns from the years 1594–5. He says that 'Most household goods left as pawns were articles of bedlinen, sheets, rugs, curtains, napkins and tablecloths', p. 90.

12. Meads, p. 65; p. 49.

13. Heal, p. 7; p. 31.

14. Peter Brears' Introduction to *The Boke of Keruynge* (Lewes: Southover Press, 2004), lays this process out in detail and includes a figure showing the different procedures, pp. 20–1; Figure 5 pp. 84–6.

15. Heal, p. 6; p. 11.

16. See Paul Schofield, *The Building of London: from the Conquest to the Great Fire*, 2nd edition (London: British Museum Publications, 1993), p. 161; Kate Giles, 'Buildings and objects: inhabiting pre-modern public buildings' in Hamling and Richardson, eds., *Everyday Objects: medieval and early modern material culture and its meanings* (Aldershot: Ashgate, 2010).

17. On urban plate collections see Llewellyn Jewitt and W. H. St John Hope, *Corporation Plate and Insignia of Office* (London: Bemrose and Sons, 1895).

18. The generically curious scene with the musicians around Juliet's marriage/deathbed offers an interesting parallel.

19. Meads passim, quote p. 3.

20. Meads, p. 75.

21. Heal p. 80.

22. For more on the way this is explored in other plays see Meads, p. 70 and *passim*.

23. This is particularly clear in domestic tragedies: see Richardson, *Domestic Life and Domestic Tragedy in Early Modern England* (Manchester: Manchester University Press, 2006).

24. Ken Albala, *The Banquet: dining in the great courts of late Renaissance Europe* (Urbana: University of Illinois Press, 2007), p. 2 and *passim*; Robert Applebaum, *Aguecheek's beef, belch's hiccup and other gastronomic interjections: literature, culture and food among the early moderns* (Chicago: University of Chicago Press, 2006), p. 13.

25. Quoted in Heal, p. 3.

26. See for more on this issue Steve Hindle, *On the parish?: the micro-politics of poor relief in rural England, c. 1550–1750* (Oxford: Oxford University Press, 2004).

27. Heal, p. 24.

28. David Scott Wilson-Okamura, 'Virgilian models of colonization in Shakespeare's *Tempest*', *ELH* 70 (2003), pp. 709–37, p. 727.

29. Vaughan and Vaughan, eds., p. 236.

30. See J. W. Lever & G. R. Proudfoot, eds., *The Wasp. From the MS. (Alnwick Castle 507)*, Malone Society (Oxford: Oxford University Press, 1974).

31. Meads, p. 182.

32. Meads, p. 181.
33. David Scott Wilson-Okamura, p. 725; in fn 58 he discusses Richard Strier's argument, in 'I am Power: Normal and Magical Politics in *The Tempest*', that Prospero functions more like a colonial administrator than an actual planter.
34. In a similar reflection in *Timon of Athens*, Timon says he has been entertained by masquers with his 'own device', and the element of reflection between elite patron and art object is a very powerful one.
35. Heal, p. 21.
36. Stephen Orgel ed., *The Tempest* (Oxford: Oxford World's Classics, 1987), p. 48.
37. Wilson-Okamura, p. 722.
38. For instance the wearing of the Irish mantle by Englishmen, on which see Stallybrass and Jones, ' "Rugges of London and the Diuell's Band": Irish Mantles and Yellow Starch as Hybrid London Fashion', in Lena Orlin ed., *Material London* (Manchester: Manchester University Press, 2000), pp. 128–49. See also, on the 'hybrid identity' of Captain Thomas Lee, and others who 'turned Irish', chapter 2 of their *Renaissance Clothing and the Materials of Memory*.
39. For more on these discourses see Graeme Murdock, 'Dress, nudity and Calvinist culture in sixteenth-century France', in Catherine Richardson, ed., *Clothing Culture 1350–1650* (Aldershot: Ashgate, 2004).

## CHAPTER 6

1. Height 21.5 cm, width 4.5 cm, depth: 9 cm.
2. In Fumerton and Hunt, eds., *Renaissance Culture and the Everyday* (Philadelphia: University of Pennsylvania Press, 1999), p. 325.
3. Adam Fox, *Oral and Literate Culture in England, 1500–1700* (Oxford: Oxford University Press, 2000), p. 189.
4. Philip Sidney, *Apologie for Poetry* (London: Thomas Nelson & Sons Ltd, 1965), p. 122.
5. Terry Eagleton, 'Base and Superstructure in Raymond Williams', in Eagleton, ed., *Raymond Williams: Critical Perspectives* (Boston: Northeastern University Press, 1989), pp. 165–75, p. 169, quoted in James Holstun 'Comment: Historical Materialism and Early Modern Studies', in *Early Modern Culture*, an electronic seminar, http://emc.eserver. org. He is also, of course, talking about the abandonment of the Marxist sense of materiality which rejects 'notions of both the autonomy and the primacy of *ideas* in social life' in favour of the ways in which 'human labour and its organization transform physical nature

into products and mediate social relations'. Ivo Kamps, ed., *Materialist Shakespeare, A History* (London, New York: Verso, 1995), p. 2.

6. Louis Montrose, *The Purpose of Playing: Shakespeare and the Cultural Politics of the Elizabethan Theatre* (Chicago: University of Chicago Press, 1996), pp. 138–9; C. L. Barber, *Shakespeare's Festive Comedy*, p. 137.

7. Margo Hendricks, '"Obscured by dreams": Race, Empire, and Shakespeare's *A Midsummer Night's Dream*', *Shakespeare Quarterly* 47 (1996), pp. 37–60, pp. 52–3.

8. Hendricks, p. 52.

9. Quoted in W. T. Mitchell, 'Space, Ideology and Literary Representation', *Poetics Today* 10 (1989), pp. 91–102, p. 92.

10. Quoted in Lee A. Sonnino, *A Handbook to Sixteenth-Century Rhetoric* (London: Routledge and Kegan Paul, 1968), p. 216.

11. Patricia Parker, *Literary Fat Ladies*, p. 19.

12. Lina Perkins Wilder, 'Towards a Shakespearean Memory Theater', *Shakespeare Quarterly* 56 (2005), pp. 156–75, p. 167, in relation to Romeo's memory of the apothecary's shop.

13. Sidney, p. 114.

14. Conrad Gessner, *Historiae Animalium I*, Cv, quoted in William N. West, *Theatres and Encyclopedias in Early Modern Europe* (Cambridge: Cambridge University Press, 2002), p. 102, where West concludes that Gessner, 'knows that representations let us take pleasure from looking at what would in reality be unpleasant to see'.

15. Parker, *Literary Fat Ladies*, p. 129, quoting Nancy Vickers.

16. Sidney, p. 124, p. 102.

17. Sidney, p. 101.

18. Mary Ellen Lamb, 'Taken by the Fairies: Fairy Practices and the Production of Popular Culture in *A Midsummer Night's Dream*' *Shakespeare Quarterly* 51 (2000), pp. 277–312, p. 297, p. 300, p. 308.

19. The inventory, taken in 1598 but subsequently lost, is reproduced in R. A. Foakes, ed., *Henslowe's Diary*, second edition (Cambridge: Cambridge University Press, 2002), p. 319.

20. Fox, p. 102.

21. Quoted in Harris and Korda eds., *Staged Properties*, pp. 10–11.

22. Wilder, p. 164.

23. Fox, pp. 32–4.

24. The phrase is Juliet Fleming's, p. 136.

25. Kelly Quinn, 'Ecphrasis and Reading Practices' *SEL* 44 (2004), p. 24; Lisa Jardine and Anthony Grafton, '"Studied for Action": How Gabriel Harvey Read His Livy', *Past & Present* 129 (1990), pp. 30–78, p. 30, p. 32.

26. Tiffany Stern, *Rehearsal from Shakespeare to Sheridan* (Oxford: Oxford University Press, 2000), p. 10, p. 54; p. 122, p. 11; p. 13, p. 12, p. 99.

27. Stern, *Rehearsals*, p. 14, p. 61; Stern, *Documents of Perfromance in Early Modern England* (Cambridge: Cambridge University Press, 2009) pp. 4,2.

28. Work on the anatomized body shows how complex and significant the relational qualities of parts can be: 'The relations between bodily and cognitive systems of organization are in many ways most powerfully encoded by the symbolics of any given part, where tensions between the metaphoric and the metonymic, between the floating and the firmly contextualized, or more generally between conditions of autonomy and dependence are powerfully articulated.' David Hillman and Carla Mazzio, *The Body in Parts, Fantasies of Corporeality in Early Modern Europe* (New York, London: Routledge, 1997), p. xii.

29. Quinn, p. 27.

30. Stephen Greenblatt, 'Fiction and Friction,' in Thomas C. Heller et al., eds., *Reconstructing Individualism* (Stanford University Press, 1986), pp. 39, 49, quoted in Parker, *Literary Fat Ladies*, p. 95.

# Further Reading

Much of the argument presented in this volume depends upon an understanding of the basic social divisions of early modern England. These are laid out in Chapter 1 of Keith Wrightson's *English Society 1580–1680* (London: Hutchinson, 1982), and their complexities and consequences explored further in other work: questions of poverty and lower status are outlined in Steve Hindle's *On the parish?: the micro-politics of poor relief in rural England, c. 1550–1750*, (Oxford: Oxford University Press, 2004); middling status is explored in Jonathan Barry, C. W. Brooks, *The Middling Sort of People: culture, society, and politics in England, 1550–1800* (Basingstoke: Macmillan, 1994); and upper status is surveyed in Felicity Heal and Clive Holmes, *The Gentry in England and Wales 1500–1700* (Stanford University Press, 1994). The economic implications of status are explored in Wrightson's very readable economic history, *Earthly Necessities, Economic Lives in Early Modern Britain* (Harmondsworth: Penguin, 2002) and in Craig Muldrew's, *The Economy of Obligation: the culture of credit and social relations in early modern England* (Basingstoke: Macmillan, 1998), and the effect of purchasing power on the material objects which people owned is addressed, at very different social levels, in Mark Overton et al., *Production and Consumption in English Households 1600–1750* (London: Routledge, 2004) and Linda Levy Peck, *Consuming Splendor: society and culture in seventeenth-century England* (Cambridge: Cambridge University Press, 2005). For engaging specific examples of the range of goods purchased, which survive mainly for the elite, see account books such as Lloyd Bowen, ed., *Family and Society in Early Stuart Glamorgan: The Household Accounts of Sir Thomas Aubrey of Llantrithyd, c. 1565–1641* (Cardiff: South Wales Record Society, 2006), or Mark Merry and Catherine Richardson, eds., *The Account Book and Inventory of Sir Thomas Puckering of Warwick and London* (Stratford-upon-Avon: Dugdale Society, 2011). Kathleen McLuskie's account of the relationship between elite material and theatrical purchases in 'Materiality and the Market: The Lady Elizabeth's Men and the Challenge of Theatre History' in Richard Dutton, ed., *The Oxford Handbook of Early Modern Theatre* (Oxford: Oxford University Press, 2009) usefully ties things to plays, and Andrew Gurr discusses the disparate nature of early modern audiences in *Playgoing in Shakespeare's London, Third Edition* (Cambridge, New York: Cambridge University Press, 2004).

There are comparatively few general introductions to material culture in this period. For the period leading up to the Renaissance, see David Hinton, *Gold & Gilt, Pots and Pins* (Oxford: Oxford University Press, 2005), and the broad chronological sweep of objects found in London offered by Geoff Egan in *Material culture in London in an age of transition: Tudor and Stuart period finds c.1450–c.1700 from excavations at riverside sites in Southwark* (London: Museum of London Archaeology Service, 2005), along with the rich and wonderful range of other publications of the Museum of London Archaeology Service focused on specific categories of find. Comparison of objects and practices in the Old and New Worlds, especially useful for a study of *The Tempest*, is to be found in Geoff Egan and R. L. Michael eds., *Old and New Worlds* (Oxford: Oxbow Books, 1999); lists of objects which settlers in the New World were advised to take with them are given in 'Supplies for Virginia Colonists, 1622', *http://www.learnnc.org/lp/editions/nchist-colonial/5338*, and for what they left behind in archaeological deposits see *http://www.virtualjamestown.org/images/artifacts/jamestown.html*. For what we hope is an inspiring range of interpretive approaches to material culture studies in this period see Tara Hamling and Catherine Richardson, eds., *Everyday Objects: medieval and early modern material culture and its meanings* (Aldershot: Ashgate, 2010).

Publications dealing with the specific areas addressed in this volume will also be helpful in pursuing the use to which early modern men and women put their possessions. On rings see Diana Scarisbrick, *Tudor and Jacobean Jewellery* (London: Tate Publications, 1995), and Diana O'Hara, *Courtship and Constraint: rethinking the making of marriage in Tudor England* (Manchester: Manchester University Press, 2000) especially Chapter 2 on courtship tokens. For more on the actual objects themselves as discovered by metal detectorists see the Portable Antiquities Scheme website: *www.finds.org.uk*. For overviews of elite portraiture see David Piper, *The English Face* (London: Thames and Hudson, 1957), Roy Strong, *The English Icon: Elizabethan and Jacobean Portraiture* (London: Routledge & Kegan Paul, 1969) and Ellis Waterhouse, *Painting in Britain 1530–1790*, fifth edition (New Haven and London: Yale University Press, 1994), and, for vernacular works see Robert Tittler, *The Face of the City* (Manchester University Press, 2008) and Tarnya Cooper, 'The Enchantment of the Familiar Face, Portraits as Domestic Objects in Elizabethan and Jacobean England' in Hamling and Richardson, eds., *Everyday Objects* (Aldershot: Ashgate, 2010). For interpretations of individual works of art and elements of representation in the period, see the essays in Lucy Gent and Nigel Llewellyn, eds., *Renaissance Bodies, the Human Figure in English Culture c.1540–1660* (London: Reaktion Books, 1990).

On aristocratic dining and the international nature of banqueting cuisine, see Ken Albala, *The Banquet: dining in the great courts of late Renaissance Europe* (Urbana: University of Illinois Press, 2007), and on the development from medieval to early modern cuisine and other delights Robert Applebaum, *Aguecheek's beef, belch's hiccup and other gastronomic interjections: literature, culture and food among the early moderns* (Chicago: University of Chicago Press, 2006). For an overview of early modern silverware C.C. Oman, *English Domestic Silver* (London: A & C Black, 1934), part 1, is useful and, for a more focused discussion, Philippa Glanville, *Silver in Tudor and Early Stuart England: a social history and catalogue of the national collection, 1480–1660* (London: Victoria and Albert Museum, 1990). Joan Fitzpatrick explores the ways in which food finds its way onto the stage, *Food in Shakespeare* (Aldershot: Ashgate, 2007), dealing with the contrasts between ordinary and exotic fare, and Chris Meads, *Banquets Set Forth. Banqueting in English Renaissance Drama* (Manchester and New York: Manchester University Press, 2001) and the several articles on the subject in *Shakespeare Jahrbuch* Band 145 (2009) are useful too.

There is a good deal written about early modern clothing: for instance the wonderful patterns drawn from extant garments by Janet Arnold in the *Patterns of Fashion* series, especially *The Cut and Construction of Clothes for Men and Women c.1560–1620* (London: Macmillan, 1985) and *The cut and construction of linen shirts, smocks, neckware, headware and accessories for men and women, c.1540–1660* (London: Macmillan, 2008). Both Christopher Breward, *The Culture of Fashion* (Manchester: Manchester University Press, 1995), Chapters 2 and 3, and Jane Ashelford, *Dress in the Age of Elizabeth I* (London: Batsford, 1988) offer a narrative history of dress in the period, or see the more focused cultural work by David Kuchta on 'The Semiotics of Masculinity in Renaissance England' in James Grantham Turner ed., *Sexuality and Gender in Early Modern Europe* (Cambridge: Cambridge University Press, 1993), pp. 233–46, and the essays in Catherine Richardson ed., *Clothing Culture 1350–1650* (Aldershot: Ashgate, 2004). For a detailed history of lace see Santina M. Levey, *Lace: A History* (Leeds: W.S. Maney, 1983), and for elite dress more generally Susan Vincent, *Dressing the Elite* (Oxford and New York: Berg, 2003). For clothing on the stage see especially Jean MacIntyre, *Costumes and Scripts on the Elizabethan Stage* (Alberta: University of Alberta Press, 1992) and the latter part of Peter Stallybrass and Ann Rosalind Jones, *Renaissance Clothing and the Materials of Memory* (Cambridge University Press, 2000).

For a sense of the relationship between proscriptive domestic discourses and actual material practice in the early modern household see Catherine Richardson, *Domestic Life and Domestic Tragedy in Early Modern England: the material life of the household* (Manchester: Manchester University Press, 2006), Chapters 1 and 2, and for its visual aspects see Tara Hamling, *Decorating the Godly Household: Religious Art in Post-Reformation Britain* (Newhaven and London: Yale University Press, 2010). Felicity Heal explores the changing nature of domestic hospitality in *Hospitality in Early Modern England* (Oxford: Clarendon Press, 1990) and Lena Cowen Orlin unravels some of the complex moral and physical issues surrounding domestic privacy in *Locating Privacy in Tudor London* (Oxford University Press, 2008), as does Erica Longfellow in 'Public, Private, and the Household in Early Seventeenth-Century England', *Journal of British Studies* 45 (2006), pp. 313–34. The furniture of the early modern household is lavishly depicted and fully explained in Victor Chinnery, *Oak Furniture, the British Tradition* (Woodbridge: Antique Collectors' Club, 1979) and Tobias Jellinek, *Early British Chairs and Seats 1500 to 1700* (Woodbridge: Antique Collectors Club, 2009), and the goods which filled it can be investigated first hand in printed collections of inventories such as J.M. Bestall and D.V. Fowkes eds., *Chesterfield Wills and Inventories* (Derbyshire Record Society, Vol I, 1977), or Michael Reed ed., *The Ipswich Probate Inventories 1583–1631* (Woodbridge: Boydell Press for Suffolk Records Society, Vol XXII, 1981). This kind of information helps to reconstruct early modern audiences' sense of the domestic interior. Natasha Korda deals with the household's stage presence in Shakespeare's plays in *Shakespeare's Domestic Economies* (Philadelphia: University of Pennsylvania Press, 2002), and Wendy Wall's dramatic focus is a little wider in *Staging Domesticity: Household Work and English Identity in Early Modern Drama* (Cambridge: Cambridge University Press, 2002). Various articles deal with the staging of particular aspects of the household, for instance Lena Cowen Orlin, 'Gertrude's Closet', *Shakespeare Jahrbuch* 134 (1998), pp. 44–67; Sasha Roberts, '"Let me the curtains draw": the dramatic and symbolic properties of the bed in Shakespearean tragedy', in *Staged Properties*, eds. Jonathan Gil Harris, Natasha Korda (Cambridge: Cambridge University Press, 2002), pp. 153–76; and Alan Stewart, 'The early modern closet discovered', *Representations*, 50 (1995), pp. 76–100. Orlin and Stewart are especially useful for *Hamlet*, and Roberts for tragedy more generally.

Felicity Dunworth charts the relationship between women and the household on stage in *Mothers and Meaning on the Early Modern English Stage* (Manchester: Manchester University Press, 2010), especially Chapter 6 on *Hamlet*, and several scholars address the productive connections between gender and material culture, for instance Will Fisher, *Materializing Gender in Early Modern English Literature and Culture* (Cambridge: Cambridge University Press, 2006) and Amanda Bailey, *Flaunting, Style and the Subversive Male Body in Renaissance England* (Toronto: University of Toronto Press, 2007), and, on the sensory nature of early modern female identity, Laura Gowing,

*Common Bodies, Women, Touch and Power in Seventeenth Century England* (Newhaven and London: Yale, 2003). Collections of essays with a longer time-frame include Moira Donald and Linda Hurcombe eds., *Gender and Material Culture in Historical Perspective* (London: Macmillan, 2000), and Jennie Batchelor and Cora Kaplan eds., *Women and Material Culture 1660–1830* (Basingstoke: Palgrave Macmillan, 2007).

Various more general attitudes towards material culture provide a useful context for work in this area and help to sketch out details of the particular early modern engagement with things. Alan Hunt lays out the details of sumptuary legislation in a wider geographical perspective in *Governance of the Consuming Passions* (New York: St. Martin's Press, 1996), and a more focused study is provided by N. B. Harte's 'State control of dress and social change in pre-industrial England', in Donald Coleman, A. H. John eds., *Trade, Government and Economy in Pre-industrial England* (London: Weidenfeld and Nicolson, 1976). Joan Thirsk's work on the moralized economic discourses of consumption is also useful here, in *Economic Policy and Projects, the Development of a Consumer Society in Early Modern England* (Oxford: Clarendon Press, 1978). Thomas Laqueur explores contemporary gender theory, *Making Sex: Body and Gender from the Greeks to Freud* (Cambridge, MA: Harvard University Press, 1990), and Anna Bryson's *From Courtesy to Civility: changing codes of conduct in early modern England* (Oxford: Oxford University Press, 1998) situates material practices within the prescriptive and often amusing genre of conduct literature. Juliet Fleming's work, especially *Graffiti and the Writing Arts of Early Modern England* (London: Reaktion Books, 2001), examines the early modern practice of writing on things, and a series of writings explore the memory theatres which used things and places to structure remembrance: for instance Mary Carruthers, *The Book of Memory* (Cambridge University Press, 1990), Frances A. Yates, *The Art of Memory* (Harmondsworth: Penguin, 1969) or, for Shakespeare's use of the idea, Lina Perkins Wilder, 'Towards a Shakespearean Memory Theater', *Shakespeare Quarterly* 56 (2005), pp. 156–75.

Finally, writing specifically about the theatre and material culture is broad and inspiring: it addresses the excavations of the archaeological sites of the Rose and the Globe on London's South Bank, for instance, in Julian Bowsher and Pat Miller, *The Rose & the Globe – Playhouses of Shakespeare's Bankside, Southwark* (Museum of London Archaeology 48, 2009), and Reginald Foakes's edition of *Henslowe's Diary* (Cambridge University Press, second edition, 2002) lists the theatrical accounts and inventories of props and costumes of the Rose's owner. In terms of sensory perception, Bruce Smith's *The Acoustic World of Early Modern England* (Chicago, London: University of Chicago Press, 1999) offers a thought-provoking reconstruction of an early modern soundscape.

Writing on the practices of cross-dressing on and off the stage abounds: see for instance the work of historians such as Natalie Zemon Davis, *Society and Culture in Early Modern France* (Stanford University Press, 1975), David Cressy, 'Gender Trouble and Cross-Dressing in Early Modern England', *Journal of British Studies*, 35 (1996), pp. 438–65, and Rudolf Dekker and Lotte Van de Pol, *The Tradition of Female Transvestitism in Early Modern Europe* (Basingstoke: Macmillan, 1989). On theatrical practice see Peter Stallybrass and Ann Rosalind Jones, *Renaissance Clothing and the Materials of Memory* (Cambridge University Press, 2000), chapter 8, Jean E. Howard, 'Crossdressing, The Theatre, and Gender Struggle in Early Modern England', *Shakespeare Quarterly*, 39 (1988), pp. 418–40, and Laura Levine, 'Men in women's clothing: anti-theatricality and effeminization from 1579 to 1642', *Criticism* 28 (1986) pp. 121–41, and, for a broader history of the cultures of transvestitism Marjorie Garber, *Vested Interests, Cross-dressing and Cultural Anxiety* (London: Routledge, 1997).

Alan Dessen's work on stage directions underpins a good deal of the material history of stage practice: see his *Elizabethan Stage Conventions and Modern Interpreters* (Cambridge: Cambridge University Press, 1984) and also Dessen and Thompson, *A Dictionary of Stage Directions in English Drama 1580–1642* (Cambridge: Cambridge University Press, 1999). On stage properties, Jonathan Gil Harris and Natasha Korda's edited collection *Staged Properties in Early Modern English Drama* (Cambridge: Cambridge University Press, 2002) contains a wealth of useful essays, and Andrew Sofer also writes thoughtfully on this subject in *The Stage Life of Props* (University of Michigan Press, 2003). Articles on props in individual Shakespeare plays, apart from those in *Staged Properties* which cover *Cymbeline* and *Othello*, include Richard Helgerson's 'The Buck Basket, the Witch and the Queen of Fairies: The Women's World of Shakespeare's Windsor' in *Renaissance Culture and the Everyday*, eds. Patricia Fumerton, Simon Hunt (Philadelphia: University of Pennsylvania Press, 1999), pp. 162–82, Karen Newman's 'Portia's Ring: Unruly Women and Structures of Exchange in *The Merchant of Venice*', *Shakespeare Quarterly*, 38 (1987), pp. 19–33, and Sofer's 'The Skull on the Renaissance Stage: Imagination and the Erotic Life of Props', *English Literary Renaissance* 28 (1998), pp. 47–75. For important critiques of the way literary critics study the material culture of the past, see Harris's 'The New New Historicism's Wunderkammer of Objects', *European Journal of English Studies* 4 (2000), pp. 111–23, and 'Shakespeare's Hair: Staging the Object of Material Culture', *Shakespeare Quarterly* 52 (2001), pp. 479–91.

# Index